American Chess Masters
from Morphy to Fischer

Other books by Andrew Soltis

THE BEST GAMES OF BORIS SPASSKY

MORPHY CHESS MASTERPIECES
(with Fred Reinfeld)

American Chess Masters from Morphy to Fischer

ARTHUR BISGUIER

ANDREW SOLTIS

MACMILLAN PUBLISHING CO., INC.
New York
COLLIER MACMILLAN PUBLISHERS
London

Copyright © 1974 by Arthur Bisguier and
Andrew Soltis

Macmillan Publishing Co., Inc.
866 Third Avenue, New York, N.Y. 10022
Collier-Macmillan Canada Ltd.

Library of Congress Cataloging in Publication Data

Bisguier, Arthur.
    American chess masters from Morphy to
       Fischer.
    1. Chess—Biography. 2. Chess—History.
I. Soltis, Andrew, joint author. II. Title.
GV1438.B57   794.1'0973   73-18510
ISBN 0-02-511050-0

First Printing 1974

Printed in the United States of America

CONTENTS

PREFACE

American chess from Paul Charles Morphy to Robert James Fischer is a long, eventful story for anyone to retell. Perhaps only Hermann Helms could personally recall all the major characters and put the details into perspective. Helms was born in Brooklyn in 1870, a year after Morphy's last recorded game. He first became interested in chess after coming across a small collection of Morphy's games in 1887.

Helms saw Captain Mackenzie play briefly and knew both Steinitz and Emanuel Lasker during the two world champions' stay in New York. He played on the same Brooklyn Chess Club team as his good friend Harry Pillsbury and once defeated Frank Marshall twice in a New York State championship game. "Mr. Marshall was very polite to me from then on," Helms recalled.

Helms was also the organizer of the 1908 Capablanca-

Marshall match, the editor and publisher of the New York 1924 tournament book, an international FIDE judge, and the promoter of simultaneous exhibitions by Lasker, Capablanca, Alekhine, Marshall, Maroczy, Reshevsky, and others.

Helms was, finally, the preeminent chess journalist. For seventy years he contributed news to New York newspapers—six papers altogether—and published his own *American Chess Bulletin*, which began as the round-by-round bulletin reports of the Cambridge Springs tournament of 1904. As columnist for the *Brooklyn Eagle*, Helms' span stretched from reporting Pillsbury's win at Hastings 1895 to advising Mrs. Regina Fischer where her eight-year-old son Bobby could find an opponent in 1951.

Hermann Helms is one of the many fascinating chess-master figures that we couldn't discuss at length in these pages. In a volume of unlimited size we could talk more about Ben Franklin and Lubosh Kavalek, of Louis Paulsen and Ken Rogoff, and so on, but our space is more restricted.

This book tries to do three things. First, it provides a series of biographical sketches of the great players the United States has produced. Second, it recounts how the game developed in strength and popularity since the days of Benjamin Franklin. Finally, it analyzes the playing styles of the masters to see what changes Americans have brought to the game and whether there is a uniquely American style.

Many of the more brilliant games of these masters have been left out in favor of the most representative examples of style. Besides the games contained in each chapter, there is an Appendix with twenty-five additional games. If we only partly succeed in acquainting new players of today with the rich heritage of American chess, we will have accomplished something.

Arthur Bisguier
Andrew Soltis

American Chess Masters
from Morphy to Fischer

INTRODUCTION

American Chess Before Morphy

♛ *My general impression of chess in America was that there was great latent ability in their players, but a deficiency in theoretical knowledge and a want of a high standard of play . . . The people had in them at once the logical calculating power of the northern races and the quick perception and warm impulses of the South, and they required only opportunity and practice to take a high place in the world of chess.*

J. Loewenthal, after his American tour in 1851

On April 13, 1826, a curious exhibition was opened in the National Hotel in New York City. An Austrian music teacher, Johann Nepomuk Maelzel, was to demonstrate for the first time in the New World the scientific marvel that had mystified the courts and learned men of Europe: the Automaton Chessplayer. Barely a hundred New Yorkers came that day to witness the event. What they saw was a robed Turkish figure seated behind a wooden chest with a chessboard placed on top of it. The large-as-life Turk sat upright and held a long-stemmed pipe with a tiny bowl in his left hand. The masked, ominous Turk was deathly still and his appearance created a sensation among the spectators.

Maelzel let the public examine the Turk from a distance at

first. Then he began to open the doors of the compartments to reveal the Automaton's inner workings. All the spectators could see was a confusing array of wheels, wires, and pistons. Then to make his case complete, Maelzel wheeled the Automaton around so that the Turk's back faced the audience. Maelzel pulled away the stolid figure's oriental robe, revealing only more wires and wheels. There was no human concealed in the Turk, the spectators assured themselves.

Finally, when the sight had sunk in, Maelzel returned the Turk to its original position and selected a chessplayer from the audience. The showman seated the New Yorker opposite the chessboard from the Turk and showed him a complex position. Did he want White or Black, Maelzel asked, adding that the Turk reserved the right to make the first move no matter which color was chosen. After the participant had made his choice and the board was arranged, the stage was set.

Having made a few adjustments and imparting mechanical instructions to the machine, Maelzel began the show. Slowly the Turk scanned the board as its head shifted from side to side. Its left hand no longer held the pipe but began to rise jerkily from the table top. The crowd was thunderstruck. The left hand moved mechanically forward until it rested above a piece. Then it fell upon the piece, picked it up, and moved it to another square—beginning a combination that won the game in a few moves!

The effect of the Automaton's first performance was electric. Word of the amazing figure spread instantly. Maelzel and his mysterious exhibit became front-page news every day not only in New York but in Boston, Philadelphia, Charleston, and wherever else they traveled. Maelzel had to turn away thousands of people. Boston newspapers claimed their chessplayers were the nation's best because one of them was the first to defeat the Turk. Not so, replied the *New York American*, claiming that the Automaton had lost twice there. Everyone had a theory of how the machine, or whatever it was, worked. Edgar Allan Poe published his own theory (not only wrong, but plagiarized from a European magazine). It was a nationwide sensation.

Thus, the first chess craze swept America. Its impact on the game's popularity was greater than the chess fever that followed Paul Morphy's 1857–60 adventures in Europe and the events in Reykjavik, Iceland in the summer of 1972.

Incredibly, it was a cleverly conceived hoax. With a neatly designed series of panels the Automaton's operator could hide inside the contraption and move from one compartment to another when they were exposed to the eyes of spectators. This amazing fraud had been dazzling Europeans since its inventor, Baron Wolfgang von Kempelen, chief engineer to the Hapsburgs, first demonstrated it to Maria Theresa and her court at the Royal Palace in 1770. After von Kempelen died, Maelzel took it over and toured Europe, America, and Cuba with it before he died in 1838.

In America the Turk at first did not play full games but only continued from positions that were easily won for the player who made the first move. This was because the strong masters who had secretly performed as the Turk in Europe refused to voyage across the Atlantic. Maelzel's first operator in America was, in fact, a woman who played just well enough to win when a queen ahead. Later in 1826 a new operator arrived from Europe and he defeated the best American players of the day easily. After the operator and Maelzel died, the Turk was left in the Chinese Museum in Philadelphia, where on July 5, 1854, it was destroyed by a fire.

But by then American chess had taken off, and within three years it had chosen a national champion who would soon prove he was a world champion. In less than thirty years the development of chess in the United States was nothing short of revolutionary. In 1826 no one could defeat an unknown master concealed in a fake contraption. By 1857 it had produced Paul Morphy.

Before introducing the first great American champion, a few points of historical background should be mentioned. Benjamin

Franklin is credited with giving the game its biggest early push. The multitalented Franklin was apparently the first American chess fanatic. He organized a chess club out of a circle of Philadelphia friends who frequented his home. The "club" met regularly and sometimes Franklin became so wrapped up in an evening of chess that the evening lasted until sunrise.

During the third year of the Revolutionary War Franklin was serving as American minister to France. Yet the seventy-three-year-old ambassador found time to lay down some basic rules of etiquette in his "Morals of Chess." "No false move should ever be made to extricate yourself out of difficulty, or to gain an advantage," he warned. "There can be no pleasure in playing with a person once detected in such unfair practice."

As an indication of the level of play at the time, the following is a game played by Franklin (White) against a friend, John Bartram, in Germantown, Pa., in 1762: 1 P-K4, P-K4; 2 N-KB3, N-QB3; 3 B-B4, B-B4; 4 P-Q3, N-B3; 5 N-B3, P-KR3; 6 N-K2?, P-Q3; 7 P-KR3, 0-0; 8 P-B3, K-R1; 9 N-N3, N-R2; 10 Q-B2, P-B4!; 11 PxP, P-Q4; 12 B-N3, P-K5; 13 PxP, PxP; 14 N-N1?, N-K4; 15 B-K3, N-Q6ch; 16 K-K2, BxB; 17 PxB, Q-R5!; 18 NxP, QxN; 19 QxN, QxNPch; 20 K-Q1, BxP; 21 Q-K2, QxR; and Franklin resigned.

The first chess club in America with formal quarters was established in the City Hotel on Broadway near Trinity Church in New York City in 1801. But under the Franklin influence chess thrived most in Philadelphia, the chess capital of the country until the late nineteenth century. The first chess book was published there in 1802, and ten years later the first foreign master, Charles Vezin, took up residence in the city, holding court at the chess room of the Philadelphia Atheneum.

"At that time," wrote an early chronicler, "the various chess openings or 'gambits' were almost unknown to American votaries of the game." There were few books, no magazines, no newspaper columns, nothing to facilitate the development of chess enthusiasm. "From the time of the Revolution to 1826," one chess historian wrote in the 1880s, "chess may be said to have been a game known to the choice few in America." But 1826 meant the arrival of the Automaton. It should be remembered that Maelzel's exhibition had little competition in the entertainment field when it arrived. There was no radio, no television, little theater, few musical amusements. The mechanical chessplayer filled an entertainment void, and with it came enthusiasm for the game itself.

During the next two decades books by the leading European authors—Philidor, Cochrane, and Lewis—appeared on American bookstalls. A strong master, Charles Henry Stanley, arrived from England in the 1840s to write a chess column in the *Spirit of the Times*, a sporting newspaper, and later to edit his own publication, *Stanley's Chess Magazine*. Both were relatively short-lived.

The following is a typical game of the period from a consultation match between two New Yorkers, Thompson and Mead, and two Virginians, Green and Newton. James Thompson, a restauranteer, was considered one of the better players of the day, but in 1859 he lost a short match to Morphy—at odds of a knight.

CORRESPONDENCE, 1842

	NORFOLK	NEW YORK
1	**P-K4**	**P-K4**
2	**B-B4**	**B-B4**
3	**P-QB3**	**. . .**

No one had access to theoretical opening books in the 1840s, so Americans were on their own. The Southerners knew the value of building a pawn center and they prepare for P-Q4.

3	**. . .**	**Q-N4!?**

This violates several opening principles (too early movement of the queen, delaying development of the minor pieces) but still is quite good. The queen will attack both the king pawn and the kingside from KN3. The Lewis Counter Gambit, 3 . . . P-Q4!; 4 PxP, BxPch!; 5 KxB, Q-R5ch; or 4 BxP, N-KB3; 5 Q-B3, 0-0 was, of course, unknown in America.

| | 4 | Q-B3 | Q-N3 |
| | 5 | N-K2 | P-Q3! |

Not 5 . . . N-KB3 because Black must give up the center after 6 P-Q4, PxP; 7 PxP, B-N5ch; 8 B-Q2.

| | 6 | P-Q4 | B-N3 |
| | 7 | 0-0 | N-KB3 |

Now how does White protect his king pawn? 8 N-Q2, B-N5 leads to 9 Q-N3, BxN; or 9 Q-Q3, BxN, costing a pawn, and 9 Q-K3, N-B3 puts White's queen pawn in a bad pin.

| | 8 | PxP? | . . . |

Black has no problems after this. Perhaps 8 N-N3, PxP; 9 N-B5 was White's best.

	8	. . .	PxP
	9	N-N3	B-N5
	10	Q-Q3	QN-Q2

All of Black's pieces are well positioned and all White's are misplaced. With their next move, the Virginians stop . . . N-B4 and prepare a queenside pawn storm if Black should castle queenside.

| | 11 | P-N4 | N-R4 |
| | 12 | B-K3 | 0-0-0 |

Which Black naturally intended. The New Yorkers' play is very logical. They exchange off the only White piece defending the kingside and the only one effectively protecting the king pawn. On 13 BxB Black might follow with 13 . . . N-B5; 14 Q moves, NxB; and . . . P-KR4-5.

	13	**NxN**	**BxN**

White does not realize it yet but he is almost lost. He can't play 14 BxB, NxB; 15 B-Q5, P-QB3, and he must defend against the threats of 14 . . . N-B3 hitting the king pawn and 14 . . . B-B6. His best try is 14 P-B3, N-B3; 15 Q-K2, NxP; 16 P-N4, although on 16 . . . BxP; 17 PxB, BxBch; 18 QxB, QxPch; Black's chances are still strong.

	14	**N-Q2**	**N-B3**

	15	**Q-B2**	**RxN!**

Busting open White's fragile position. He can't capture with the bishop because of 16 BxR, B-B6; 17 P-N3, Q-N5, followed by . . . Q-R6.

	16	**QxR**	**NxP**
	17	**Q-B1**	**B-B6**
	18	**P-N3**	**P-KR4**

There is little White can do about a general advance of Black's kingside pawns, which must open a deadly file.

	19	**B-Q5**	**P-R5**
	20	**BxN**	**QxB**
	21	**BxB**	**RPxB**
	22	**Q-K3?**	**. . .**

22 Q-N5, hoping for 22 . . . B-R8; 23 P-B3, BxP; 24 QR-K1 with counterplay was an active defense.

22	. . .	Q-N5
23	KR-N1	P-K5
24	Q-K1	. . .

Or 24 Q-B4, QxQ; 25 PxQ, R-R3, followed by . . . R-N3ch-N7, and . . . RxRP, winning. After 24 Q-K1, Black finished off neatly with 24 . . . P-KB4; 25 R-N2, P-B5; 26 QR-N1, Q-R6; 27 Q-KB1, QxRPch!; 28 KxQ, RPxPch; 29 K-N1, R-R8 mate.

Not great chess—just simple and direct with no great positional subtleties. Inaccurate opening play got White into trouble and he underestimated the depth of his predicament. From chess, Franklin wrote, the educated American could learn foresight, circumspection, caution, and "the habit of not being discouraged by the present bad appearances in the state of affairs." Even in these early days U.S. chessplayers were learning to live with bad positions.

1. PAUL MORPHY:

The First Champion

♛ *His only devotion to the game, if it may be so termed, lay in his ambition to meet and defeat the best players and great masters of this country and of Europe. He felt his enormous strength, and never for a moment doubted the outcome . . . This one ambition satisfied, he appeared to have lost all interest in the game.*

From Morphy's obituary written in the New Orleans Times-Democrat *by his lifelong friend, Charles Maurian*

Johann Jakob Loewenthal was a successful Budapest merchant who dabbled in politics and experimented in chess. He loved to occupy his free hours pitching pawns at a cafe near the Danube where chessplayers and political activists met. Loewenthal had learned the moves from the illustrious Josef Szen, founder of the Budapest Chess Club, and by 1842 had risen to the level where he, Szen, and Grimm collaborated to win a Paris-Budapest correspondence match against the famous Frenchmen Saint-Amant, Kieseritsky, and Deschapelles.

But in 1848 Loewenthal directed his energies toward the republican cause of Lajos Kossuth. When the Austrian army crushed Kossuth's revolt against the Dual Monarchy, Loewenthal judiciously fled the country and decided upon a chess tour of the United States. He won a few exhibition matches, including Charles Henry Stanley, the unofficial American champion, among his victims. In fact, Loewenthal won wherever he went. Then he traveled down the Mississippi to New Orleans and met a twelve-year-old boy named Paul Charles Morphy. He lost.

After his stay in New Orleans Loewenthal headed north, intending to open a "smoking and chess divan" in Cincinnati. But before he could settle down, Loewenthal was invited to the first international chess tournament which was being held in conjunction with the Great Exhibition of London in 1851. Loewenthal was eliminated in the first round of that historic event but decided to remain in England. He eventually became a leading magazine editor and manager of the British Chess Association.

Yet Loewenthal may be best remembered for a prediction. In the *London Era* of October 5, 1856, he wrote, "The progress Chess has made in America is almost, if not quite, equal to that which it has achieved in England . . . We must pay some attention to chess in America if we mean to keep our laurels green. The men of the New World are not apt to lag behind when they throw themselves into any pursuit, and if we do not take care, we may have the next chess champion from the far west."

This appeared barely a year before Paul Morphy won the first American Chess Congress and less than two years before he began his incredible series of European match victories that would establish him as the best player of the world before he was twenty-two years of age. And, equally incredible, Morphy retired from serious chess in 1860 at the height of his powers after only fifty-five tournament and match games.

How can we judge Paul Morphy today, more than a century after his sensational victories? The game has been revolutionized by analysts like Steinitz, Nimzovich, and Tarrasch, who injected a scientific sophistication into chess that no one in the 1850s could imagine. Few players today can appreciate how much chess has changed since Morphy's time, when the Evans Gambit and Boden-Kieseritsky Gambit were king.

Before Morphy, chess was essentially a kind of trench warfare occasionally punctuated by brilliant sacrifices. On the highest levels games were slow-moving and the moves were often randomly chosen. Morphy was the first player (not counting Philidor of the early eighteenth century, who was too far ahead of his contemporaries) to understand and communicate to others the idea that chess had an underlying logic to it. There was a reason why a chess game was won. Brilliancy didn't just happen—there were conditions that had to be present to make tactical ideas possible.

This is the position in an offhand game between Louis Paulsen and Morphy played shortly before the First American Chess Congress. Paulsen, a German immigrant who was then living in Dubuque, Iowa, and raising potatoes, was noted for his blindfold play. This was one of four games he played simultaneously *sans voir*; Morphy played just this game blindfolded.

Black has a considerable positional advantage because of his powerful knight, which cannot be driven away by pawns, and because of his control of central squares. White has played 15 P-KR3 (after 1 P-K4, P-K4; 2 N-KB3, N-QB3; 3 N-B3, B-B4; 4 B-N5, P-Q3; 5 P-Q4, PxP; 6 NxP, B-Q2; 7 NxN, PxN; 8 B-R4?, Q-B3!; 9 0-0, N-K2; 10 B-K3?, BxB; 11 PxB, Q-R3; 12 Q-Q3?, N-N3; 13 QR-K1, N-K4; 14 Q-K2, 0-0).

The problem facing Black is how to exploit a demonstrably superior position. He can take control of the queen knight file, but after White's B-N3 Black has problems making progress. He has no immediate central action. Rather, Black's advantage is partly due to the blocked situation in the center, which incapacitates White's two minor pieces. Any of Morphy's contemporaries might have been stumped by this problem. But even blindfolded Morphy played:

15	. . .	**K-R1!**
16	**N-Q1**	**P-N4!!**

A magnificent idea. There is no way White can stop . . . P-N5, opening up the dangerous file. White's heavy pieces are meaningless attackers because of the powerful Black knight at K4 containing them. Black has established a powerful attack with just two moves. So simple, we say.

17	**N-B2**	**R-KN1**
18	**N-Q3**	**P-N5!**
19	**NxN**	**PxN**

The knight is eliminated, but White must still defend against Black's plan to double rooks on the knight file and add the pressure of the queen or bishop to the assault on KN7.

20	**PxP**	**BxP**
21	**Q-B2**	**R-N3!**

Stops 22 Q-B6ch and threatens 22 . . . B-R6. Paulsen has nothing better than gobbling pawns.

22	**QxP**	**B-K3**
23	**QxP**	. . .

Here 23 Q-B3 would be met by 23 . . . QR-KN1; 24 R-B2, B-R6; 25 R(1)-K2, B-N5. At this point Black announced mate in five, beginning with 23 . . . RxPch!; 24 KxR, R-N1ch. After 23 QxP it seems inevitable that there is a combinational decision at Black's disposal because there is no White piece in a

position to defend the kingside, whereas there are four Black pieces ready to attack it.

The lesson here is that although his contemporaries praised the final mate in five, they didn't understand, as Morphy did, why Black's position in the diagram was so much better and how he should proceed. Blindfolded, Morphy could *sense* what to do.

When Morphy was twelve years old he was already one of the best players in the United States. Loewenthal must have been shocked to find himself losing two games and drawing one during the Hungarian's stay in New Orleans. This was especially remarkable because Morphy had learned the moves just two years before. Morphy was the first prodigy in a series that includes Capablanca, Reshevsky, and Fischer.

Paul Charles Morphy was born on June 22, 1837, into a wealthy New Orleans family with traces of French, Spanish, and Irish ancestry. His father, a lawyer who later served on the highest court in Louisiana, left his eldest son more than $146,000 at his death. Morphy attended the better schools, including St. Joseph's College, a Jesuit institution near Mobile, Alabama, and the University of Louisiana. Morphy graduated so quickly that he won admittance to the bar in 1857, when he was a year too young to actually practice in the state's courts. So Paul Morphy turned to chess.

Years later when Morphy was in self-imposed retirement and Steinitz, that terribly dull Austrian, was world champion, Morphy's supporters began to exaggerate the Morphy story. Morphy, they said, was a natural player. He never read a book, they insisted. The truth was quite different.

Morphy was a keen student of the game. In New York and later in Europe his detractors accused him of winning because he was better prepared with "book" openings, a very modern criticism! With an enormous power of memory Morphy knew by heart hundreds of games by the European masters. When arrangements had finally been worked out for Morphy and Adolph Anderssen, the unofficial world champion, to play a match in Paris in December 1858, Morphy's confidant, Frederick Milne Edge, recalls how Morphy pulled out a chess board and began to show off several of the German champion's best games.

So when the best players in the country were invited to the Descombes Rooms in New York in the fall of 1857, Morphy jumped at the opportunity. The organizer of this remarkable event—remarkable because no one had ever organized anything like it in America and because it was put together during one of the worst business panics of the nineteenth century—was Daniel Willard Fiske. Fiske was an author, diplomat, librarian, businessman, and later founder of a short-lived magazine, *Chess Monthly*, which contained some of Morphy's few written articles on the game.

The tournament, based on the knockout rules*, was a breeze for Morphy, as he allowed only one draw in his first three matches. Then he silenced his only serious rival, Paulsen, 5-1 with two draws. Here is one of his simpler games.

FIRST AMERICAN CHESS CONGRESS,
New York, 1857

	A. B. MEEK	MORPHY
1	**P-K4**	**P-K4**
2	**N-KB3**	**N-QB3**

* One of the oldest controversies of chess tournaments is: Who plays whom? And how is a winner determined? In Morphy's day players were paired randomly for the first round. The contestants then played one game or a short match—the best of three games, for example—and the losers were eliminated. The winners were again paired for single games or short matches in the second round and the losers were again dropped from the race for prizes. This knockout procedure continued until there were only two players left and the winner of this finale took home first prize.

Although still popular in some sports—American college basketball tournaments, for example—the knockout system has been replaced for nearly a century in international chess by the round robin (whereby each player plays every opponent in the tourney).

3	**P-Q4**	**PxP**
4	**P-B3**	**PxP**

It was considered almost unsportsmanlike to decline a gambit in this era. More in keeping with Morphy's style is 4 . . . N-B3; 5 P-K5, N-K5; 6 Q-K2, P-B4; 7 NxP, B-B4!

5	**NxP**	**B-B4**

This bishop does better work on QN5: for example, 5 . . . B-N5; 6 B-QB4, N-B3; 7 0-0, BxN; 8 PxB, P-Q3.

6	**B-QB4**	**P-Q3**
7	**P-KR3?**	**. . .**

This demonstrates that Meek did not understand one of the keystones of Morphy's style. Morphy saw that the game was an equilibrium between material and time. You could be way ahead of your opponent in material but lose because he has marshaled his forces into a quick mating attack. It doesn't matter whether or not you're two pawns ahead of an opponent if his pieces are swarming over your king. Moreover, the relative nature of this equilibrium meant that the more development (time) you had, the less significant material was.

White has offered an opening gambit, a perfect illustration of Morphy's material-time equilibrium. But then Meek plays too much in the style of his name. 7 Q-N3! or 7 0-0 is called for, rather than the wasteful (in time) 7 P-KR3.

By comparison, we should mention another Meek-Morphy game played two years earlier in Mobile, Morphy playing Black: 1 P-K4, P-K4; 2 N-KB3, N-QB3; 3 P-Q4, PxP; 4 B-QB4, B-B4; 5 N-N5? (again misreading the nature of a gambit), N-R3!; 6 NxBP, NxN; 7 BxNch, KxB; 8 Q-R5ch, P-N3; 9 QxB (and here Black takes the initiative), P-Q3; 10 Q-QN5, R-K1; 11 Q-N3ch?, P-Q4!; 12 P-KB3, N-R4!; 13 Q-Q3, PxP; 14 PxP, Q-R5ch; 15 P-N3, RxPch; 16 K-B2, Q-K2; 17 N-Q2, R-K6; 18 Q-N5, P-B3! (if 19 QxN, R-K7ch); 19 Q-B1, B-R6!; 20 Q-Q1, R-KB1!; 21 N-B3, K-K1!; and White resigned.

	7 . . .	**B-K3**

Naturally Black seizes a chance to neutralize the most obnoxious White piece. 8 BxB, PxB; 9 Q-N3, Q-B1; 10 N-KN5, N-Q1 holds Black's pawn. Therefore, Meek tries to complicate matters.

8	**B-QN5**	**KN-K2**
9	**N-N5**	**0-0!**
10	**Q-R5**	**P-KR3**

Another principle that Morphy followed—and like the time-material equilibrium it was new to the chess world—was that it takes more than two isolated pieces to mate a well-developed opponent. Meek's concept is actually deeper than it appears. He forces . . . P-KR3 so that he can open the knight file with P-KN4-5 (à la Paulsen-Morphy!). But White mistakes the nature of the position. You can't get away with things like that if the center is fluid and you are behind in development.

11	**N-B3**	**N-N3**

So that 12 BxP, PxB; 13 QxP can be met by 13 . . . Q-B3; 14 N-N5, Q-N2.

12	**P-KN4?**	**QN-K4!**

This makes way for the entrance of the Black queen by preparing . . . P-QB3 or . . . Q-R5 after an exchange of knights. The attack is over for White but is just beginning for Black.

| 13 | NxN | PxN! |
| 14 | P-N5 | Q-Q5! |

A brilliant idea that involves an attack-extinguishing sacrifice of the Exchange.

15	B-K3	Q-N5
16	BxB	QxP!
17	0-0	QxN
18	BxR	RxB

Black has two pawns for the Exchange, which would be compensation enough. But he has more. Morphy threatens 19 . . . QxP and 19 . . . N-B5 very strongly. 19 PxP, for example, would lose elegantly to 19 . . . N-B5; 20 Q-R4, P-QB3!; 21 KR-B1, QxP!; or 21 B-R4, Q-B6; 22 Q-N3, N-K7ch. The theme of diverting White's bishop from control of his K2 occurs in the game as well as in the notes.

19	QR-B1	Q-N7!
20	B-B4	N-B5
21	Q-Q1	. . .

Immediate disaster follows 21 Q-R4, PxP; 22 Q-N3, BxB, threatening 23 . . . N-K7ch.

21	. . .	NxPch
22	K-N2	N-B5ch
23	K-R1	Q-N3!

With this crushing move, Black swings his queen over to the kingside and wins quickly. The rest of the game was not significant: 24 PxP, BxB; 25 P-R7ch, KxP; 26 Q-N4, Q-R3ch; 27 K-N1, BxR; 28 RxB, R-Q1; 29 P-R4, R-Q3; 30 P-B3, R-KN3; 31 K-B2, and Black announced mate in three.

It was this principle of development, equally useful in attack and defense, that separated Morphy from the better players of the day. Consider this position in the Evans Gambit: 1 P-K4, P-K4; 2 N-KB3, N-QB3; 3 B-B4, B-B4; 4 P-QN4, BxP; 5 P-B3, B-B4; 6 0-0, P-Q3; 7 P-Q4, PxP; 8 PxP, B-N3.

This so-called normal position of the gambit was something of a controversy in Morphy's day. Anderssen claimed that White's best move was 9 P-Q5 so that if 9 . . . QN-K2; 10 P-K5!. Other players suggested 9 B-N2, threatening 10 P-Q5 might be stronger. (In 1971 the young Italian master Mariotti defeated one of the world's strongest players, Svetozar Gligorich, with 9 P-KR3!?)

But Morphy intuitively thought that 9 N-B3 must be the right move because it added an additional piece to the attack and tempted Black into 9 . . . N-B3?; 10 P-K5!, PxP; 11 B-R3!, with a virulent attack. Another Morphy brilliancy (versus Schulten, New York, 1857) began with 9 . . . B-N5; 10 B-QN5, BxN?!; 11 PxB, K-B1; 12 B-K3, QN-K2; 13 K-R1, and White eventually had a strong attack on the knight file.

One of the clearest demonstrations of the novelty of Morphy's use of development was a casual game with Jules Arnous de Riviere, a frequent punching bag for Morphy who nevertheless was strong enough to lose narrowly to Mikhail Tchigorin in an 1883 match. The game, played in Paris in 1858 during Morphy's first tour of the French capital, went as follows:

9	**N-B3**	**Q-B3?**

A stupendously naive move. It is hard to believe that this attempt to attack the queen pawn was made by one of the stronger players of Morphy's day.

10	**N-Q5**	**Q-N3?**

Pride, not chess ability, prevents him from returning the queen to Q1. From here on Morphy does nothing but attack the queen and make threats.

11	**N-B4**	**Q-B3**
12	**P-K5!**	**PxP**
13	**PxP**	**Q-B4**
14	**P-K6!**	**P-B3**

To keep the file closed (14 . . . PxP; 15 NxP, BxN; 16 BxB, QxB?; 17 R-K1).

15	**N-R4**	**Q-B4**
16	**B-K3!**	**Q-KN4**

Not 16 . . . QxKB; 17 Q-R5ch, with a fast mate. Now 17 N(B)-N6 would fail to 17 . . . BxB.

17	**N-B3!**	**Q-QR4**
18	**BxB**	**QxB**
19	**N-Q5**	**Q-R4**
20	**N-Q2**	**. . .**

Threatening one more attack, 21 N-N3.

20	**. . .**	**N-Q5**
21	**N-N3!**	**NxN**
22	**PxN**	**Q-B4**
23	**Q-R5ch!**	**K-Q1**

Anything else mates or loses the queen to 24 NxKBPch.

24	**QR-Q1!**	**Resigns**

Black, who has made ten of his last fifteen moves with one clumsy piece, will collapse with one discovered check.

To repeat, it is hard to assess how strong Morphy really was. Bobby Fischer more than a hundred years later said Morphy could beat anyone today (excluding Fischer, of course) if given the right preparation. Certainly in his own time the Louisianan was king. After winning the New York tournament he played a short match with Stanley, the unofficial U.S. champion. Morphy won four of the first five games and Stanley conceded the match. He received odds of pawn and move!

Two years later during his European tour Morphy gave an exhibition against five of the strongest players of the era: Thomas Barnes, Henry Edward Bird, Loewenthal, Stanley Boden, and de Riviere. There was no time limit and so it took most of a day. Morphy won two games, drew two, and lost only one. An astonishing performance.

Morphy had left for England in June 1858 with the hopes of wresting the title of chess supremacy from the Europeans. His fans weren't disappointed. He was clearly the best in the better British clubs, even though Howard Staunton, the imperious former world champion, refused Morphy's challenges. Morphy had to be content by beating everyone else. First there was Loewenthal, much improved since 1849. But Morphy won easily, 9-3 with two draws. He then gave pawn and move odds to one of the leading Englishmen, Rev. John Owen, and won with five wins and two draws in a short match.

After crossing the Channel in the fall, Morphy trounced Daniel Harrwitz. Harrwitz was the main attraction at the Cafe de la Regence, the famous Parisian center for intellectuals and chess fanatics. Among its customers over the years were Voltaire, Rousseau, Benjamin Franklin, Napoleon, Robespierre, and Philidor. Morphy lost the first two games and then won three in a row. Harrwitz began to plead illness, although on one occasion his supporters found him offering gambits at the Cafe when he had reported sickness to Morphy. Morphy eventually won 5-2 with one draw. In these matches Morphy's play was often strikingly modern.

MATCH, London, 1858

	MORPHY	J. LOEWENTHAL
1	**P-K4**	**P-K4**
2	**N-KB3**	**N-QB3**
3	**B-N5**	**. . .**

"That disgusting arrangement, the Ruy Lopez" is how Morphy's traveling companion, Frederick Milne Edge, termed this opening in contrast to the rollicking Evans Gambit. The move 3 . . . P-QR3, incidentally, was popularized by Morphy and later established as the main line by Steinitz.

3	**. . .**	**P-QR3**
4	**B-R4**	**N-B3**
5	**P-Q4**	**PxP**
6	**P-K5**	**. . .**

Morphy's choice is not particularly dangerous, and Black can equalize quickly after this. More popular these days is the variation 6 0-0, B-K2; 7 R-K1, P-QN4; 8 P-K5, NxP; 9 RxN, P-Q3! (not 9 . . . PxB; 10 NxP, and 11 N-B5); 10 R-K1!, PxB; 11 NxP, B-Q2; 12 Q-B3!, as played by the young Hungarian masters of today.

6	**. . .**	**N-K5**
7	**0-0**	**N-B4**
8	**BxN**	**QPxB**
9	**NxP**	**N-K3**
10	**NxN**	**BxN**

Black has the dynamic equality that occurs often in variations of the Lopez in which White gives up his bishop. Black has a doubled pawn formation and therefore his queenside majority is not as valuable as White's kingside majority. But he also has the two bishops. To make progress in this position White must contain Black's minor pieces and mobilize his majority.

11	**Q-K2**	**B-QB4?**

Wrong on two counts. First, Black could play the far superior 11 . . . Q-Q5!, threatening 12 . . . B-KN5 or 12 . . . B-B5. White may be forced into an uncomfortable endgame in which the bishops are too strong. The second criticism of 11 . . . B-QB4 is that it encourages a trade of bishops after B-K3.

12	**N-B3**	**Q-K2**

Probably intending . . . 0-0-0. But 12 . . . 0-0; 13 N-K4, B-K2; 14 B-K3, P-QN3; 15 QR-Q1, Q-B1 was much better.

13	**N-K4**	**P-R3**
14	**B-K3!**	. . .

A very fine idea. In the bishops-of-opposite-color middle game that follows 14 NxB, Black finds it easier to blockade the White pawn majority on white squares. Morphy sees that his knight is more valuable than his queen bishop to further his plan.

14	. . .	**BxB**
15	**QxB**	**B-B4**

On 15 . . . 0-0 (not 15 . . . 0-0-0; 16 Q-R7!); 16 P-KB4, B-B4; 17 N-N3!, BxP; 18 P-B5, QR-K1; 19 QR-K1, White has a very strong attack. Morphy now plays an elegant pawn sacrifice that gives him decisive control of the open files.

16	**N-N3!**	**BxP**
17	**P-B4**	**P-KN3**

Otherwise 18 P-B5 is crushing.

18	**P-K6!**	**B-B4**

The threat was 19 Q-QB3. If 18 . . . 0-0 White forces . . . B-B4 by playing 19 R-B2!

19	**NxB**	**PxN**
20	**PxPch**	**KxP**
21	**Q-KR3**	**Q-B3**
22	**QR-K1**	**KR-K1**
23	**R-K5!**	. . .

Since Black cannot play 23 . . . RxR because it opens up the bishop file, White will win control of the king file. In the resulting heavy piece ending Black is virtually in *zugzwang* because of the dominance of White's pieces and the weakness of the Black king. The extra Black pawn is meaningless.

23	. . .	K-N3
24	KR-K1	RxR
25	RxR	R-Q1
26	Q-N3ch	K-R2
27	P-KR3!	. . .

A pleasing move that is both useful in providing *luft* for the king and in forcing Black to find a move in a difficult position.

For example, 27 . . . R-Q4 leads to a virtual *zugzwang* after 28 R-K8!, Q-N2 (28 . . . Q-N3??; 29 R-K7ch); 29 Q-K3!, R-Q2; 30 Q-K6, R-B2; 31 P-QN4!; and now 31 . . . Q-N3?; 32 R-R8ch or 31 . . . R-B3; 32 Q-K5, R-B2; 33 QxQch, KxQ; 34 R-QN8 should win. Note also that 28 . . . Q-B2 instead of 28 . . . Q-N2 is very similar after 29 Q-K3, R-Q2; 30 Q-K5!

27	. . .	R-Q2
28	Q-K3	P-N3

Having been prevented from 28 . . . R-K2, Black bides his time.

29	K-R2	P-B4
30	Q-K2	Q-N3

A typical Loewenthal trap: 31 QxP??, R-Q7.

31	R-K6!	Q-N2
32	Q-R5	R-Q4

No better was 32 . . . R-B2; 33 RxPch. Several annotators have said that now, on 33 . . . Q-B1, White wins with 34 P-KN4, but one suspects that 34 Q-N6ch and 35 R-K8 is more effective.

33	P-QN3	P-N4
34	RxP	R-Q3

Desperation. After 34 . . . P-N5; 35 R-K6, he runs out of moves.

35	**QxBPch**	**Q-N3**
36	**QxQch**	**KxQ**
37	**R-R5**	**R-N3**

On 37 . . . P-B3 White wins with 38 P-KN4!, followed by P-QR4. The rest of the game was a good example of Morphy's endgame technique: 38 P-KN4!, P-B3; 39 K-N3, P-R4?; 40 R-R7, PxP; 41 PxP, K-B3; 42 P-B5, K-K4; 43 R-K7ch, K-Q3; 44 P-B6, R-N1; 45 P-N5, R-KB1; 46 K-B4, P-B5; 47 PxP, PxP; 48 K-B5, P-B6; 49 R-K3, Resigns. Ruthlessly following a plan throughout—the cultivation of the mobile majority.

This showed that Morphy was not just the brilliant combinational master that his fans thought he was. He was, in Reti's words, the first positional player. He laid down principles for the obtaining of advantages—a relatively new idea. This was especially true in open positions. "Another of Morphy's perceptions," wrote Reti, "which becomes clear in a large number of his games, is that superior development increases in value, in proportion as the game is more open." Morphy ridiculed closed positions—he played 3 PxP in the French Defense to avoid a closed center—and it was the task of Steinitz to take Morphy's scientific approach and adopt it by laying down principles for closed games.

It should be no secret, considering this and what we've seen from the Paulsen-Morphy game, that Morphy was exceptionally good at opening lines. Consider this game against Stanley Boden (Black) in a casual 1858 game at one of the London clubs. After obtaining a sizable opening advantage because of Boden's miscues (1 P-K4, P-K4; 2 N-KB3, N-QB3; 3 P-Q4, PxP; 4 B-QB4, B-B4; 5 0-0, P-Q3; 6 P-B3, N-B3?; 7 PxP, B-N3; 8 N-B3, 0-0; 9 P-Q5, N-QR4?; 10 B-Q3, P-B4), Morphy examined weaknesses on both sides of the board (11 B-KN5!, P-KR3; 12 B-R4, B-N5; 13 P-KR3, B-R4?!; 14 P-KN4!, B-N3; 15 Q-Q2, R-K1; 16 QR-K1, B-B2; 17 N-QN5!?, K-R2 [better 17 . . . B-N1 so that 18 BxN, QxB; 19 QxN, QxN]) and took aim at the kingside (18 BxN, PxB; 19 NxB, QxN; 20 Q-B3!, Q-Q1; 21 N-R4, P-N3; 22 P-B4!, K-N2).

Many of Morphy's competitors wouldn't have wasted a second's thought before playing 23 P-B5 further embarrasing the bishop. But Morphy is thinking about bigger game.

23   **NxB!!**   . . .

The point of this fine move is based on the realization that Black's weakest spot is KN6. This may be hard to see from the diagramed position but consider how quickly White will mobilize an attack on that square after B-N1 or B-B2 in coordination with Q-Q3 and P-K5. Black's remaining pieces have no method of controlling events on KN6.

We often see Morphy sacrificing material advantages to gain decisive attacks, but here he is sacrificing *positional* advantages, for example, correcting Black's doubled pawns and giving up a good knight for a bad bishop.

23   . . .   **PxN**
24   **P-K5!**   **QR-B1**

Black dare not open up the lines by exchanges: 24 . . . QPxP; 25 PxP, QxP; 26 B-K4, or 25 . . . PxP; 26 RxP, RxR; 27 QxRch. Black's king has no place to hide on the kingside because . . . K-R2 will allow R-B7ch in many cases.

25   **B-N1!**   **K-B2**

And here the threat of 26 Q-Q3 or Q-B2 is unstoppable. For example, 25 . . . Q-K2; 26 Q-B2, Q-KB2; 27 P-K6 distracts the defender. Just as bad is 25 . . . QPxP; 26 PxP, QxP; 27 PxPch, K-B2; 28 BxPch!, KxB; 29 Q-B2ch.

26   **P-K6ch**   **K-N2**
27   **Q-Q3**   **P-B4**
28   **PxP**   **Q-B3**

Black allows White a crushing phalanx of pawns because 28 . . . PxP; 29 QxP, Q-B3; 30 Q-R7ch, K-B1 hangs a rook to 31 P-K7ch, RxP; 32 RxR, QxR; 33 Q-R8ch.

29   **PxP**   **QxQNP**
30   **P-B5**   **. . .**

And since 30 . . . R-B1; 31 P-K7, or 30 . . . R-K2; 31 P-B6ch is unpalatable, Boden played 30 . . . Q-B3; 31 P-K7!, P-B5; 32 Q-KN3, P-B6; 33 R-K6, Q-Q5ch; 34 Q-B2, QxP; 35 P-B6ch, and then Resigned in face of 35 . . . K-R1; 36 P-N7ch, K-N1; 37 P-B7ch.

The climax of Morphy's European travel was his match with Anderssen, the winner of the famous "Evergreen" and "Immortal" games.* They agreed to a thirteen-game match with nothing at stake but honor. Morphy was prickly about any suspicion that he played chess for money. He refused to play Ignatz Kolisch, who later became a millionaire and a baron, because Morphy refused to play for money and Kolisch refused to play for fun. In fact, according to Edge, on his arrival in England Morphy had disdained offers from English well-wishers

* In the age of the Romantics, two games were hailed as the most beautiful ever played. Anderssen's 23-move victory over Kieseritzky at a London club in 1851 was acclaimed "The Immortal Game" because of its many sacrifices, including the offer of two rooks and a queen. Two years later against J. Dufresne in Berlin, Anderssen played a spectacular five-move mating combination which began with the most innocent of moves but finished with a flurry of sacrifices. It was immediately dubbed "The Evergreen Game" because, contemporaries said, its beauty would shine forever.

to finance his expedition because he didn't want to be considered a professional. When the match was concluded, 7-2 with two draws in Morphy's favor, one of Anderssen's supporters asked why he wasn't playing as brilliantly as he had against Dufresne and Kieseritzky. The amiable Anderssen explained that Morphy simply wouldn't let him.

This is the key point of brilliancy. Immortal combinations do not take place unless one of the players makes several mistakes. When two more or less evenly matched players meet there will probably not be sparkling combinations if they play up to their level. Only Anderssen approached Morphy in ability and that is why their match was so devoid of brilliancy. Often Morphy played the uncharacteristic role of the positional defender, as in the following.

MATCH, Paris, 1858

	ANDERSSEN	MORPHY
1	**P-K4**	**P-K4**
2	**N-KB3**	**N-QB3**
3	**B-N5**	**P-QR3**
4	**B-R4**	**N-B3**
5	**P-Q3**	. . .

A characteristic difference between Morphy on one side and the Anderssen imitators and Steinitz students on the other was the preference to keep the center closed in the early stages. As we've seen, Morphy never failed to play the more active variations, such as 5 P-Q4. Speaking of the "period of close games," which he said extended from about 1843 to some time after 1851, Morphy wrote, "It was an epoch of uninteresting games and dreary analytical labours, and . . . afforded but comparatively few specimens of brilliant play."

5	. . .	**B-B4**
6	**P-B3**	**P-QN4**

7	B-B2	P-Q4
8	PxP?!	. . .

Black's development has been natural and free, whereas White has deliberately chosen a somewhat constricted course. Nevertheless, Steinitz took on such positions regularly and scored great victories (for example, versus Lasker, match, 1894: 1 P-K4, P-K4; 2 N-KB3, N-QB3; 3 B-N5, N-B3; 4 P-Q3, P-Q3; 5 P-B3, B-Q2; 6 B-R4!?, P-KN3; 7 QN-Q2, B-N2; 8 N-B4, 0-0; 9 N-K3, N-K2; 10 B-N3, P-B3; 11 P-KR4!, Q-B2; 12 N-N5, P-Q4; 13 P-B3, QR-Q1; 14 P-KN4, and won with a fierce attack). The difference, however, is that Steinitz understood that he could maneuver the White pieces for extensive periods without risk as long as he held firm in the center. But 8 PxP?! surrenders the strong point.

8	. . .	NxP
9	P-KR3	. . .

This has a place in the opening, when White plans P-Q4 and wants to avoid . . . B-KN5. Here it could be neglected in favor of, need we say it, development.

9	. . .	0-0
10	0-0	P-KR3?

An inexact move that allows 11 NxP!, NxN; 12 P-Q4, freeing White's game: 12 . . . B-Q3; 13 PxN, BxKP; 14 P-KB4!, B-B3; 15 Q-Q3!; or 12 . . . Q-R5; 13 PxN!, B-K3; 14 N-Q2 and 15 N-B3. Black wanted to anticipate N-KN5 and Q-R5 or P-Q4. Best was 10 . . . B-N3.

11	P-Q4?!	PxP
12	PxP	B-N3
13	N-B3	N(4)-N5
14	B-N1	. . .

In a sense, Anderssen has been very consistent. He placed his bishop at QB2 at move 7, when almost every other player would automatically play 7 B-N3. But now this bishop enjoys a fine attacking line. White also threatens to embarrass Black's knights with 15 P-Q5 and 16 P-QR3.

The fly in the ointment would appear to be White's queen pawn. It is the most obvious weakness. But Anderssen has set several of the traps that had made him the unofficial champion. On 14 . . . BxQP, White plays 15 N-K2!, followed by 16 P-QR3 and 17 Q-B2, winning a piece. Also 14 . . . NxQP; 15 NxN, QxN is dubious because of 16 Q-B3, B-K3; 17 P-QR3, N-Q4; 18 R-Q1.

The best method is 14 . . . NxQP; 15 NxN, BxN!; 16 Q-B3, B-K3; 17 B-K4 P-QB3; (Maroczy offers a long variation beginning with 17 Q-K4, R-K1; 18 R-Q1, P-QB4; 19 Q-R7ch, K-B1; 20 B-K3, Q-B3, and ending in Black's favor. 17 B-K4, R-N1; 18 R-Q1, Q-B3; 19 B-KB4 is also complex.) 18 B-KB4 with complex chances not unwelcome to Anderssen.

14   . . .   **B-K3!**

Morphy plays the simplest move, stopping P-Q5 and reinforcing the Nimzovichian blockade on Q4 twenty-eight years before Nimzovich was born.

15   **P-R3**   **N-Q4**
16   **B-K3**   . . .

This was Anderssen's improvement on 16 N-K2 (threatening 17 Q-B2), N-B3; 17 B-K3, R-K1; 18 N-N3, B-B5!, after which Black had a superior position in the second match game. Here in the fourth game he protects his queen pawn so that 17 NxP, PxN; 18 Q-B2 is threatened.

16   . . .   **N-B3!**

A very thoughtful regrouping that would elude many players today. Morphy seeks a more dynamic blockade on Q4. He brings his knight back to defend the kingside and places a bishop on Q4, where it threatens to win the *isolani*.

17   **Q-Q2**   **R-K1**

At the same time Black must anticipate threats such as 18 BxP, PxB; 19 QxP, which would be met here by 19 . . . NxP!; 20 N-N5, N-B4.

18   **R-Q1**   **B-Q4**

Again, Morphy has a more aggressive idea in 18 . . . N-QR4, threatening 19 . . . N-N6 and 19 . . . N-B5. But this would allow the 19 BxP sacrifice. White's pressure in promoting P-Q5 should not be discounted. Consider 18 . . . B-N6; 19 R-QB1, B-Q4 (to drive the rook off Q1); 20 NxB, QxN; 21 B-R2, Q-Q3; 22 RxN, QxR; 23 N-K5!, as given by Sergeant.

19   **N-K5**   . . .

Another little trap that Sergeant suggests Morphy did not accept because he had a simpler line of play and didn't want to waste energy over the dangerous 19 . . . NxN; 20 PxN, RxP. The defense given was 21 BxB, PxB; 22 B-R2, Q-K1; but Reti offers 23 NxB, NxN; 24 P-B4 and wins.

19   . . .   **Q-Q3**
20   **Q-B2**   . . .

Once more threatening the Black queen knight indirectly (21 NxB and 22 NxN). The move is firmly handled by Morphy who now can accept the offered pawn with impunity. But White's position has already reached a difficult stage. He is denied 20 BxP, PxB; 21 QxP because of 21 . . . NxN; 22 PxN, BxPch!; 23 K-R1, RxP; or 22 NxB, QxN; 23 QxN, BxP. On the more conservative 21 NxB, KNxN; 22 NxN, QxN; 23 Q-Q3, White has play but Black need not fear the advance of the queen pawn: for example, 23 . . . N-B3; 24 P-Q5, Q-Q3; 25 BxB, QxB; 26 P-Q6, QR-Q1.

20	. . .	NxP!
21	BxN	BxB
22	NxB	. . .

Black doesn't have to fear 22 N-N4, P-B3!; 23 NxNch, QxN; 24 Q-R7ch, K-B1; 25 Q-R8ch, K-K2; 26 NxBch, PxN; 27 R-K1ch, K-Q3; 28 RxR because of 28 . . . QxPch, with a familiar mating attack. The last Anderssen trap was 22 NxB so that if 22 . . . QxN(Q4); 23 N-B6, R-K5; 24 RxB, RxR; 25 N-K7ch, grabbing the queen.

22	. . .	QxN(K4)
23	NxNch	QxN
24	Q-R7ch	K-B1

And there was no more of the feared Anderssen attack after 25 B-K4, QR-Q1; 26 K-R1, BxNP; 27 QR-N1, RxRch; 28

RxR, QxP; 29 Q-R8ch, K-K2. The endgame was misplayed on both sides but Morphy's pawns scored eventually.

Like Fischer, Capablanca, and every super-grandmaster who followed him, Morphy was called a chessplaying "machine" by his awed contemporaries. "It is no use struggling against him," Anderssen said in defeat. "He is like a piece of machinery which is sure to come to a certain conclusion."

And yet on December 28, 1858, when Anderssen conceded the match, the machine was making his last serious test. The following spring Morphy played an informal match against the president of the London Chess Club, Augustus Mongredien. He allowed one draw in eight games. On his return to New York Morphy took on James Thompson, the New York restauranteer who was considered so qualified that he was invited to the First American Congress. Morphy offered odds of *knight* and won the series 5-3 with one draw.

But by the time Morphy made his next Atlantic voyage, the Civil War had erupted. After a long series of offhand games with de Riviere, Morphy returned to New Orleans and his law practice in 1863. He continued to play occasionally with his old friend Charles Amedee Maurian but insisted on giving him odds. Zukertort and Steinitz came to visit him in the 1880s but Morphy refused to talk chess with them. His chess career was over. We have no recorded Morphy games after 1869.

What happened to Paul Charles Morphy after his great European successes has been the subject of novelists, psychologists, biographers, and, of course, chessplayers. No one knows for certain. When presented with a fabulous gold and silver chess set and an ebony and mother-of-pearl board on his return in May 1859, Morphy reacted strangely. He said he felt insulted to be characterized as a professional chessplayer. "Chess has never been and can never be aught but a recreation," Morphy declared. But it was only in this recreation that he excelled. In the period after Appomattox Morphy began to develop feelings of persecution. He was certain he was going to be poisoned or that someone would set fire to his clothing.

He began a lawsuit against his brother-in-law, the executor of his father's will, claiming that he was being cheated of Alonzo Morphy's estate. The case was apparently unjustifiable on any legal grounds, although Morphy spent years acquiring "evidence" before it was thrown out of court.

By this time the mere mention of chess would drive him into a frenzy. What was wrong? One theory suggests that his mind was crushed by the inability to dethrone Staunton from the world championship. This is rather speculative, considering that Anderssen was regarded as the best player in the world from the London 1851 tournament until the arrival of Morphy. Another theory is that his decline dated from the time a Louisiana woman turned down his proposal of marriage because he was "a mere chessplayer." Perhaps it was that his preparation to become a prominent lawyer like his father was blunted by his chess success. Clients couldn't take his law practice seriously and only thought of him as an erratic genius. Perhaps Morphy would have overcome his mental troubles at any other time in American history except during the chaos of antebellum New Orleans. Who knows?

It came to an end on July 10, 1884, when Morphy took a long walk and then relaxed afterward in a cold bath. His mother found him dead of an apparent "brain congestion." Only a few relatives attended the funeral the following day.

2. THE MORPHY EXCITEMENT

♛ *Morphy's brilliant achievements in Europe attracted such attention to chess in this country that . . . a perfect furore for the game set in, and it continued until chess became thoroughly naturalized among us.*

An unknown chess historian quoted in H. E. Bird's The Chess Openings *(1880)*

Captain Mackenzie

So powerfully did chess take hold of the public imagination in the post–Civil War era that we have this paradox: the game made its greatest strides *after* Morphy retired. Chess clubs sprouted everywhere. In New York before 1855 only one club could maintain a healthy membership. By 1880 there were five in Manhattan alone. The city began to replace Philadelphia as the nation's chess capital. The Manhattan Chess Club was opened in 1877 and nine years later was the local sponsor of the Steinitz-Zukertort match, the first competition that was recognized as a World Championship.

Chess literature also multiplied overnight. The first American chess magazine, *The Chess Palladium*, was founded in 1846 under the editorship of Napoleon Marache—loser in a famous Morphy brilliancy—but lasted only a few months. Yet even after *Fiske's Chess Monthly* stopped publication in 1861, state and regional periodicals popped up all over. Before Morphy there had been only ten chess columns appearing in newspapers in North America, including one Cuban and three Canadian papers. In the final issue of *Chess Monthly* Fiske listed eighty-seven regular columns.

Ironically, it was a European immigrant who assumed Morphy's crown. George Henry Mackenzie was indeed a remarkable figure. Born in Scotland in 1837, he tried a business career in France and served in Ireland, India, and the Cape of Good Hope as an ensign in the King's 60th Rifles. Professional soldier was the calling he chose, and so in 1861 Mackenzie resigned his commission and sailed for America. He signed on as a private in the federal army and had risen to captain by the time of his discharge in 1864.

Captain Mackenzie, as he was known for the rest of his life, had played with moderate success in Europe's minor-league tournaments. He won a first prize in a handicap tournament in London in 1861 by successfully accepting pawn-and-move odds from Anderssen. Before emigrating, Mackenzie had defeated the leading British amateur, Rev. G. A. MacDonell, in a match.

In New York the captain assumed a new profession, chess-player, which proved very successful. He won the strong New York Chess Club championship four years in a row and then registered his biggest successes at the Second American Chess Congress in Cleveland in 1871, at the Third Congress in Chicago in 1874, and at the Fifth Congress in New York in 1880. Only at the Fourth Congress (Philadelphia, 1876) was he nosed out, and then by another British immigrant, James Mason of Ireland.

As the strongest pretender to Morphy's crown, Mackenzie was financed to a series of European tournaments. He was almost always a high placer, although he took first only at Frankfurt 1887. In matches he defeated Bird and Blackburne and drew with Amos Burn.

Tall, handsome, with a distinguished Van Dyke beard, Mackenzie dominated American chess until his death from pneumonia at the Cooper Union Hotel in 1891. His last career was his most successful one, but it wasn't enough. Like Steinitz who died as a charity case on Wards Island nine years later, Mackenzie passed away in poverty.

Mackenzie was a vigorous attacker without any pretensions of positional depth. The following game could easily be mistaken for a Morphy masterpiece.

PARIS, 1887

	MACKENZIE	MASON
1	**P-K4**	**P-K3**
2	**P-Q4**	**P-Q4**
3	**N-QB3**	**N-KB3**
4	**PxP**	**. . .**

A la Morphy. In the 1860s the Exchange Variation often worked well because during this early period rapid development of Black's pieces was not a recognized principle. Even in the 1880s the center exchange was thought of as a simple, solid bid for initiative rather than the deadly road to tedious symmetry that it is known as today.

Remember that the openings were relatively uncharted in Europe, let alone the primitive United States. Steinitz was experimenting with 2 P-K5 in the French Defense at this time. And Bird, in an opening text published after his American tour in 1877, recommended 2 B-N5?!, P-QR3; 3 B-R4, P-QN4; 4 B-N3, P-QB4; 5 P-Q3, P-Q4; 6 P-QR4, P-B5; 7 B-R2, with "the sounder game" for White!

4	**. . .**	**PxP**
5	**N-B3**	**B-Q3**
6	**B-Q3**	**0-0**
7	**0-0**	**N-B3**

Black could play 7 . . . P-B3 with a more solid center, but after 8 N-K5, QN-Q2; 9 B-KB4, Q-B2; 10 R-K1, R-K1; 11 Q-K2 he has no way of continuing the pressure against White's outpost knight. Usually symmetry is a bad policy for Black, but here 7 . . . N-B3 is perfectly safe. 7 . . . P-KR3 also suggests itself.

8	**B-KN5**	**N-K2??**

A horrible move that allows Black's kingside to be perforated without compensation. On 8 . . . B-KN5; 9 NxP, NxP; 10 BxN, BxN; 11 BxPch, Black's symmetrical policy fails; but he can do much better with 9 . . . BxPch; 10 KxB, QxN. Even the passive 8 . . . B-K3 was far superior to 8 . . . N-K2.

9	**BxN**	**PxB**
10	**N-KR4!**	**K-N2**
11	**Q-R5**	**. . .**

White has the makings of a murderous attack because of the speed with which his pieces hop to the kingside. Mason, who later returned to live in England and write chess books, delays . . . N-N3 because he fears N-B5 or, even better, B-B5, followed by BxB and N-B5.

11	**. . .**	**R-R1**
12	**P-B4**	**P-B3**
13	**R-B3**	**N-N3**
14	**QR-KB1**	**Q-B2**

Black has an impotently passive position. The addition of one more attacking piece—that is, the only one not now participating—will crack the kingside open.

15	**N-K2!**	**B-Q2**
16	**N-N3**	**QR-KN1**

The threat was 17 N(4)-B5ch, BxN; 18 NxBch, K-R1; 19 Q-R6ch, K-K1; 20 Q-N7, winning a pawn. But it wasn't the only idea, as Mackenzie demonstrates in one of the prettiest mates of American chess annals.

17	**Q-R6ch!!**	**KxQ**
18	**N(4)-B5ch**	**BxN**
19	**NxBch**	**K-R4**
20	**P-N4ch**	**. . .**

The fancy way compared with the direct 20 R-R3ch, K-N5; 21 N-R6 mate, or 20 . . . N-R5; 21 RxNch, K-N3; 22 R-R6 mate.

20	**. . .**	**KxP**
21	**R-N3ch**	**K-R4**
22	**B-K2 mate**	

Mackenzie reveled in king hunts. Lacking the subtle sense of positional balance that Morphy alone exercised in the previous generation, Mackenzie just went for the opposing king. The following memorable quickie was played against Morphy's old punching bag, James Thompson (White): 1 P-K4, P-K4; 2 P-KB4, PxP; 3 N-KB3, P-KN4; 4 P-Q4, P-N5; 5 N-K5?, Q-R5ch; 6 K-Q2?, Q-B7ch; 7 K-B3, N-QB3; 8 P-QR3, P-Q3; 9 NxN, PxN; 10 B-Q3, R-N1; 11 R-B1, and now Black mated elegantly with 11 . . . QxQPch!; 12 KxQ, B-N2ch; 13 P-K5, BxPch; 14 K-K4, N-B3.

When forced to play defensive chess, Mackenzie played combinational defensive chess. Amos Burn (White) exerted too much energy in the opening of their meeting at Frankfurt 1887: 1 P-Q4, P-K3; 2 P-QB4, P-Q4; 3 N-QB3, N-KB3; 4 B-B4, B-Q3; 5 B-N3, P-QN3; 6 P-K3, B-N2; 7 N-B3, 0-0;

8 R-B1, P-QR3; 9 PxP, PxP; 10 B-Q3, R-K1; 11 B-R4, QN-Q2; 12 N-KN5?!, N-B1; 13 Q-B3, N-N3; 14 BxN?, RPxB; 15 N-R3, B-K2; 16 BxN, BxB; 17 0-0.

Burn apparently intended to use his two knights against Black's central pawns with 17 N-B4 but noticed that it would drop a pawn immediately. Mackenzie reacted correctly.

17   . . .   **P-KN4!!**

Not simply to prevent the knight's entrance into the game via KB4, but to prepare an attack on the king rook file with . . . P-N3 and . . . K-N2. With two bishops and a mobile queenside Black has excellent winning chances.

18	**K-R1**	**R-QB1**
19	**N-KN1**	**P-N3**
20	**N(1)-K2**	**K-N2**
21	**Q-N3**	**Q-K2**
22	**R-B2**	**P-B4!**

Intending to pressure the bishop file, to force White into QPxP, which gives Black strong mobile pawns, and perhaps to offer a queen trade with . . . Q-B2. Black holds all trumps in the ending, as Burn becomes too optimistic about the bishop file.

23	KR-B1	PxP
24	QNxP?	. . .

White had to recapture with a pawn so that he only has a bad game after 24 . . . R-B5; 25 P-KR3 (*luft*, not 25 P-N3, RxP), KR-QB1.

24	. . .	RxR!
25	NxQ	QRxN!

The White knight is trapped and Black will win two pieces and a rook for his sacrificed queen. The vulnerable haven of White's king seals Burn's fate.

The game continued 26 P-KR4, RxN; 27 RPxP, B-K4; 28 Q-R4, PxP; 29 P-B3 (29 PxP, RxKNP; 30 Q-R6ch, K-N1 is a faster loss), R-Q7; 30 R-K1, P-K7; 31 P-B4, BxNP; 32 P-B5, PxP; 33 P-N6, R-Q8!, and White resigned after a few futile checks.

Sam Loyd and the American Chess Problem

When Morphy, the unrivaled American champion, was annotating games for Fiske's *Chess Monthly*, the boy wonder was neither the youngest nor most imaginative contributor. The problems editor was a sixteen-year-old New Yorker whose reputation as a problemist would rival Morphy's as a competitive chessplayer.

Sam Loyd was an authentic American genius who at various times was a plumbing contractor, the owner of a chain of music stores, a newspaper columnist, an associate of P. T. Barnum, and a chess problemist and tournament player; he was best known as "The Puzzle King." Loyd modified an Oriental board game and gave America Parcheesi. He devised the world-famous "14-15" puzzle in which one tries to shift small numbered tiles around a square board so that they fall in numerical order. Loyd's mathematical puzzles were internationally renowned.

Born in Philadelphia of "wealthy but honest parents" in 1841, Loyd was the youngest of eight children. Two of his brothers also turned out to be occasional problemists. Although he only first started to play chess regularly with his brothers in 1855, Loyd exploded into problem composition during the next two years. Loyd created delightful mates and other chessboard tasks for more than fifty years until his death in 1911.

The formulating of problems, much more than competitive chess, can be defined in terms of distinctive styles. National "schools" of problem composition are easily detected, with one nation's problemists hailed for their originality, another for their difficulty of solution, and another for their economy of pieces and intricacy of theme. The American school is generally defined as having two main attributes: neatness of theme and uniqueness, surprise, or humor.

Later these attributes would be developed by Eugene B. Cook, a Loyd contemporary, by William A. Shinkman, and Otto Wurzburg. But it was Loyd who starred in the formulation of the humorous American style of problem. Loyd would offer mates in half a move that required the completion of castling or of en passant capture. Or they called on the solver to retract a move and force mate. Or there was an intriguing story concerning the problem. For example, try the following two problems.

In the first, the classic Excelsior Theme—a mate in five moves—the reader is asked to guess before attempting a solution which of the White pieces delivers the final coup. The second problem was set in the war camp of King Charles XII of Sweden during the Battle of Bender. One day in 1713, while playing with his minister, a Turkish bullet zipped through the king's tent and smashed the White knight just after King Charles (White) had announced mate in three. Before the minister could search for the other knight, Charles said proudly that he didn't need it. It was a mate in four even then. And instantly a second bullet pierced through the night and smashed the pawn at KR2. Another pause by the king, who thereupon astounded his opponent by announcing another mate, this time in five moves. This three-part problem was enjoyed widely. In fact, in 1900 a German problemist found an additional wrinkle. If the first bullet had smashed the rook instead of the knight, Charles would still be able to force mate—in six! (Solutions are on pp. 290-91.)

As a player, Loyd was never a threat to Mackenzie or his successors. This didn't stop him from claiming that problemists would defeat tournament competitors in a large match. To prove this, Loyd challenged Eugene Delmar, then one of the best players in the country, to a match and lost miserably, 5-1 with two draws.

Search for a Champion

Mackenzie's death opened up a chaotic period during which no fewer than four men claimed the national championship in a space of eight years. And for the first time there was a championship.

No one questioned the superiority of Morphy or Captain Mackenzie during their day, but neither of them claimed an official title of U.S. Champion. This wasn't as odd as it seems. International chess was still in its infancy and titles were a mere formality that didn't seem necessary at the time. Remember that the first world title match wasn't held until 1886, even though we can name the "best player in the world" at various points over the past five centuries.

American chess was soaring in interest in the 1880s, and the European masters discovered the U.S. chess fever. Steinitz toured the United States in 1882 and Zukertort a year later. Both tried to meet Morphy but were unsatisfied. While the Steinitz-Zukertort match was being held, the leading organizers here decided upon the first international tournament held on American soil. Led by Max Judd of St. Louis, F. M. Teed of Brooklyn, and Sam Loyd, then president of the prestigious New York Chess Club, they arranged for the Sixth American Congress to start in New York in early 1889.

Tchigorin of Russia made the trip, as did Max Weiss of Vienna. The English contingent included John Henry Blackburne, H. E. Bird, and Amos Burn. J. Taubenhaus of Paris and N. Macleod of Canada also were invited. The prize list totaled $5,000, and an expensive tournament book, authored by world champion Steinitz, was commissioned.

No one expected an American would take one of the top prizes and there was little surprise when Tchigorin and Weiss tied for first. But Solomon Lipschutz finished a respectable sixth with victories over Tchigorin, Blackburne, Gunsberg, and James Mason. Lipschutz followed this a year later by winning a strong tournament organized by the new U.S. Chess Association. Thus, he claimed the title of U.S. Champion.

Napier recalled Lipschutz as a "frail little man, with a gentlemanly mien and manners and an extravagantly long, pointed nose—the Cyrano of Chess." He was a methodical attacker with some strikingly good positional ideas—and some terrible ones. Steinitz praised his "excellent and novel idea" in the Ruy Lopez. After 1 P-K4, P-K4; 2 N-KB3, N-QB3; 3 B-N5, P-Q3; 4 BxNch, PxB; 5 P-Q4, Lipschutz played 5 . . . P-B3!, strengthening the center. Obvious today, this was original in 1889.

On the other hand, Lipschutz was capable of positional folly. His game with D. G. Baird from the 1889 tournament went as follows: 1 P-K4, P-K4; 2 N-QB3, B-B4; 3 P-B4, P-Q3; 4 N-B3, N-QB3; 5 N-QR4, B-N3; 6 NxB, RPxN; 7 B-N5, N-B3; 8 P-Q3, Q-K2; 9 0-0, 0-0; 10 BxN??, with absolutely no reason for giving up the two bishops.

Here is an example of Lipschutz' fighting style. Against Taubenhaus' Ruy Lopez, Lipschutz' position with Black is not pleasant.

White now continued.

15	**QR-Q1**	**PxP**
16	**RxKP**	**B-Q3!**

Forced by the threat of 17 RxN and 18 NxP. Now 17 NxB, PxN; 18 RxP? loses to 18 . . . Q-B3. White must avoid . . . Q-B3 here.

17	**R-R5**	**B-QB1**
18	**B-K3**	**R-B3**
19	**N-K4**	**. . .**

19 RxP, RxR; 20 BxR, R-N3; 21 Q-QB4, Q-N4; 22 N-N3 could have been played because 22 . . . P-QB4 is met by 23 QN-K4. Taubenhaus' move encourages Black to set a trap.

19	**. . .**	**R-N3**
20	**Q-B3**	**B-B1!**
21	**Q-R5**	**P-Q4!?**

Tricky but inferior if White could find 22 P-QB4!, Q-K1; 23 N(4)-N3, PxP; 24 N-R4. Objectively, the best was 21 . . . P-Q3.

22	**N-R4?**	**N-B5!!**

A brilliant chance that threatens 23 . . . B-KN5 and completely upsets White's game. White falls apart quickly; for example, 23 Q-B3, QxN; 24 QxN, R-N5!

23	**BxN**	**B-KN5**
24	**R(1)xP**	**. . .**

One last gasp. 24 Q-K5, BxR; 25 B-N5 is handled by 25 . . . Q-K1!; 26 NxR, RPxN; or 25 N-QB3 is met by 25 . . . QxN; 26 NxB, B-Q3.

24	**. . .**	**PxR**
25	**QxQPch**	**QxQ**
26	**RxQ**	**R-QB3**
27	**P-KR3?!**	**. . .**

Better was 27 R-Q7. Black now wins a pawn and the game: 27 . . . B-K3; 28 R-Q2, BxP; 29 P-QN3, B-N8 and White resigned in a few moves.

Before Lipschutz could make his claim stand he was challenged by Jackson Whipps Showalter, the "Kentucky Lion." Showalter was a flamboyant attacker who won his nickname from his Minerva, Kentucky, birthplace and his long mane of red hair. Besides being a consistent tournament player, Showalter was also something of a baseball player. When he died in 1935 at the age of 75, *Chess Review* noted that Showalter was "the first person to pitch a curveball in Kentucky."

Showalter's match challenge led to the first head-to-head U.S. Championship. The Manhattan Chess Club, quickly winning recognition as one of the best clubs in the Western Hemisphere, was the scene of the 1892 confrontation, which ended in an easy Lipschutz victory, 7-1 with seven draws. But Lipschutz left the Eastern chess circles for California in the following year to regain his faltering health. (Incidentally, the *first* great master of the West Coast was none other than Charles Fournier St. Amant, who lost a famous match to Staunton in 1843. St. Amant visited California after the Gold Rush and stayed two years as French consul before returning to Europe.)

With Lipschutz gone, who was U.S. champion? Why, Showalter of course, said Jackson W. Showalter. This claim was quickly disputed by a fellow son of Kentucky, Albert Beauragard Hodges. Hodges was a witty attacker who once conducted Ajeeb, one of the many successors to von Kempelen's Automaton. Hodges moved north, settled in New York's Staten Island, and ran a prosperous business in Brooklyn. A frequent Manhattan Chess Club champion, Hodges outfought Showalter 5-3 with one draw in an 1894 title match. Then, having accomplished what he wanted to do in the world of chess, Hodges retired from competitive play and devoted himself to business.

Naturally Showalter once again claimed the title. To everyone's surprise Lipschutz returned from California to announce that he never abdicated and that Showalter would have to beat him in a match if he wanted the title. This was arranged in 1895 and ended, finally, in a Showalter victory, 7-4 with three draws. Showalter then polished off two more challengers before losing to the man who had taken first place in his first foreign tournament, Hastings in 1895—Harry Nelson Pillsbury.

Showalter was the last of the minor American masters before

the golden age of Pillsbury and Marshall. But he was not a weak player, although never achieving any foreign prizes. In his first match with Pillsbury he scored several fine wins and lost only by a margin of 10-8 with four draws. One of these games is a classic.

MATCH, New York, 1897

	SHOWALTER	PILLSBURY
1	**P-K4**	**P-K4**
2	**N-KB3**	**N-QB3**
3	**B-N5**	**N-B3**
4	**0-0**	**NxP**
5	**P-Q4**	**N-Q3**
6	**B-R4?!**	**. . .**

This was a Showalter specialty but has disappeared from tournament play today. The more common endgame after 6 BxN, QPxB; 7 PxP, N-B4; 8 QxQch, KxQ is fairly level although Bisguier is the only grandmaster to continually play this position with Black nowadays. The more speculative 6 PxP, NxB; 7 P-QR4, P-Q3; 8 P-K6!? is not considered dangerous for Black after 8 . . . PxP; 9 PxN, N-K2; 10 N-B3, N-B4.

6   . . .   **PxP**

In another game Pillsbury played the equalizing 6 . . . P-K5!; 7 R-K1, B-K2; 8 N-K5, 0-0; 9 N-B3, N-B4; 10 B-K3, NxN; 11 PxN, P-Q3, which put 6 B-R4 to sleep.

7   **P-B3!**   **PxP?**

Showalter's gambit is probably best refused with 6 . . . P-K5 or handled by 7 . . . B-K2; 8 PxP, 0-0; 9 P-Q5, N-R4; 10 B-B2, B-B3. Acceptance of the second pawn gives White a fierce initiative.

8   **NxP**   **B-K2**
9   **N-Q5**   **0-0**
10   **R-K1**   . . .

Black's misplaced knight on Q3 will cost Black at least two tempi. Add that to the tempi that White already has won out of the opening and you can say that White's double pawn gambit is sound. Pillsbury's problems are revealed by the simple and direct consolidation 10 . . . R-K1; 11 B-B4, B-B1, which White would answer with 12 Q-Q3!, followed by B-B2 or N-N5.

10   . . .   **B-B3**
11   **B-B4!**   . . .

With 12 NxP threatened, Black has no time for 11 . . . BxP. On 11 . . . R-K1 Showalter could try either 12 NxP, RxRch; 13 NxR; or 12 QBxN, RxRch; 13 QxR, PxB; 14 NxBch. In each case White has excellent compensation.

11   . . .   **N-K1?**

This invites a handsome refutation, typical of the rough-and-ready chess played in Teddy Roosevelt's days. Showalter is in his element and performs well. His recurrent problem in other tournaments and matches was the temptation to launch into unsound attacks. (His game with Weiss from the Sixth American Congress shows his inability to play simple positions with White: 1 P-K4, P-K4; 2 N-KB3, N-QB3; 3 B-N5, N-B3; 4

0-0, B-K2; 5 P-Q3, P-Q3; 6 P-KR3?!, 0-0; 7 N-B3, P-QR3; 8 B-R4, P-R3; 9 N-K2, N-KR2; 10 P-KN4?, and Black had a winning counterattack after 10 . . . P-KR4; 11 N-R2, P-Q4; 12 KPxP?, QxP; 13 B-N3, Q-Q1; 14 P-QB3, B-Q3; 15 N-N3, Q-R5; 16 K-N2, PxP; 17 NxP?, K-R1; 18 P-KB4, P-B4.)

12	**RxN!!**	**QxR**
13	**NxP**	**Q-K5**
14	**B-Q6!**	**R-N1**
15	**B-B2!**	. . .

Driving the queen off the king file and preparing a smashing finale in deep center field.

15	. . .	**Q-KN5**
16	**BxR**	**KxB**
17	**Q-Q6ch**	**B-K2**
18	**R-K1!**	. . .

This forces one final weakness. Black can't move his bishops, his rook, or his knight. And on 18 . . . Q-N5 White wins immediately with 19 RxB! That doesn't leave much.

18	. . .	**P-KN3**
19	**Q-Q2**	**Q-R4**
20	**N-Q5**	**B-Q1**

Or else 21 NxB and 22 Q-Q6 with an easy win. Now Showalter capitalizes on Black's move 18.

21	Q-B3!	P-B3
22	NxP	B-R4

And Showalter announced mate in five beginning with 23 NxQPch, BxN; 24 Q-B6ch, and 25 B-N3ch.

Mackenzie, Lipschutz, Hodges, and Showalter—only one of the pretenders to Morphy's legacy could claim the unofficial rank of grandmaster. They were generally aggressive players whose positional ideas were unformed. Ignorance of the openings was another handicap. Gunsberg answered 1 P-K4 with 1 . . . P-QN3 against four Americans in the Sixth Congress and allowed only one draw. Even Showalter, who was better "booked" than most Americans, was capable of the grotesque: As Black against Weiss he once played 1 P-K4, P-K4; 2 N-KB3, N-QB3; 3 B-N5, B-K2; 4 N-B3, B-KB3?; 5 P-Q3, QN-K2? Still, American chess was undergoing its fastest period of growth during the so-called Morphy Excitement (1860–90).

Before we get to Morphy's true heirs, one last footnote should be added. Pillsbury died in 1906 and Marshall assumed the title on the basis of his fine results (first at Cambridge Springs, Pennsylvania, 1904, for example). The Western Chess Association, which was sponsoring the first Western Opens in the previous decade, and the Brooklyn Chess Club tried to organize a match or tournament to certify Marshall's claim to the title. But by this time (1907) the Great Swindler was playing—and losing badly—to Lasker for the world championship. Two years later Marshall lost a similar lopsided match to Capablanca. Capablanca then claimed the title of U.S. champion!

Marshall charged that the Cuban had no claim because he was not an American citizen. Capablanca's supporters said Marshall was trying to outtalk his rival after being outplayed. While this controversy was going on with both players lining up supporters and publishing broadsides aimed at the other man, another voice was heard from.

Walter Penn Shipley was one of the better amateurs of the day. From his organizing efforts in Pennsylvania and his respected editorship of the *Philadelphia Enquirer* chess column, Shipley held the kind of unofficial dean of American chess position that Hermann Helms would fulfill half a century later.

Shipley studied the claims of both sides in the dispute and soberly evaluated their legal status. His verdict was a minor bombshell. Marshall was not the champ, he said, and neither was Capablanca. The only man who had a legitimate claim to the title was the last one to hold it—Jackson Whipps Showalter. Marshall lost no time in arranging a match with Showalter in Lexington, Kentucky, and disposed of the "Lion" 7-2 with three draws.

3. PILLSBURY, MARSHALL, AND THE SPIRIT OF MORPHY

♛ *There was nothing else I wanted to do. Chess began to absorb my whole life. My head was full of it, from morning to night—and in my dreams as well. Gradually, it crowded out every other interest. I knew that I was going to devote my life to chess.*

Frank Marshall in My Fifty Years of Chess

The greatest tournament of the nineteenth century began on August 5, 1895, at the Brassey Institute in Hastings, England. Unlike its Christmastime successors, the first Hastings was played in the late summer when the breeze off the Channel breaks through the heat of a British afternoon.

Enormous attention was paid to the Hastings event for several reasons. First, it had a roster rich in superstars—one former world champion, the current world champion, and the champions of England, France, Germany, Austria, Russia, and Italy. It was also the first time that the new champion, Emanuel Lasker, 27, would meet in a tournament with the man he dethroned, Wilhelm Steinitz. It was, in fact, Lasker's first major international tournament. Was his match victory just a fluke? Finally, would the new players—Lasker, Tarrasch, Janowski—outdistance the old masters—Bird, Mason, Blackburne, Tchigorin —some of whom had been Morphy's contemporaries?

But as the rounds mounted in number at the Brassey Institute the hundreds of spectators there and thousands of fans of the chess world who followed the games in print became fascinated with another phenomenon. It all started naturally enough. In the first round Tchigorin, the Czarist representative, offered the young American, Pillsbury, a rook on the ninth move and eventually forced resignation on the fifty-first. Bad luck for the twenty-two-year-old from Somerville, Mass., but after all, the fans said, he was lucky to have been invited in the first place. Then a strange thing began to happen—Pillsbury started to win. And not just win in an ordinary manner. Tchigorin had humbled him with a forceful attack that paralleled Pillsbury's own style. But in the second round Pillsbury mounted a brilliant sustained initiative against Tarrasch, the master of the initiative in semiclosed positions.

After the doctrinaire doctor, Pillsbury trounced Steinitz, the great positional mind, by exploiting the former champion's pawn weaknesses and containing his two bishops. Against Janowski, the champion of two-bishop play, the American obtained the two bishops and won again, this time in fifty-four moves. The tricky tactician Mieses fell to a countersacrifice that scored in twenty-two moves. Clearly, Pillsbury was the tournament sensation. With two rounds to go it seemed sure he would take one of the top three places, although first was unlikely.

But in the semifinal round, August 31, Pillsbury won while both his rivals lost unexpectedly—Lasker to Blackburne and Tchigorin (in sixteen moves!) to Janowski. Leading by a half point, Pillsbury had only to handle Isidor Gunsberg. He did little with the White pieces in the opening and, with his competitors winning, the pressure was on the young American as the following endgame appeared.

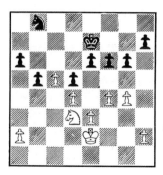

Although White has a protected passed pawn, Black is ready to blockade it with . . . N-B3 and then work for . . . P-K4 or . . . P-QR4. Yet Pillsbury shows the position is a forced win.

27	**P-B5!**	**P-N4**

Black cannot allow White two connected passed pawns, as would happen after 27 . . . KPxP; 28 PxP, PxP; 29 N-B4; or 28 . . . P-N4; 29 N-N4.

28	**N-N4!**	**P-QR4**

This does not stop White's threat but averts immediate loss. Now it becomes a matter of arithmetic.

29	**P-B6!**	**K-Q3**
30	**PxP**	**NxP**

Naturally 29 . . . PxN lost to 30 P-B7, and 30 . . . PxN to 31 P-K7, KxKP; 32 P-B7.

31	**NxN**	**KxN**
32	**P-K4!!**	**. . .**

Finally securing the two connected pawns.

The game continued 32 . . . PxP; 33 P-Q5ch, K-Q3; 34 K-K3, P-N5; 35 KxP, P-R5; 36 K-Q4, and here Black lost quickly with 36 . . . P-R4?; 37 PxP, P-R6; 38 K-B4, P-B4; 39 P-R6, P-B5; 40 P-R7, but was still lost in the beautiful line 36 . . . K-K2!; 37 K-B4, P-N6!; 38 PxP, P-R6; 39 K-B3, P-B4!; 40 PxP, P-R4; 41 P-N4, P-R7; 42 K-N2, P-R8(Q)ch; 43 KxQ, P-N5; 44 P-N5, P-R5; 45 P-N6, P-N6; 46 PxP, PxP; 47 P-Q6ch!!, KxP; 48 P-N7, and White will queen with check and scoop up the Black pawn.

As Gunsberg conceded, Pillsbury established himself as Morphy's successor, the de facto American champion and one of the strongest players in the world.

The next period in American chess lasted, in effect, from that September day in 1895 until March 1924, when the great New York tournament began in the Japanese Room of the Alamac Hotel. This era starred two remarkable individuals who owed their style to Morphy and yet reflected the basic schism that separates modern masters from the pre-Morphy Romantics.

Harry Nelson Pillsbury was the first American to excel in positional play in forty years. He was a dynamic figure whose skill and new ideas changed the tempo of international chess as much as did Lasker or Tarrasch. His games, with their textbook demonstration of the attack on both wings and of dynamic play against static weaknesses, influenced twentieth-century play considerably. Before Pillsbury, for example, the Queen's Gambit was a somewhat stodgy closed opening and the Ruy Lopez was one of several open game openings, not demonstrably better than the King's or Evans Gambit. After Pillsbury the Queen's Gambit Declined was the dominant opening in chess for nearly thirty years. (So much so, that in the Alekhine-Capablanca match of 1927 there were thirty-two Queen's Gambit Declined openings in thirty-four games, and some time later Capablanca feared that concentration on this one opening had caused the ancient game to be played out.) The Ruy Lopez eclipsed all other 1 P-K4, P-K4 openings and became, in Tartakover's words, "The Spanish Torture." We must credit Pillsbury with being the key influence on these changes.

Frank James Marshall was, on the other hand, the ultimate extension of what we call the natural player. He was positionally primitive and frequently was mauled by better-rounded players. (Capablanca, for example, had a career record against

Marshall of 20 wins, 2 losses, and 29 draws.) But Marshall possessed enormous talent and imagination in the clash of pieces. Combinations were his meat and he was as brilliant in this respect as anyone before or after. Again, it was the case of not always being able to obtain the positions that made combinations happen that was his main problem. For both Marshall and Pillsbury, impatience in an inferior or simply constricted position was their worst enemy. Although Pillsbury's early death left Marshall as the leading American until the 1930s, Pillsbury was the true successor of Morphy. Marshall was more in the Anderssen-Kieseritsky tradition.

One of Pillsbury's virtues was his being a student of chess. Born December 5, 1872, he was a comparatively late starter—he learned the game at age sixteen. But during the next five years he devoured everything that was written on the game. He acquired a sound theoretical knowledge of the openings—something that few of his U.S. contemporaries could claim.

Naturally he studied the games of the best European players and, most of all, was influenced by Steinitz. The maneuvering behind closed positions, the preparation of the decisive pawn-break, the cultivation of advantages that explode into quick victories—these lessons that Morphy had not completely understood, Pillsbury absorbed from Steinitz. Here in this encounter from Nuremberg in 1896, where he tied for third with Tarrasch behind Lasker and Maroczy, the world champion may have felt he was playing the old Austrian himself.

NUREMBERG, 1896

	PILLSBURY	EMANUEL LASKER
1	**P-K4**	**P-K3**
2	**P-Q4**	**P-Q4**
3	**N-QB3**	**N-KB3**
4	**P-K5**	. . .

First introduced by Steinitz against Fleissig at Vienna 1873, the key point of this opening is White's sixth move, which seeks to play off of Q4, an ideal outpost. In Anderssen's day 4 P-K5, KN-Q2; 5 QN-K2?!, P-QB4; 6 P-QB3, N-QB3; 7 P-KB4, Q-N3; 8 N-B3 was tried but Steinitz was the first to add the modern positional touch and bring it to life in international chess.

4	. . .	**KN-Q2**
5	**P-B4**	**P-QB4**
6	**PxP!?**	. . .

Today 6 N-B3, N-QB3; 7 B-K3! has proven quite good for White.

6	. . .	**N-QB3**

The main feature of White's system is the use of the Q4 square and other black squares for outposts. For this reason 6 . . . BxP or 6 . . . N-QB3; 7 P-QR3, BxP; 8 Q-N4, 0-0 is considered safe for Black. The followup of the text ignores White's center idea.

7	**P-QR3**	**NxBP?**
8	**P-QN4!**	**N-Q2**
9	**B-Q3**	**P-QR4**

You might say à la Morphy, comparing this with his game with Owen.* Black wins QB4 back for his pieces but has lost time and space on the queenside. The backward White pawn on the bishop file cannot be easily exploited.

10	**P-N5**	**QN-N1**
11	**N-B3**	**N-B4**
12	**B-K3**	**QN-Q2**
13	**0-0**	**P-KN3**

* In Owen-Morphy, London, 1858, Black introduced the idea with 1 P-Q4, P-K3; 2 P-QB4, P-Q4; 3 P-K3, N-KB3; 4 N-KB3, P-B4; 5 N-B3, N-B3; 6 P-QR3, B-Q3; 7 PxBP, BxBP; 8 P-QN4, B-Q3; 9 PxP, PxP; 10 B-K2, 0-0; 11 0-0, and now 11 . . . P-QR4!

To stop 14 P-B5. White has a considerable edge in time and space, which he may convert into more tangible advantages with the breaks P-QB4 and P-KB5 (after P-KN4), with proper preparation.

14	**N-K2!**	**B-K2**
15	**Q-K1**	**N-N3**

Black is experiencing great difficulties completing his development. Sergeant and Watts recommend 14 . . . B-N2, but after 15 Q-K1 and 16 Q-B2 or 16 Q-N3 or even B-B2-KR4, White is comfortably better. The bishop on K2 would support 15 . . . NxB; 16 PxN, N-B4 in the current position, but again White has a beautiful game after 17 Q-B3.

16	**KN-Q4**	**B-Q2**
17	**Q-B2**	**N(3)-R5?**

One provocation too many. 17 . . . R-QB1 met the threatened 18 NxP with more economy. If then 18 N-N3, Black can play 18 . . . N(3)-R5 with safer prospects.

18	**QR-N1**	**P-R4**

For better or worse Black had to try 18 . . . 0-0; 19 P-N4, P-B4. Now the roof caves in.

19	**P-N6!**	**NxB**
20	**PxN**	**BxP**

White intended 21 P-B5!, NPxP; 22 Q-N3 anyway. What follows is a combination that could have run to a mate at move 39!

21	**P-B5!**	**NPxP**
22	**N-B4**	**P-R5**

To stop 23 Q-N3. White might also play 23 NxBP, PxN; 24 NxP here, but he has a nicer point.

23	**R-R1**	**B-K2**
24	**RxN!**	**BxR**
25	**QNxKP!!**	**PxN**
26	**NxKP**	**. . .**

At this point Lasker surrendered the queen with 26 . . . B-Q2; 27 NxQ, RxN, but after 28 B-B5, R-QB1; 29 BxB, KxB; 30 Q-K3, R-B3; 31 Q-N5ch, K-B2; 32 R-B1, RxRch; 33 QxR, he was quite lost and eventually conceded at move 50.

The main line of Pillsbury's combination was 26 . . . Q-B1; 27 QxBP, Q-B3 (27 . . . R-KN1; 28 N-B7ch, K-Q1; 29 P-K6!, B-QB3; 30 Q-B7, and either 30 . . . R-B1; 31 QxR!, BxQ; 32 RxBch, or 30 . . . R-K1; 31 Q-N7, followed by 32 R-B7 and 33 RxB!); 28 B-N5!, QxPch; 29 P-Q4, Q-N5; 30 Q-B7ch, K-Q2; 31 BxB, QxB; 32 N-B5ch, K-Q1; 33 NxPch, K-Q2; 34 N-B5ch, K-Q1; 35 QxPch, K-B2; 36 Q-N7ch, K-Q1; 37 QxRch, K-B2; 38 Q-N7ch, K-Q1; 39 Q-N8 mate!

Before the Hastings invitation Pillsbury had made little impression on the chess world. In 1892 he began a match with John Barry of Boston (who later lost a U.S. championship match to Showalter) by losing the first four games and then suddenly winning the next five games and the match. A few mediocre results in New York tournaments preceded his first trip to Europe.

When he returned, Pillsbury was the man of the hour. For

the first time since the Morphy days, newspapers printed chess news on the front page. At a banquet at the Pouch Gallery in Brooklyn, the twenty-two-year-old was given an engraved gold watch. The banquet menus showed positions from the Hastings games with Tarrasch and Gunsberg on their covers. On the inside there were diagrams of his queen sacrifice against Janowski. Dessert was flavored ice in the form of chess pieces served on paper chessboards.

Hardly a month passed before Pillsbury was back in Europe for a grand four-man tournament with Lasker, Tchigorin, and Steinitz. Already the handsome young New Englander who smoked those awful, heavy, black cigars was considered one of the four best players in the world.

The St. Petersburg match was something of a disappointment to his fans, who had expected one tremendous success to cap the first at Hastings. He won the minimatch of six games with Lasker 3½-2½ but managed only two draws with Steinitz and had to settle for third place. Thus began a series of fifteen tournaments in which Pillsbury was always a high placer but never again solely in first place. Only in the final two years of his life, when overtaken by disease, did Pillsbury finish out of the money and glory.

In 1897 Showalter approached Pillsbury and challenged him to a match—an odd situation considering that Showalter was the U.S. Champion. "I was not seeking the match," Pillsbury said, "and even if I should win I shall leave Showalter in possession of the title. I am not in search of any title but one."

But that title was elusive. During the five-year period in which Pillsbury was as good as anyone else (1895–1900) world champion Lasker was busy studying mathematics and playing only in occasional tournaments. He didn't return to major events and championship matches until 1907, a year after Pillsbury's death. Yet Pillsbury's lifetime record against Lasker was 7-7, and one wonders what would have happened had the two men met under the kind of championship procedures that are now mandated by the world chess federation, FIDE.

The strong points in Pillsbury's chess were his combinative flair, his great originality in planning, plus talent in execution. Richard Reti would later characterize him as the forerunner of "Americanism in chess . . . free from all plodding depth of thought . . . simple in theme" but refreshing in execution of bold plans.

None of Morphy's immediate successors could, for example, appreciate how to win the position that Pillsbury achieved against Tarrasch during a short match after the 1898 Vienna tournament. The opening moves were as follows: 1 P-K4, P-K4; 2 N-KB3, N-QB3; 3 B-N5, N-B3; 4 0-0, NxP; 5 P-Q4, B-K2; 6 Q-K2, N-Q3; 7 BxN, NPxB; 8 PxP, N-N2; 9 N-B3, 0-0; 10 R-K1, N-B4; 11 N-Q4, N-K3; 12 B-K3, NxN; 13 BxN, P-Q4??.

The right move, 13 . . . P-QB4!, begins the so-called Rio de Janeiro variation, with 14 B-K3, P-Q4; 15 PxP e.p. (15 N-R4, P-Q5), BxP!; 16 N-K4 (or 16 Q-R5 or 16 QR-Q1), B-N2!, with equal play because of the open lines for the two bishops. What Tarrasch has just done, however, is to allow his queen-side pawns to be fixed and to concede control of his QB4 and Q5 squares.

14	**N-R4!**	**B-N5**

Black maneuvers his bishop to QN3 so that he can put his queen on K2 and have pressure along the king file and on his QB4.

15	**P-QB3**	**B-R4**
16	**Q-R5!**	. . .

A superb move that is not easily understood. Although White has a strong advantage, if not a bind, on the queenside, he cannot crack through Black's defenses on that side of the board. Black's queen rook pawn is easily defended and his bishop pawns cannot be attacked. But the bind gives White a free hand to attack on the kingside, which has been weakened by the removal of the black-squared bishop. How does he protect his KN2 after White brings a rook to KN3?

16	. . .	**B-N3**
17	**R-K3**	**B-K3**
18	**R-N3**	**K-R1**

This solves the first problem without further weakening, but White has one more attacking piece and Black has no more defensive pieces that can swing into action.

19	**QR-Q1!**	**Q-K2**
20	**P-N4**	. . .

He must stop 20 . . . P-QB4. But now to raise counterplay with . . . P-QR4 or with . . . P-B3, Black must exchange bishops, accentuating the bind.

20	. . .	**BxB**
21	**RxB**	**P-B3?**

Black has an ingenious defense here but it is not 21 . . . P-KR3 because of 22 R-R4, B-B4; 23 RxP!, QxR (23 . . . KxR is mate in two); 24 QxQ, KxR; 25 Q-B6ch. The right idea is 21 . . . P-R4!; 22 R-R4, B-B4, so that 23 QxB, QxR; 24 R-R3, P-N3. And if 23 R(3)-R3!, Black plays Marco's suggestion of 23 . . . P-N4!!, after which White has nothing better than 24 QxPch!, BxQ; 25 RxBch, K-N1; 26 R-R8ch, K-N2; 27 R(8)-R7ch, K-N1 (not 27 . . . K-N3; 28 R(7)-R6ch, K-B4??; 29 R-B3ch, KxP; 30 R-K3ch); 28 R-R8ch, Draw.

22	**N-B5!**	**PxP**
23	**QxP**	**Q-B3!**
24	**QxQ**	**RxQ**
25	**R-K3**	**. . .**

White has a considerable superiority in the ending, especially without rooks. White then gets his king to QB5 or K5 and wins any way he wants. Black avoids 25 . . . R-K1 for the very reason that it makes an exchange of one pair of rooks inevitable.

25	**. . .**	**B-N1**
26	**P-B3**	**P-N3**
27	**R-K7**	**R-B2**
28	**R-K6!**	**P-QR4**

Black is helpless after 28 . . . K-N2; 29 RxBP, R-K1; 30 K-B2.

29	**P-QR4!**	**. . .**

Adding one more advantage to those of White. He has the good knight versus the bad bishop, the more active rooks, the better king position, and finally the outside passed pawn. The rest is easy.

29	**. . .**	**K-N2**
30	**RxBP**	**R-K2**

31	**K-B2**	**PxP**
32	**PxP**	**B-B2**
33	**P-N5**	. . .

And Black resigned after 33 . . . R-QN1; 34 N-R6, R-N2; 35 N-N4, R-R2; 36 R-R6!, RxR; 37 NxR, K-B3; 38 R-Q2, P-B3; 39 P-N6, B-K3; 40 N-B5, B-B1; 41 P-R5.

Thus, in Reti's phrase, Pillsbury adapted the "practical results of the Steinitz theories" but not the plodding. In exploiting weaknesses he was magnificent. "Not content with storing up small advantages, he always finds the right methods for destroying his opponent's position root and branch," Reti said.

It was the same ability to manipulate events on both sides of the board that made the Pillsbury Attack in the Queen's Gambit so influential. First, examine this gamelet against the great annotator.

PARIS, 1900

	PILLSBURY	MARCO
1	**P-Q4**	**P-Q4**
2	**P-QB4**	**P-K3**
3	**N-QB3**	**N-KB3**
4	**B-N5!**	**B-K2**
5	**P-K3**	**0-0**
6	**N-B3**	**P-QN3**

An inaccurate move that should be prepared for with 6 . . . P-KR3; 7 B-R4, and then 7 . . . P-QN3, as played by Tartakover. But this finesse took some time to seep in.

7	**B-Q3**	. . .

Usually Pillsbury didn't allow Black a chance to win the tempo with 7 . . . PxP and played 7 PxP immediately.

7	. . .	B-N2?!
8	PxP	PxP
9	N-K5	. . .

This was the trademark of the Pillsbury Attack, but Marshall's 9 BxN!, BxB; 10 P-KR4 was even better. His game with Burn from this tournament went 10 . . . P-N3 (10 . . . P-QB4!?); 11 P-R5, R-K1; 12 PxP, RPxP; 13 Q-B2, B-N2?; 14 BxP!, PxB; 15 QxP, N-Q2; 16 N-KN5, Q-B3; 17 R-R8ch!, Resigns.

9	. . .	QN-Q2
10	P-B4	P-B4

Twice at Cambridge Springs, 1904, Pillsbury, playing Fox, faced the better 10 . . . N-K5! and played 11 BxB, QxB; 12 BxN!, PxB; 13 0-0, P-KB4; 14 Q-N3ch, K-R1; 15 QR-B1, N-B3; 16 KR-Q1. Fox got into a mess with 16 . . . QR-B1?; 17 N-N5!, B-Q4; 18 Q-R4, P-QR4; 19 N-R7!, R-R1; 20 N(7)-B6, but Barry equalized with 16 . . . P-B3!; 17 N-K2?!, QR-B1; 18 K-R1, N-Q4; 19 P-QR3, R-QB2.

11	0-0	P-B5?

Although this is an error, it was a logical one. It was taken for granted before Pillsbury's appearance on the chess scene that Black's queenside majority was more valuable than White's kingside play. Maroczy, Janowski, and, of course, Tarrasch all tried it against Pillsbury and were unpleasantly surprised.

12	B-B2	P-QR3
13	Q-B3!	P-N4
14	Q-R3	P-N3
15	P-B5	P-N5?

Black has made logical moves and no obvious positional errors. Yet he is already quite lost. It was games like this, called "Pillsburials," that put the Queen's Gambit on the map.

16	PxP	RPxP

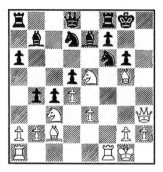

17	**Q-R4!**	**PxN**
18	**NxN**	**QxN**
19	**RxN!**	**P-R4**

To get the rook to QR3 where it anticipates 20 QR-KB1 and 21 BxNP. Or does it?

20	**QR-KB1**	**R-R3**
21	**BxP!!**	**PxB**
22	**RxRch**	**BxR**

And White announced mate in six moves, beginning with 23 RxBch, KxR; 24 Q-R8ch, K-B2; 25 Q-R7ch.

But the Queen's Gambit Declined was not a one-idea opening in Pillsbury's hands. Consider his game with Janowski (Black), Vienna, 1898, the following position of which would have been reached from the above game if White had played 9 R-QB1 and Black responded with 9 . . . QN-Q2:

10	**0-0**	**P-B4**
11	**Q-K2**	**P-B5?!**
12	**B-N1**	**P-QR3**
13	**N-K5**	**P-N4**
14	**P-B4**	**P-R3**
15	**B-R4**	**R-K1**
16	**R-B3**	**. . .**

Intending to continue 17 R-R3 and P-KN4-5. Black's response is natural, and bad.

16	. . .	N-K5
17	BxB	QxB
18	BxN!	PxB
19	R-N3	. . .

With a clear advantage because Black must answer the threat of 20 Q-N4. On 19 . . . NxN; 20 BPxN, Black has several kingside weaknesses.

19	. . .	N-B3
20	P-QR4!	P-N5
21	N-Q1	. . .

And White has quickly shifted his attention to the queenside, where the win of a pawn is inevitable. Janowski sacrificed it with 21 . . . P-B6, but after 22 PxP, PxP; 23 RxP, KR-QB1; 24 N-N4, NxN; 25 QxN, he didn't have enough counterplay and lost in forty-five moves.

Against Pillsbury at Budapest, 1896, Maroczy (Black) played normal opening moves as follows: 1 P-Q4, P-K3; 2 P-QB4, P-Q4; 3 N-QB3, N-KB3; 4 B-N5, B-K2; 5 P-K3, 0-0; 6 N-B3, P-QN3; 7 R-B1, B-N2; 8 PxP, PxP; 9 BxN, BxB; 10 B-Q3, N-Q2; 11 0-0, P-B4; 12 B-N1, P-B5?, only to discover that 13 N-Q2! threatened to win a pawn with 14 QNxP, BxN; 15 Q-R5, or 14 Q-B3 and 15 KNxP. Maroczy tried 13 . . . R-B1, but 14 QNxP, BxP; 15 PxB, BxN; 16 BxPch, KxB; 17 Q-R5ch,

K-N1; 18 QxB, N-B3; 19 QxQ left Pillsbury with an elementary endgame win. There were more than a few tricks to the Queen's Gambit.

Two more examples are especially significant, and the reader may also examine Pillsbury's wins over Wolf at Monte Carlo in 1903, over Gottschall at Munich in 1900, and over Burn at Hastings in 1895.

The most brilliant example of the Pillsbury Attack in the hands of its namesake was the meeting with Tarrasch (Black) at Hastings. After a typical opening (1 P-Q4, P-Q4; 2 P-QB4, P-K3; 3 N-QB3, N-KB3; 4 B-N5, B-K2; 5 N-B3, QN-Q2; 6 R-B1, 0-0; 7 P-K3, P-QN3; 8 PxP, PxP; 9 B-Q3, B-N2; 10 0-0, P-B4; 11 R-K1?!, P-B5?; 12 B-N1, P-QR3; 13 N-K5, P-N4; 14 P-B4, R-K1; 15 Q-B3, N-B1; 16 N-K2, N-K5; 17 BxB, RxB; 18 BxN!, PxB), the following position was reached.

19	**Q-N3!**	**P-B3**
20	**N-N4**	**K-R1**
21	**P-B5!**	. . .

Setting up the tension that continues through the next twenty-five moves. White has surrendered a major share of the board but has certain tangible values. Most of all, he has the kingside attack and the chance for P-KN4-5, which is his main attacking theme.

21	. . .	Q-Q2
22	R-B1	R-Q1
23	R-B4	Q-Q3
24	Q-R4!	R(1)-K1
25	N-B3?	. . .

While Black has been aimlessly shifting heavy pieces, White was preparing the assault that should have begun with 25 N-B2! and if 25 . . . B-Q4 then 26 P-KN4, P-R3; 27 Q-N3, P-N5; 28 P-KR4, N-R2; 29 N-R3. The text move encourages Black into his correct middlegame plan—the mobilization of the queenside.

25	. . .	B-Q4
26	N-B2	Q-B3
27	R-B1	P-N5!
28	N-K2	Q-R5

Black apparently is running riot on the queenside with 29 . . . QxP and 29 . . . Q-B7.

| 29 | N-N4! | N-Q2 |

White had 30 NxP, PxN; 31 QxBPch, R-N2; 32 R-N4 in answer to 29 . . . QxP.

| 30 | R(4)-B2! | K-N1 |

So Pillsbury survives the queenside crisis. Black would rue 30 . . . QxP; 31 N-B4, B-B2; 32 N-N6ch, BxN; 33 PxB, P-R3; 34 NxRP!!, PxN; 35 QxRPch, K-N1; 36 R-B5!, or 34 RxP!, NxR; 35 RxN!, PxR; 36 QxRPch.

31	N-B1	P-B6
32	P-QN3	Q-B3
33	P-KR3!	P-QR4!
34	N-R2	P-R5
35	P-N4	PxP
36	PxP	R-R1?

A major miscalculation. Black assumes that he need not stop
P-N5. On 36 . . . P-R3, however, 37 Q-N3, N-B1!; 38 P-R4,
N-R2 Black is more secure.

37	**P-N5!**	**R-R6**
38	**N-N4**	**BxP?**

If Black has spent so much energy to win this pawn he
should recognize the dangers and play 38 . . . RxP!. It is the
advantage of the connected passed pawns that should win for
Black if White's attack sputters. The sacrifice of the Exchange
preserves an important defense piece, which is missing now.
Pillsbury follows with a series of hammerblows.

39	**R-KN2!**	**K-R1**
40	**PxP**	**PxP**

40 . . . NxP; 41 N-K5, Q-K1; 42 N-N6ch wins.

41	**NxB**	**RxN**
42	**N-R6!**	**R-N2**
43	**RxR**	**KxR**
44	**Q-N3ch!!**	**KxN**

The rook hangs on 44 . . . K-B1; 45 Q-N8ch. Now follows the
prettiest move of the game.

45	**K-R1!**	**. . .**

Black has no defense to 46 R-KN1! The rest of the game was of no consequence: 45 . . . Q-Q4; 46 R-KN1, QxBP; 47 Q-R4ch, Q-R4; 48 Q-B4ch, Q-N4; 49 RxQ, PxR; 50 Q-Q6ch, K-R4; 51 QxN, P-B7; 52 QxP mate.

The other game of note illustrates something unique about the Pillsbury-Marshall era. American masters now prepared variations in advance, sometimes years in advance. Marshall waited ten years to spring his countergambit in the Ruy Lopez against Capablanca—and, as we'll see, still lost. Pillsbury, too, had his midnight oil.

At St. Petersburg, 1896, Lasker scored one of his more brilliant successes by evading the Pillsbury Attack and playing into Tarrasch's line, as follows: 1 P-Q4, P-Q4; 2 P-QB4, P-K3; 3 N-QB3, N-KB3; 4 N-B3, P-B4; 5 B-N5, BPxP; 6 QxP, N-B3.

The game continued 7 Q-R4, B-K2; 8 0-0-0?!, Q-R4; 9 P-K3, B-Q2; 10 K-N1, P-KR3!; 11 PxP, PxP; 12 N-Q4, 0-0!; 13 BxN, BxB; 14 Q-R5, NxN; 15 PxN, B-K3; 16 P-B4, QR-B1; 17 P-B5, RxN!, with a winning attack. After this game Pillsbury began to analyze the consequences of 7 BxN! with William Ewart Napier, a British-born player who was English Champion in 1904. He played hundreds of offhand games with Pillsbury (and later married his niece). Among those casual games were many devoted to 7 BxN! Finally at Cambridge Springs, Pennsylvania, during the great international tournament of 1904,

Pillsbury had a chance to play 7 BxN! against Emanuel Lasker, nearly nine years after the position had occurred. As Pillsbury told Napier during the game, Lasker played the only defense to 7 BxN! that Napier hadn't tried. The game went as follows:

	7	**BxN!**	**PxB**

Not 7 . . . NxQ; 8 BxQ, N-B7ch; 9 K-Q2, KxB (best); 10 KxN, PxP; 11 R-Q1ch, with advantage.

	8	**Q-R4**	**PxP**

And here 8 . . . P-Q5 confers an edge to White after 9 0-0-0!, P-K4; 10 P-K3, B-QB4; 11 PxP, PxP; 12 N-Q5.

	9	**R-Q1**	**B-Q2**
	10	**P-K3**	**N-K4!?**

A strange move but not unusual for Lasker, who sees that 10 . . . P-B4 (Tarrasch's suggestion) is clearly better for White after 11 Q-R5! There is more sense in 10 . . . B-K2; 11 BxP, Q-B2, but Black still has his problems castling and completing development.

	11	**NxN**	**PxN**
	12	**QxBP**	**Q-N3**

Black seems to have survived an early crisis (no better was 12 Q-R5, Q-B3 and . . . Q-N3 or Q-R3). Black should continue on his next move with 13 . . . B-B3 and 14 . . . Q-N5, aiming for an ending in which he has two bishops and a mobile, albeit doubled, pawn mass.

	13	**B-K2**	**QxNP?**
	14	**0-0**	**R-QB1**
	15	**Q-Q3**	**R-B2**

Black protects his second rank. Compare this with 15 . . . B-B3; 16 N-N5, BxN (16 . . . QxP; 17 N-B7ch!, K-K2; 18 P-B4!, RxN; 19 Q-Q6ch); 17 QxBch, QxQ; 18 BxQch and 19 R-Q7ch.

16	**N-K4**	**B-K2**
17	**N-Q6ch**	**K-B1**

On 17 . . . BxN; 18 QxB, White wins the king pawn because 18 . . . Q-B6, trying to protect everything, fails to 19 B-N5!.

18	**N-B4!**	**Q-N5**

Black has defensive chances on 19 NxP, B-K1; 20 R-B1, Q-Q3. Pillsbury finds a most convincing execution of the attack.

19	**P-B4!!**	**PxP?**

A bad error that makes things easy. 19 . . . P-K5; 20 Q-Q4, P-B3; 21 QxKP is strongly in White's favor, but there is no simple winning plan. The opening of this file does Black in.

20	**Q-Q4!**	**P-B3**

Of course, 20 . . . R-N1 loses a rook to 21 QxBP.

21	**QxBP**	**Q-B4**
22	**N-K5!**	**B-K1**

On 22 . . . B-B1, for example, White wins with 23 Q-R6ch, K-N1; 24 RxP!

23	**N-N4**	**P-B4**
24	**Q-R6ch**	**K-B2**

There also was a reason why 24 . . . K-N1 fails—25 QxKPch, B-B2; 26 N-R6ch, K-N2; 27 QxBch, KxN; 28 RxP and mate in a few.

	25	**B-B4!**	. . .

This in effect ends the game because 25 . . . QxB hangs the queen and 25 . . . B-Q2 allows 26 RxB. There is no defense to BxPch or RxPch.

25	. . .	**R-B3**
26	**RxPch!**	**QxR**
27	**R-KB1**	**QxRch**
28	**KxQ**	**B-Q2**
29	**Q-R5ch!**	**K-N1**
30	**N-K5**	**Resigns**

What was Pillsbury like? He was, by contemporary accounts, a genial, rather modest, unassuming, good-natured young man. In serious games he could play with machine-like concentration. "When Pillsbury sits at the board he has an absolute stony calmness in his face," an observer wrote. "Not a single muscle moves, only now and then will he wink a bit faster, when he feels himself slowly and satisfactorily nearing the goal, so finely calculated and elaborated."

On the other hand, at his spectacular exhibitions of blindfold skill it was a different story. On one occasion he was playing sixteen boards unseen and taking part in a game of whist to keep himself busy between moves. "You see I like duplicate whist about as much as I like chess. It's almost as interesting and far less fatiguing." He lit up a cigar and a table messenger arrived to announce, "Board No. 7, knight to queen's bishop fourth square." Pillsbury scratched a match on the sole of his shoe to relight his cigar, took three puffs, and said, "Pawn to king knight's fifth square. As I was saying, I would almost as soon give up chess and play whist altogether." He was interrupted then by another move, which he replied to in less than ten seconds. "I was going to say that if I ever succeed in winning twenty simultaneous games of chess I shall probably quit and play no more."

In fact, he played twenty-one games simultaneously during the Hanover, 1902, tournament on an off day. His opponents were all budding masters who were playing in lower sections of the event. He allowed his opponents to consult one another and to move the pieces! Yet Pillsbury still managed to win 3, draw 11, and lose only 7 during nearly twelve hours of play. On another occasion he played twelve games of chess and six games of checkers *sans voir*. (He insisted, however, that he be allowed to see the cards of the game of whist he played throughout the exhibition.) He did this on several occasions and would recite afterwards the moves of all the games plus a series of thirty words submitted to him before the play began.

The myth has developed that Pillsbury became mentally imbalanced because of the strain of his blindfold play. The exact nature of the disease that caused apoplexy was never publicly detailed. Some sources claim it was syphilis. Although he played in the Cambridge Spring event in 1904, he failed miserably in Marshall's great success. The Lasker game was the bright spot. A year later he tried to commit suicide by jumping from the fourth floor of a Philadelphia hospital where he was being treated for mental disorders. He spent most of the rest of the year hospitalized or at home with his wife. (He married in January 1901.) An apoplectic seizure followed in early 1906 and he died on June 27, at the age of thirty-three. In a eulogy in his magazine Lasker hailed Pillsbury as "the pathfinder in the thicket of chess theory, gifted with pleasant and loveable traits, a source of pleasure and joy and a teacher for thousands."

Marshall: The Last Romantic

Probably no American champion took more pleasure out of playing chess, as opposed to winning games, than did Frank Marshall. He would rather lose the game than lose the chance for brilliancy. In many ways, other than chess style, Marshall was another Pillsbury. He preferred strong cigars and sharp middlegames and liked to say he hadn't let a day go by since the age of ten without a game of chess. Unlike a Morphy or a Fischer, with their star quality, Marshall had an egalitarian friendliness that immediately established a rapport between him and anyone else who knew the moves.

Marshall was also one of the more psychologically perceptive players. He understood the limitations of his own style and the weaknesses of others. What he couldn't bring himself to do was to change his style to take advantage of his opponents. "As a chess player I suppose I am a little like Jack Dempsey as a fighter. Dempsey used to start slugging at the opening gong and never gave his opponent a chance to get started," Marshall wrote in *My Fifty Years of Chess.* "Sometimes he would meet a fighter who was a good boxer and who went on the defensive. He couldn't hurt Jack but he made him look bad," Marshall went on. "I have been much the same way in chess. I have always liked a wide open game and tried to knock out my opponent with a checkmate as quickly as possible. I subscribe to the old belief that offense is the best defense. However, I always had great difficulty with defensive players. Sometimes they made me 'look bad' too—but I still prefer my own style of chess!"

This was his style at Cambridge Springs, especially in his twenty-third-move mate of Pillsbury. But Marshall had also embarrassed the New Englander four years earlier, at Paris, 1900 (Pillsbury finishing second behind Lasker), in the following game.

PARIS, 1900

	PILLSBURY	MARSHALL
1	**P-K4**	**P-K4**
2	**N-KB3**	**N-KB3**
3	**P-Q4**	**P-Q4?!**

As he said, Marshall liked open games, even if he had to take a gamble to get into one. There is no reason why Black should equalize by trading off center pawns in a symmetrical position so quickly. But this was one of the many typical Marshall lines, such as the Marshall Variation of the French: 1 P-K4, P-K3; 2 P-Q4, P-Q4; 3 N-QB3, P-QB4?!; and now 4 N-B3, N-QB3; 5 B-K3?!, N-B3; 6 KPxP, KPxP; 7 PxP, B-K2; 8 B-K2, 0-0; 9 0-0, R-K1; 10 P-KR3, B-B4, and Black has the unusual pleasure of having sacrificed a pawn for play on the "wrong" side of the French Defense (Mieses-Marshall, Vienna, 1908).

4	**KPxP**	**KPxP**
5	**B-QB4?!**	. . .

Much better is 5 B-N5ch, P-B3; 6 PxP, PxP; 7 B-QB4, clearing away wood in the bishop's diagonal. Also 7 B-K2!, as played by Stein against Bronstein in the 1967 USSR Championship: 7 . . . B-QB4; 8 P-B3, PxP; 9 QxQch, KxQ; 10 NxP, K-K2; 11 0-0, with advantage.

5	. . .	**B-N5ch!**
6	**P-B3**	**Q-K2ch**

Now 7 Q-K2, QxQch; 8 KxQ, PxP; 9 NxP, 0-0 is an excellent ending for Black.

7	**B-K2**	**PxP**
8	**PxP?!**	**B-QB4**
9	**0-0**	**0-0**
10	**P-B4**	**R-K1**
11	**B-Q3**	**B-KN5**

White is evidently playing for a win (8 NxP was sounder) and has sacrificed time for space. Given a chance to breath, Pillsbury can set up a typically grandiose attacking formation with bishops bearing down on the Black kingside from QN2 and Q3. Best here is 12 QN-Q2 (not 12 R-K1, BxN, winning a piece), QN-Q2; 13 B-N2, B-QR6; 14 B-B3.

12	**B-N2**	**N-K5!**
13	**QN-Q2?**	. . .

At this point 13 BxN, QxB; 14 QN-Q2, or 13 N-B3 (13 . . .
BxN; 14 QxB, N-Q7; 15 Q-R3) was necessary to save a fragile
game. This is Marshall's chance. He begins a combination now
that couldn't have been analyzed out to the resignation. But
Black evaluated the position up to the twentieth move and saw
he had no losing chances in the ending. No further coaxing of
Marshall was necessary.

13	. . .	**NxP!**
14	**RxN**	**BxRch**
15	**KxB**	**Q-K6ch**
16	**K-N3**	. . .

Otherwise Black has won the Exchange and a pawn.

16	. . .	**QxB**
17	**KxB**	**R-K7!**

This too is part of the combination. Black threatens 18 . . .
RxPch and cuts the White queen off from defense. Notice how
quickly Black's pieces enter the attack.

18	**K-R3**	**N-Q2!**

More thematic was 18 . . . P-KR4, intending 19 . . . Q-B4ch,
but White ties up his pieces with 19 QxR!, QxQ; 20 R-K1; and
21 R-K8ch, as Marshall pointed out. Now 19 P-N4?, RxN, or
19 N-B1, QxQ loses.

19	**R-B1**	**P-KR4**
20	**Q-B2**	**N-B4!**

Marshall probably had this position in mind when he began the combination at move 13. White cannot exchange queens because after 21 QxQ, NxQ; 22 R-B2, he has 22 . . . P-KN4!!; for example, 23 NxP, N-K8; 24 R-B1, RxN; 25 B-B3, R-Q6ch, or 23 K-N3, P-N5; 24 N-R4, N-K8; 25 R-B1, RxN; 26 B-B3, R-QB7!

21	**P-N3**	**P-KN4!**

Immediately decisive, as White has no defense to 22 . . . P-N5ch. The game concluded as follows:

22	**P-N4**	**RxN**
23	**QxQ**	**RxQ**
24	**R-B3**	**P-B4!**
25	**K-N2**	**BPxP**
26	**NxP**	**R-Q7ch**
Resigns		

Marshall was then twenty-three. A year before, at the same age when Pillsbury made his triumphant debut, Marshall also went to England for his first major tournament. But on arrival in London he was told he wasn't prestigious enough to rate entry into the Masters Tournament. He settled for the minor event, which took place in tandem with the prestige tournament, and won first place ahead of Mieses and Marco. This guaranteed him the reputation, a sort of grandmasters' union card, that gained him invitations to dozens of succeeding tournaments.

Always an erratic player, Marshall was capable of winning the biggest tournament of the year and then losing a lopsided match (8-0 with 7 draws to Lasker for the world championship in 1908, 8-1 with 8 draws to Tarrasch a year later, and 8-1 with 14 draws to Capablanca also in 1909). He could also beat the tournament favorite in one round and lose to a tailender in the next.

Marshall's biggest problem was holding a positional game and restraining his imagination. Against Pillsbury at Buffalo, 1901, for example, he couldn't resist playing as Black 1 P-Q4, P-Q4; 2 N-KB3, P-QB4; 3 P-K3, P-B5?, and conceding a large advantage to White after 4 N-B3, P-B4?! (to stop 5 P-K4); 5 N-K5, N-KB3; 6 P-QN3!, PxP; 7 RPxP.

But although he was not a "complete" player, Marshall was capable of playing the "complete" game. The following game is a good example.

VIENNA, 1903

TCHIGORIN	MARSHALL
1 **P-K4**	**P-K4**
2 **P-KB4**	**PxP**
3 **B-B4**	**P-Q4**

The Bishop's Gambit's heyday was rapidly coming to an end at this time (later to be renewed by Bobby Fischer). The death blow was presumed to be 3 . . . N-KB3, sometimes attributed to Morphy after his victory over Anderssen (4 P-K5?, P-Q4; 5 B-N3, N-K5; 6 N-KB3, B-KN5; 7 0-0, N-QB3, already with an advantage) during a series of six games played while the two masters were waiting for their photograph to be taken in 1858. The point of 3 . . . P-Q4 is to open lines and gain time by later attacking the bishop. 4 PxP, Q-R5ch; 5 K-B1, B-Q3 is fine for Black.

4 **BxP**	**Q-R5ch**
5 **K-B1**	**P-KN4**

Not much better is the modern 5 . . . B-Q3; 6 N-KB3, Q-R4; 7 P-Q4, N-K2; 8 N-B3, P-QB3; 9 B-B4, P-B3; and now 10 P-K5!, PxP; 11 N-K4, B-B2; 12 PxP, with a plus. The point of Tchigorin's next move is to answer 6 . . . PxP with 7 Q-B3 or 7 K-N2?! with a pawn offered for nice open lines.

6	**P-KN3!?**	**Q-R3**
7	**N-QB3?**	. . .

Correct is 7 P-Q4, N-KB3; 8 Q-B3, NxB; 9 PxN, B-Q3; 10 P-B4!, with a central pawn mass and the use of the king file.

7	. . .	**N-KB3**
8	**P-Q4**	**N-B3**
9	**K-N2**	**B-Q2**

A great fighting draw between Tchigorin and Pillsbury from the same tournament went 9 . . . B-KN5; 10 Q-Q3, 0-0-0!; 11 BxN, PxB; 12 P-KR4! (12 Q-R6ch, K-N1; 13 QxP, B-Q2; 14 Q-B4, NxP!; 15 NxN, B-B3!), N-R4!; 13 RPxP, QxP; 14 RxN!, QxR; 15 BxP, Q-R4.

10	**P-KR4**	. . .

White must proceed with this dangerous try or face a laggard development because his best developing moves are restricted (10 N-B3, Q-R6ch, or 10 Q-B3, NxQP, or 10 Q-Q3, 0-0-0!; 11 B-Q2, N-QN5).

10	. . .	**R-KN1**
11	**N-B3**	**NPxP**
12	**N-K2!**	**P-R6ch!**
13	**K-B1**	. . .

One of the remarkably resilient features of the King's Gambit is that even after denuding his kingside of pawn protection, White could have an excellent game from the positional point of view. Given a chance for 14 BxP or 14 NxP, Black's attack will be halted and his queen will be kicked around. Marshall undoubtedly appreciated this when he played 10 . . . R-KN1! and most assuredly intended something like the storm that now breaks. Typically, he could have obtained an even better game without sacrificing: 13 . . . N-KR4!; 14 PxP, R-N7; 15 P-B5, Q-N2; 16 RxP, Q-N5.

13	. . .	**PxP!?!**
14	**BxQ**	**P-N7ch**
15	**K-N1**	**BxB!**

Black's combination is inspired but not particularly deep. He must obtain material equivalent of the queen (16 R-R2, B-K6 mate) because White cannot allow 16 . . . B-K6ch; 17 K-R2, N-N5ch; 18 KxP, N-K4ch!; 19 K-R4, NxNch and mates.

16	**Q-Q3**	**N-KN5**
17	**RxP**	**B-K6ch**
18	**KxP**	**N-B7ch**
19	**R-N3**	**RxRch**
20	**KxR**	**NxQ**
21	**PxN**	. . .

A fairly even endgame is reached by a series of more-or-less forced moves (19 K-R2?, BxR! mates). But White has a chronic problem in the ending because of Black's two bishops. The rest of the game is perhaps more impressive than the first part.

21	. . .	**N-N5!**

Winning the "Two Bees" because 22 BxP, R-N1; 23 B-Q5, NxB; 24 PxN, RxP activates Black's rook too quickly.

22	**R-KB1**	. . .

Marshall notes he had worked out the following variation against 22 R-KR1: 22 . . . NxB!; 23 RxP, K-K2; 24 PxN, R-N1ch; 25 K-R2, B-N5; 26 N(3)-N1, B-B4; 27 R-R5, K-B3, and White is all tied up.

22	. . .	NxB
23	PxN	K-K2
24	N-K5	R-N1ch
25	K-B3	B-R6!

There now followed slow penetration by the Black pieces: 26 R-Q1, B-N4; 27 R-KR1, B-B4; 28 N-N3, B-N3; 29 N-K4, P-KR3; 30 N-B5, P-N3; 31 N-K4, P-KB3!; 32 NxBch, RxN; 33 K-N4, B-K6ch; 34 K-B5, R-N8!; 35 RxR, BxR. Seeing that 36 NxP, BxP; 37 N-N8ch, K-Q3; 38 K-K4, B-N2; 39 P-Q4, P-KR4 puts him at a loss to stop the rook pawn or protect his knight, Tchigorin meets the challenge by forcing Black to occupy Q3 with a pawn.

White played 36 P-Q6ch!!, PxP; 37 NxBP, BxP; 38 N-N8ch, K-Q2; 39 NxP (39 P-N3, P-KR4; 40 K-N5, K-K3!; 41 KxP, B-K6; 42 K-N6, K-Q4; 43 N-K7ch, K-Q5; 44 N-B6ch, KxP; 45 NxP, P-Q4 wins, according to Marshall), BxP; 40 K-K4, K-B3; 41 P-Q4, P-N4; 42 N-B5, P-N5; 43 N-K7ch, K-Q2; 44 N-Q5, P-R4; 45 K-Q3, K-B3; 46 K-B4, B-B8; 47 N-K7ch, K-Q2; 48 N-Q5, K-K3; 49 N-N6, B-Q7; 50 K-Q3, B-B6; 51 K-B4, B-K8; 52 N-Q5, K-B4; 53 N-N6.

On 53 K-Q3 Black would penetrate with his king: 53 . . . K-N5; 54 N-N6, K-B6; 55 N-Q5, P-R5; 56 K-B4, P-N6!, followed by . . . P-R6, or 54 K-B4, K-B6; 55 N-B6, K-K6; 56 N-Q5ch, K-Q7, and . . . K-B7-N7.

53	. . .	**K-K5**
54	**N-B8**	**P-Q4ch**
55	**K-B5**	**P-R5**
56	**N-Q6ch**	**K-Q6!**

Now 57 KxP, P-N6; 58 PxP, P-R6 again wins.

57	**N-N5**	**P-R6!**
	Resigns	

Nothing to stop . . . P-N6! A great Marshall game. His skill in endgames, which are, after all, the stark interplay of pieces, was much greater than players today give him credit for. Tchigorin, by the way, was considered the premier endgame player of his day.

Marshall was born on August 10, 1877, on the West Side of Manhattan but learned chess in Montreal, where his family moved when he was eight. He played in coffeehouses at the age of eleven to find stronger players, graduated to the Montreal Chess Club (winning the championship at seventeen), and then returned to New York, where he took up residence at the Manhattan and Brooklyn Chess Clubs. Twenty years later, when he was an established star and the reigning American champion, Marshall, through the help of wealthy patrons, set up his own "chess divan," which eventually became the Marshall Chess Club. For the succeeding half century the Marshall Chess Club was in the forefront of U.S. chess, being the early breeding ground for such masters as Fine, Evans, and Sherwin.

Marshall made periodic visits to Europe during the years 1900–1903 with minor successes, but his triumph at the Pennsylvania resort, Cambridge Springs, elevated him to grandmaster status. He allowed only four draws (Lasker, Marco,

Tchigorin, and Napier) in the strongest American tournament since 1889. By finishing a point and a half ahead of Lasker, Marshall laid the basis for the championship match three years later. But before that Marshall had also topped the strong fields at Scheveningen, 1905, and Nuremberg, 1906, and had also married.

After the Capablanca match Marshall returned to Europe in 1910 and played constantly until 1914. He began that last year by competing against ten other top players of the day at a tournament sponsored by the St. Petersburg Chess Society. After finishing in a tie for fourth, Marshall and four others advanced to a double-round final section. Although he came in last in this playoff with Capablanca, Lasker, Alekhine, and Tarrasch— three world champions and one who easily might have been— Marshall was dubbed one of the five original Grandmasters of Chess by Czar Nicholas.

But then, after a series of exhibitions in Russia and Germany, Marshall entered the ill-fated Mannheim tournament. Midway through the event war was declared and the foreign masters, including Janowski, a nominal Frenchman, and Alekhine of Russia, were arrested by the Kaiser's troops. Marshall was allowed to head for Holland and escape to neutral America. But in effect this meant the end of international chess for five years; for Marshall, an exile of a full decade. The only major competition he faced before the New York 1924 tournament was a U.S. championship challenge match from Edward Lasker. Out of practice and aided by Lasker's ill health, Marshall defeated the German émigré, 5-4 with 9 draws.

In playing over Marshall games, one gets a tremendous sense of risk. In Pillsbury's games one gets a similar feeling that he is gambling when the position becomes tactical. But that is deceptive. Pillsbury rarely gambled when he could plan. Marshall's play, by definition, involved risks.

Take his game with Amos Burn, a familiar catalyst to Marshall's brilliance, at Ostend, 1907: 1 P-Q4, N-KB3; 2 N-KB3, P-Q3; 3 B-B4, QN-Q2; 4 P-K3, P-KN3; 5 B-Q3, B-N2; 6 QN-Q2, 0-0; 7 P-KR4!?, R-K1.

Black appears ready to push White backward with 8 . . . P-K4. This is especially troublesome to White because then . . . P-K5 will cost a piece. There is only one consistent method of continuing the attack:

8	**P-R5**	**NxP!**

On 8 . . . P-K4 White can play 9 B-KN5, P-KR3; 10 BxN, QxB; 11 QPxP, QPxP; 12 Q-K2, or 9 PxNP, PxB; 10 PxBPch, KxP; 11 N-N5ch, K-B1; 12 NxPch, with interesting chances. Now 9 B-KN5, KN-B3 is harmless to Black.

9	**RxN?!**	**PxR**
10	**BxPch**	**KxB??**

And frequently the gambles paid off. Here 10 . . . K-B1 leaves White without a meaningful followup; for example, 11 N-N5, P-K4; 12 QxP, Q-K2, or even simpler with 11 . . . N-B3 and Black is ahead the Exchange.

But after 10 . . . KxB?? Marshall finished off snappily with 11 N-N5ch, K-N3 (11 . . . K-N1; 12 QxP, N-B1; 13 QxPch, K-R1; 14 0-0-0!); 12 QN-B3, P-K4; 13 N-R4ch, K-B3; 14 N-R7ch, K-K2; 15 N-B5ch, K-K3; 16 NxBch!, K-K2; 17 N-B5ch, K-K3; 18 P-Q5ch, KxN; 19 QxPch, K-K5; 20 0-0-0, and Burn resigned in face of 20 . . . PxB; 21 R-Q4 mate.

This was, in Marshall's term, a "swindle." Today the term is usually used to mean a tactical trick that saves a lost position. Better players are apt to demean swindles, but they continue to be a recurring fact of chess at all levels. (Similar is the popular term, "cheapo," invented by master Karl Burger in the 1950s to mean a cheap threat that is so obvious that your opponent could never miss it—but he usually does.)

Marshall's swindles were notorious and springing them gave him as much pleasure as some of his finest masterpieces. He even published an early collection of his games titled *Marshall's Chess "Swindles."* One of the more respectable examples was this position against H. E. Atkins, a nine-times British Champion. Black (Atkins) had played very effectively in the opening and held a considerable advantage: 1 P-Q4, P-Q4; 2 P-QB4, P-QB3; 3 N-QB3, N-B3; 4 PxP, PxP; 5 B-B4, N-B3; 6 P-K3, P-K3; 7 B-Q3, B-K2; 8 N-B3, 0-0; 9 N-K5?!, NxN; 10 PxN, N-Q2; 11 Q-B2, P-KN3; 12 P-KR4?, N-B4!; 13 P-R5, NxBch; 14 QxN, P-KN4; 15 B-N3, P-B4; 16 PxP e.p., BxP; 17 R-Q1, Q-N3; 18 R-Q2, B-Q2; 19 0-0, QR-B1; 20 R-B1, B-N4; 21 Q-B2, R-B5; 22 Q-N3, Q-B3; 23 R(2)-B2, R-B1; 24 Q-R3, B-R3.

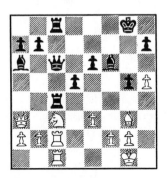

White's premature attack is repulsed and Black is ready for the positional execution beginning with . . . P-N4-5. However, White's last move prepared for an ingenious attempt at swindle:

25   **P-N3!!**   . . .

What makes this move so enjoyable is that years later some of the finest annotators in the world still didn't understand it. Mieses, for example, wrote, "A charming combination. 25 . . . RxN is followed by 26 RxR, BxR; 27 B-K5 and White stands better." But Pachman, who noted White's move as 25 P-N3?, saw that Black must win then with 27 . . . BxB!; 28 RxQ, RxR, because Black has two excellent bishops and a rook for the queen. He also threatens mate and can consolidate with 29 . . . K-B2.

But Marshall, in his game collection, demonstrates the real point behind 25 P-N3!!: 25 . . . RxN; 26 RxR, BxR; 27 RxB!, QxR; 28 Q-K7!, and White, a rook behind, can at least draw because of the threats of B-K5 and QxKPch. For instance, 28 . . . R-B3; 29 P-R6! wins. Black has no better than a draw with 28 . . . R-B1; 29 QxKPch, R-B2; 30 Q-K8ch, R-B1; 31 Q-K6ch, R-B2. In fact, with 27 Q-K7! instead of 27 RxB White can play for a win.

Atkins, perhaps thinking that 25 . . . RxN lost, played:

25	. . .	R-B4?
26	NxP!	RxR
27	RxR	QxR
28	NxBch	K-B2

Otherwise the White queen invades: 28 . . . K-N2; 29 Q-K7ch, K-R3; 30 Q-KB7, Q-Q8ch; 31 K-R2, R-KR1; 32 P-B3! and 33 N-N4 mate.

29	Q-Q6!!	KxN

The key points were 29 . . . Q-B2; 30 N-K4!, and 29 . . . R-B3; 30 Q-Q7ch!, KxN; 31 B-K5ch, K-B4 (31 . . . KxB; 32 Q-Q4ch and 33 P-KN4 mate); 32 P-B3!! Atkins could have made it last longer with 29 . . . Q-B3.

30	B-K5ch	K-B4

Or 30 . . . K-B2; 31 Q-Q7ch, K-B1; 32 B-Q6ch and mates.

                31   **P-B3!**   **Resigns**

The New York in which Marshall lived was just beginning to assume the status of the nation's chess capital. Steinitz had published his *International Chess Magazine* in the city. It folded in 1891 after six years, but in 1904 Lasker began to publish another highly respected journal, *Lasker's Chess Magazine*, in New York. Lasker had the help of Sam Loyd, then in his seventies, Harold M. Phillips, president of the Manhattan Chess Club, and Prof. Isaac L. Rice, a wealthy patron who stumbled upon (actually blundered into) a novel piece sacrifice in the King's Gambit and paid Lasker and several other players a small fortune to analyze the "Rice Gambit."

In December 1923 a group of well-to-do chess fans put in motion the steps that led to one of the strongest tournaments ever held, New York, 1924. The invitees were Emanuel Lasker, Capablanca, Alekhine, Richard Reti of Czechoslovakia, Geza Maroczy of Hungary, the ubiquitous Janowski, Edward Lasker, two strong Russian-born masters, Bogolyubov and Tartakover, and finally many-time British Champion Frederick Dewhurst Yates.

But most of all this was Marshall's reintroduction to big-league chess after ten years. The new postwar theories of Reti, Tartakover, and Nimzovich were revolutionizing the game in Europe with their concentration on attack from the wings. Marshall's *va banque* style was dying out in the growing science of the game. By the end of the next war Marshall was dead and so was Rudolph Spielmann, "The Last Knight of the King's Gambit," and with them the neo-Romantic element of chess.

But when the prizes were handed out on West 72d Street in April 1924, Marshall proved he was still a vital force, finishing in fourth place, behind the three world champions, Lasker of the past, Capablanca of the present, and Alekhine of the near future. And he took home the second brilliancy prize for the following game.

New York, 1924

	MARSHALL	BOGOLYUBOV
1	**P-Q4**	**N-KB3**
2	**N-KB3**	**P-K3**
3	**B-N5**	**P-Q4**

3 . . . P-B4 would constitute the attack of Mexican master Carlos Torre. White may try 4 P-K3, Q-N3; 5 QN-Q2, QxP; 6 B-Q3 in gambit style. A spectacular game from the 1954–55 Rosenwald tournament, Bisguier-Sherwin, went 4 P-K3, Q-N3; 5 N-B3, after which Black considered the old aphorisms about taking the queen knight pawn. Sherwin asked, "Why should I labor under antedeluvian prejudices?" and won after 5 . . . QxP!; 6 N-N5, Q-N5ch; 7 P-B3, Q-R4; 8 N-Q2, P-QR3!!; 9 N-B4, QxN; 10 N-Q6ch, BxN; 11 BxQ, PxB, with a material plus.

4	**P-K3**	**QN-Q2**
5	**P-B4**	**P-B3**
6	**PxP**	**KPxP**

Without much ado the game became a Queen's Gambit Declined and entered into one of Marshall's favorite variations, the Exchange Variation. Experience has shown this to be a most solid and yet resourceful variation for White.

7	**N-B3**	**Q-R4?**

Black confuses this with the variation named after the site of Marshall's greatest success, 6 N-B3, Q-R4, the Cambridge Springs Defense. In the blocked center Black's move is a waste of time and inferior to 7 . . . B-K2; 8 B-Q3, N-K5!, simplifying.

8	**B-Q3**	**N-K5**
9	**Q-B2**	**. . .**

Two rounds later Janowski tried the more Marshall-like 9 0-0 against Bogolyubov, who shied away from 9 . . . NxN; 10 PxN, QxBP; 11 P-K4!, PxP; 12 R-K1, P-KB4; 13 R-QB1, Q-R6; 14 N-R4, N-B3; 15 BxN, PxB; 16 Q-R5ch, K-Q1; 17 B-B4, with excellent play according to Alekhine.

9	. . .	NxB
10	NxN	P-KR3

This drives the knight back to KB3, where it hops to K5. The pawn move also encourages White to rearrange the position of his queen and bishop after Black has castled. Better is 10 . . . N-B3.

11	N-B3	B-K2
12	0-0	0-0
13	P-QR3	Q-Q1

The queen was about to be driven back by P-QN4 (. . . Q-B2 meets NxP). Now White shifts gears. Instead of proceeding with the well-known Minority Attack beginning with P-QN4-5, he directs attention to the kingside. A dubious choice but typical of Marshall.

14	QR-K1?!	P-QR4

Obviously a wasted move, considering White's announced intention to attack on the other flank.

15	Q-K2	N-B3?

White prepared for 16 B-N1 and 17 Q-B2 to force a further hole around the Black king. Bogolyubov anticipates this but surrenders K5 prematurely. The right idea was 15 . . . B-Q3 and 16 . . . R-K1 first.

16	N-K5	B-Q3
17	P-B4	. . .

This attacking formation should be known as Pillsbury's Legacy. Aside from the assault theme that Marshall chooses,

White might also play K-R1 and P-KN4-5. Black's only counter-play is in the center.

17	. . .	**P-B4**
18	**B-N1!**	**B-Q2**
19	**Q-QB2**	**B-B3**

Bogolyubov meets the threatened 20 NxQP and prepares his own attack-squelching . . . N-K5. The Ukrainian was an all-out attacker in the Marshall style. But here he is Black in the kind of game in which *he* won brilliancy prizes as White. Bogolyubov (which translates as God's beloved) was also an almost infuriating optimist. Three years later when the New York organizers wished to repeat their great tournament by inviting Bogolyubov, Capablanca, Marshall, Vidmar, Nimzovich, Alekhine, and Spielmann, he wired back, "Instead of mediocre tournament propose match myself and Capablanca."

| 20 | **PxP!** | **BxP** |
| 21 | **K-R1!** | . . . |

Now 22 P-K4 and 22 N-N4 are threatened; for example, 21 . . . R-B1; 22 N-N4, P-KN3 (22 . . . N-K5; 23 NxN wins a piece); 23 NxPch!, K-N2; 24 NxBP, RxN; 25 QxPch, K-B1, and we have a position in which Marshall and Alekhine agree that Black is not happy but has better chances than in the game.

21	. . .	**R-K1**
22	**P-K4!**	**B-Q5**

Because 22 . . . PxP unleashes White's pieces after 23 NxB, PxN; 24 NxP, NxN; 25 RxN, RxR; 26 QxR, P-N3; 27 P-B5!

23	**NxB**	**PxN**
24	**P-K5**	**N-N5**

Finally this knight defender is driven away and the White queen penetrates. There is still life in Black, however, on play such as 25 Q-R7ch, K-B1; 26 Q-R8ch, K-K2; 27 QxNP, R-KN1. White would sacrifice the Exchange as in the game.

25	**Q-R7ch**	**K-B1**
26	**P-KN3!**	**Q-N3**
27	**B-B5!**	. . .

The major function of this move is to prevent Black's king from escaping to the queenside via Q2. The minor function is to provoke a knight move.

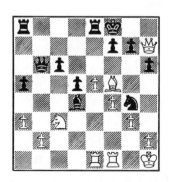

27	. . .	**N-B7ch**
28	**RxN!**	. . .

Of course, 28 K-N2 also wins (28 . . . N-K5; 29 NxN, PxN; 30 Q-R8ch, K-K2; 31 QxNP, QxPch; 32 K-R1), but Marshall is true to his forcing style.

28	. . .	**BxR**
29	**Q-R8ch**	**K-K2**
30	**QxNP!**	**K-Q1**

There is a simple mate after 30 . . . BxR; 31 Q-B6ch, K-B1; 32 QxRPch.

31	**Q-B6ch**	**R-K2**
32	**P-K6!**	. . .

The final touch. Black cannot allow 33 PxP and yet can't play 32 . . . PxP; 33 RxP, or 32 . . . Q-Q5; 33 R-K5.

Bogolyubov played 32 . . . B-Q5 and after 33 PxP!, BxQ; 34 P-B8(Q)ch, K-B2; 35 RxRch, BxR; 36 QxR, K-Q3; 37 Q-R8, Q-Q1, White announced a mate in five: 38 Q-K5ch, K-B4; 39 N-R4ch, K-B5; 40 Q-B3ch, K-N4; 41 B-Q3ch, KxN; 42 Q-B2 mate.

Altogether, Marshall won seven international tournaments without loss of a game. In the 1930s he settled down to managing his club, captaining the world champion U.S. Olympiade team four times and regaling friends with his great stories about the game. The stories included the time the spectators showered the table with gold pieces after a particularly brilliant Marshall win; the time Amos Burn never got a chance to get his pipe going before mate; the time Dus-Chotimirsky told onlookers in broken English, "Poor Marshall dead," only to return, find he had lost a piece, and then toss the pieces back shouting, "Oh, oh, Marshall not dead, I dead."

Marshall resigned the U.S. championship in 1936, after twenty-nine years. There were several strong contenders but no one could finance a match challenge during the early Depression years. Marshall's grand gesture established the series of championship tournaments that have continued until today. Frank J. Marshall died on November 10, 1944, outliving Lasker by two years and Capablanca by one.

4. CAPABLANCA AND THE AGE OF PERFECTIONISM

♛ *I know at sight what a position contains. What could happen? What is going to happen? You figure it out.* I know it!

J. R. Capablanca

The great tournament that opened in New York's Alamac Hotel on March 16, 1924, signaled the end of the Pillsbury-Marshall era. Marshall would play in foreign events into the early 1930s, but by that time there was a whole new crop of Americans—Fine, Reshevsky, Kashdan—proving their worth in Europe. But first there was José Raoul Capablanca.

"Capa" was a Cuban by birth but was easily mistaken for an American, and we consider him an American chessplayer. He learned the moves in his native Havana, where he was born in 1888, a year before the Steinitz-Tchigorin match was held in the Cuban capital. But it was in the United States that Capa grew into one of the world's greatest players. From age seventeen, when he first visited New York before entering Columbia University, to age fifty-four, when he was fatally stricken by a heart attack during a skittles game at the Manhattan Chess Club, Capablanca was identified with American chess.

His ideas are pivotal in the development of the American style. Capablanca arrived on the scene after a century of attacking masters, few of whom understood the positional superstructure of Morphy's brilliancies. Capablanca preceded half a century of essentially positional masters who copied and perfected his technique. Bobby Fischer is the postwar Capablanca.

Like the technicians who came after him, Capa was a realist. He accepted the idea of Pillsbury and Marshall that what mattered most in chess was the practical. He didn't lose himself in the complications of the Europeans, who tried to win the perfect game or complete the unattainable strategic masterpiece. "He is a realist," said Euwe, "who has banished the romantic and the experimental completely." Or as Capa himself explained, "Inclined to simplicity, I always play carefully and try to avoid unnecessary risks. I consider my method to be right," he said, "as any superfluous 'daring' runs counter to the essential character of chess *which is not a gamble but a purely intellectual combat conducted in accordance with exact rules of logic*" (emphasis added).

Capablanca rose above the earlier Americans and repeatedly defeated Marshall because he achieved another kind of perfection—the perfection of a technique. Efficiency was the hallmark of his play. "Americanism is doubtless beginning to penetrate triumphantly into the realms of art," Reti wrote with a tinge of disappointment. "Of course it is a type of charm that we marvel at rather than feel the glow of . . . We have today a worldwide art of efficiency and practicability."

Perhaps Capa's greatest contribution was showing that chess was really an easy game after all. You didn't have to be an eccentric genius like Nimzovich, a doctrinaire classicist like Tarrasch, or a mad attacker like Marshall to beat strong players.

Typical of this attitude was the combination. Capa didn't concentrate on lengthy combinations, which might win or might also lose through miscalculation. There were simpler methods. He used tactics the way an engineer used his implements—sometimes ropes, sometimes pulleys, and sometimes dynamite.

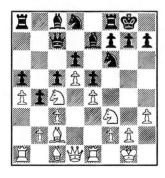

Dr. Milan Vidmar had the Black pieces in this game from the New York, 1927, tournament and has just erred with 15 . . . P-QR4, which allows a minicombination. The natural advantages of White's game (his outpost knight on QB4, aggressive pieces, greater space) permit this.

16	KNxP!	B-R3
17	B-N3	PxN
18	P-Q6	. . .

Regaining the piece, of course, but also opening the bishop's line and procuring an ending in which White is heavily favored.

18	. . .	BxP
19	QxB!	QxQ
20	NxQ	N-N2

Black has several problems with his weak pawns. For example, 20 . . . R-N1 is met by 21 N-N5!, BxN; 22 PxB, RxP; 23 B-QB4, regaining a pawn and obtaining the two bishops in what should then be an easy win.

21	NxN	BxN
22	PxP	BPxP
23	P-B3	KR-Q1
24	B-K3	P-KR3

25	KR-Q1	B-B3
26	QR-B1	B-K1
27	K-B2	RxR
28	RxR	R-B1
29	P-N4!	. . .

With the final winning idea of driving the knight off via P-R4 and P-N5. Black was lost anyway because of his hopeless queen rook pawn. 29 P-N4!, maintaining the pressure, is much better than 29 B-N6, N-Q2; 30 BxP, N-B4, with counterplay.

Vidmar played 29 . . . B-Q2, occupying the knight's good square, and Capablanca won soon, after 30 B-N6, B-K3; 31 BxB, PxB; 32 R-Q8ch!, RxR; 32 BxR.

The opening was important to Capablanca, but it was not something to be studied for hours and hours in preparation for a surprise novelty. In his later years Capa finished out of first place in some tournaments because of his habit of drawing the first few games in each event. By taking quick draws he could study the other games being played and be well armed on all the latest theoretical wrinkles when he started to win in the later rounds.

Rather, Capablanca treated the opening the same way as the hypermoderns: The middle game begins with the first move. It was a matter of timing. He who holds the initiative will probably have the winning chances. Morphy got the initiative by developing his pieces quickly. Many of his successes were due to the inability of his opponents to think of moving anything off the first two ranks except the queen. Remember de Riviere.

But development for the sake of development, Capa said, was wasteful. The pieces you bring out randomly will cost you time later on when you have to redevelop them to better squares. The quicker you find the best squares for the pieces, the better off you are.

Here is one example of this theme, Janowski-Capablanca, New York, 1916.

Black (Capablanca), on the move, seems to have a slight disadvantage. His queenside pawns are weakened because of a . . . Q-N3 trade. Any of the prominent masters of the day might have continued 10 . . . P-K3 to equalize development. But Capa appreciates the situation better. In this position, an ending, time is not as important as piece placement.

10	. . .	**B-Q2!!**
11	**B-K2**	**P-K3!**

Instead of the garden-variety developers, Black has begun his middlegame plan. He intends . . . N-R4, . . . P-QN4, and . . . N-B5, with the beginning of a strong queenside assault. White is completely oblivious to Black's strategy and refuses to play for the draw with 11 B-N5. Note how important the white-squared bishop is to Black's attack and how useless it would be on KB4 in connection with that strategy.

12	**0-0**	**B-Q3**
13	**KR-B1**	**K-K2**
14	**B-B3**	**KR-QB1**
15	**P-QR3?**	**N-R4**
16	**N-Q2**	**P-B4!**

Black enjoys a very strong endgame initiative. His opponent's move 15 not only weakens QN3 but also makes . . . N-B5 powerful. White is stopped from his intended P-K4 by Black's last move. Now that the opening is over, we can see the advantages of correct piece placement. The game continued 17 P-KN3, P-QN4; 18 P-B3, N-B5!; 19 BxN, NPxB; 20 P-K4, K-B2; 21 P-K5, B-K2; 22 P-B4, P-QN4; 23 K-B2, R-R5; 24 K-K3, KR-QR1; 25 QR-N1, P-R3!, signaling an attack on the kingside via . . . P-KN4. The kingside phase proceeded with 26 N-B3, P-N4; 27 N-K1, R-KN1; 28 K-B3, PxP; 29 PxP, R(5)-R1; 30 N-N2, R-N5; 31 R-N1, QR-N1; 32 B-K1.

And here, with all White's material attention directed at the kingside . . .

32	. . .	**P-N5!!**
33	**PxP**	**B-R5**

Black makes way for this bishop to enter the game. After even the best defense (34 R-QB1, stopping . . . B-B7) Black wins by returning his heavy pieces to the queenside and winning both knight pawns.

34	**R-QR1?**	**B-B7!**
35	**B-N3**	**B-K5ch**
36	**K-B2**	**P-R4!**

And won in a few moves.

According to Capablanca, you develop your pieces with a middlegame plan already in view. Where does the king bishop belong to participate in the queenside attack? Where does the queen knight belong in a particular semiopen game?

Against Alekhine at St. Petersburg 1913 he played 1 P-Q4, P-Q4; 2 P-QB4, P-QB3; 3 P-K3, N-B3; 4 N-KB3, P-K3; 5 QN-Q2, during a period when everyone automatically developed the knight on QB3. If Alekhine had appreciated the difference he would have played 5 . . . P-B4. Even with a lost tempo Black stands well in a Tarrasch Defense to the Queen's Gambit in which QN-Q2 is played. Black doesn't need to support the strong point on his Q4 if no White knight is there to assault it.

Instead, Black played 5 . . . QN-Q2; 6 B-Q3, B-K2; 7 0-0, 0-0; 8 Q-B2, PxP?!, which gives White just what he wanted—an opportunity to bring this queen knight to the dominating K5 square. After 9 NxP, P-B4; 10 QN-K5, PxP; 11 PxP, N-N3, Capablanca again came up with a fine idea. He can play routinely with 12 B-KN5 or 12 R-Q1. But instead he chose 12 N-KN5!, P-KN3; 13 N(N)-B3, which allows him to develop his bishop with a gain of time on a more aggressive square, KR6.

White finished off with a crushing penetration on the queen's bishop file: 13 . . . K-N2; 14 B-KN5, QN-Q4; 15 R-B1, B-Q2; 16 Q-Q2, N-N1; 17 BxB, QxB; 18 B-K4!, B-N4? (18 . . . KN-B3; 19 BxN, NxB is better); 19 KR-K1!, Q-Q3; 20 BxN, PxB; 21 Q-R5!, P-QR3; 22 Q-B7!, QxQ; 23 RxQ, P-R3; 24 RxP, QR-B1; 25 P-QN3, R-B7; 26 P-QR4, B-K7; 27 N-R4!, P-KR4; 28 N(R4)xP, R-K1; 29 RxPch, K-R3; 30 P-B4, P-R4; 31 N-R4, RxN; 32 BPxR, K-N4; 33 P-N3, K-N5; 34 R-N7ch, K-R6; 35 N-N2!, Resigns.

The queenside bind was a common theme in Capa's games. It gave him the kind of position he loved to play—one that didn't suffer from exchanges, that didn't involve any risks, and that he played so much better than the average opponent. The following is an example.

New York, 1916

	CAPABLANCA	SCHROEDER
1	**P-Q4**	**P-Q4**
2	**N-KB3**	**P-K3**
3	**P-B4**	**N-KB3**
4	**B-N5**	**QN-Q2**
5	**N-B3**	**B-K2**
6	**P-K3**	**0-0**
7	**R-B1**	**P-QR3**

The Swiss Variation, a not particularly good alternative to the orthodox 7 . . . P-B3. Many a player would assume that because . . . P-QB3 has to be played eventually, Black has lost a move on normal lines if White enters the Exchange Variation with PxP here. In fact, Black may be one move *ahead* of normal Exchange lines. If White plays the minority attack, he will have to play R-QN1 after he has already played R-QB1. And in that case Black's . . . P-QR3 is very useful. On the other hand, if White plays for the attack on the kingside or in the center, he will find that 7 R-B1 is a waste of time.

Capablanca often played 8 Q-B2 or 8 P-QR3.

8	**Q-B2**	**R-K1**
9	**B-Q3**	**PxP**
10	**BxP**	**P-N4**
11	**B-Q3**	**B-N2**

Black wants to solve his queenside problems with . . . P-B4 but can't do it immediately because of 12 BxN, NxB; 13 N-K4, NxN; 14 BxN. The game now centers on . . . P-QB4. If Black can play it safely, he is equal.

12	**P-QR4!**	**P-N5**

Black would like to try something like 12 . . . PxP; 13 NxP, P-B4, but he has little compensation after 14 NxP. White's uncastled king is very safe—another contrast to Morphy and the principle of rapid development.

13	BxN!	NxB
14	N-K4	NxN
15	BxN	BxB
16	QxB	. . .

White has secured a small but very certain advantage on the queenside. He threatens to stop mechanically the liberating . . . P-QB4 with 17 R-B6. Note that Black couldn't avoid the many exchanges that preceded. He had to stop 15 N-B5.

16	. . .	P-QB4
17	PxP	Q-R4
18	P-QN3	BxP
19	N-N5!	P-R3

Black has paid a price for liberation. He must accept the smashing knight sacrifice because 19 . . . P-N3 is met by 20 Q-B3! and now (a) 20 . . . R-R2; 21 Q-QB6; (b) 20 . . . R-KB1; 21 Q-R3, P-R4; 22 NxKP, PxN; 23 QxPch, K-R2; 24 Q-Q7ch, K-R1; 25 Q-B6, QR-B1; 26 QxNP, with an overwhelming position; and (c) 20 . . . P-B4; 21 NxKP. The position of Black's queen is felt.

20	Q-R7ch	K-B1

21	Q-R8ch!	K-K2
22	QxNP	PxN
23	QxNPch	K-Q3
24	K-K2!	. . .

Now with the heavy pieces coming to the queen bishop file, Black can just bring his king to safety. But the name of the game is "catch the king rook pawn." With everything mixed into a traffic jam on the queenside, there is little opposition to Capa's simple pawn march.

24	. . .	QR-B1
25	R-B4	K-B3
26	KR-QB1	K-N3
27	P-R4!	P-B4

This loses to a nice finishing combination. But Capa offers this alternative line: 27 . . . R-B2; 28 P-R5, KR-QB1; 29 P-R6, B-Q3; 30 QxQch, KxQ; 31 RxR, RxR; 32 RxR, BxR; 33 P-B4, B-Q1; 34 P-N4, B-B3; 35 P-N5, B-R1; 36 P-K4, K-N3; 37 P-B5, followed by P-N6-7.

28	Q-N7	R-K2
29	Q-K5	R-B3
30	RxB	Resigns

This was a game of Capablanca's early period when he was eager to mix it up with any opponent. Many analysts have noted that his play was much sharper before his loss of the world title to Alekhine. But this is a misreading of his style. Capablanca could, like Reshevsky who followed him, play all kinds of positions. But he found that certain types of game—clear, simple games where open files and good bishops proved decisive— were the ones he could win with the greatest of ease. The risky complex games did not have "Capablanca positions."

Here is another demonstration of Capablanca simplicity.

New York, 1927

	NIMZOVICH	CAPABLANCA
1	**P-QB4**	**N-KB3**
2	**N-KB3**	**P-K3**
3	**P-Q4**	**P-Q4**
4	**P-K3**	**B-K2**
5	**QN-Q2**	. . .

Here is Capablanca's own system being used against him. There is, however, a difference. Black has not played . . . P-QB3 and therefore he will not lose a tempo by later playing . . . P-QB4.

5	. . .	**0-0**
6	**B-Q3**	**P-B4**
7	**QPxP?**	**N-R3!**

Already Black has a good game because of White's poor seventh move. White would not be criticized now for heading into a drawish ending via 8 N-N3, PxP; 9 BxP, QxQch; 10 KxQ.

8	**0-0**	**NxP**
9	**B-K2**	. . .

And this abject retreat is no worse than 9 B-B2, P-QN3; 10 Q-K2, B-R3. From now on Nimzovich is fighting to maintain the balance in a somewhat symmetrical position. That Black can maintain his initiative in the face of White's efforts to draw is very instructive.

9	. . .	**P-QN3**
10	**PxP**	**NxP**
11	**N-N3**	**B-N2**
12	**NxN**	**BxN**
13	**Q-R4**	**Q-B3!**

An excellent square for the queen. White is restrained from completing development on the queenside for a while and this gain in time gives Black an opportunity to take control of the only open files.

14	B-R6	BxB
15	QxB	N-N5
16	Q-K2	KR-Q1
17	P-QR3	N-Q6
18	N-K1	NxN!

The strong temptation to maintain support of the knight or to avoid exchanges is resisted by Black. He sees that as the pieces are removed from the board the natural advantages of Black—his open lines—increase in value. Also, by acquiescing to the exchange, Black keeps the momentum, which now allows him to centralize his pieces. His target: placing the rook on the seventh rank.

19	RxN	QR-B1
20	R-N1	Q-K4!

To meet 21 P-QN4 with 21 . . . B-Q3; 22 P-N3, Q-K5, with great control of key squares. Now this queen heads for a square from which it exercises great restraining power—QR7!

21	P-N3	Q-Q4
22	P-QN4	B-B1
23	B-N2	Q-R7

Alekhine, who was inordinately critical of Capablanca's opponents in the tournament book because of his bitter passion to see him defeated, suggested that White could draw with 24 QR-Q1, RxR; 25 RxR, P-QR4; 26 PxP, PxP; 27 Q-R6, R-B7; 28 R-Q8. But Black then wins simply with 28 . . . Q-N8ch! (not 28 . . . RxB; 29 RxBch!, drawing); 29 K-N2, QxB and . . . RxPch.

24	R-R1	Q-N6
25	B-Q4	R-B7

Black must either get this move in or the alternative . . . P-QR4. Either the weak queenside or the seventh rank must be exploited. Otherwise White will be able to challenge control of the bishop file and draw. Best here is 26 Q-Q1.

26	Q-R6?!	P-K4!

27	BxKP	R(1)-Q7

The decisive shot. There are few forces in nature as powerful as doubled rooks on the seventh rank. On 28 R-KB1 Black scores with the pretty 28 . . . QxKP!; 29 B-B4, RxP! More difficult but also lost is 28 Q-B1, Q-Q4!; 29 B-B4, Q-KR4; 30

P-KR4, P-KR3!, followed by 31 . . . RxP, winning the queen, and then . . . P-KN4.

28	**Q-N7**	**RxP**
29	**P-N4**	**Q-K3**
30	**B-N3**	**RxP!**

And Black will mate after 31 BxR, QxNPch and . . . Q-R6. Nimzovich actually played 31 Q-B3, but after 31 . . . R(R)-N7ch; 32 QxR, RxQch; 33 KxR, QxNP; 34 QR-Q1, P-KR4, he resigned after a few hopeless moves. Again—initiative, open lines, the rook on the seventh rank, and centralization—all parts of a "Capablanca position."

Separated by more than three decades from his death, we don't see Capablanca as the enigma he was to the chess public of his era. He was at once boastful and rigidly objective about his marvelous talent. In a 1913 tournament in Cuba he asked the mayor of Havana to clear the room of spectators so that few would be present to see him concede a game to Marshall.

Yet when he decided that his adjourned position in the thirty-fourth and last game of his championship match with Alekhine was lost, Capa simultaneously drafted a notice of resignation to the tournament committee and a newspaper report to the *New York Times*, which was thus able to announce before anyone else that Capablanca was no longer world champion. He must have seen it as a duty to make the result known quickly no matter how painful it was to him.

Tall, dark, and handsome, Capa was called the Don Juan of chess by Reuben Fine in his psychological analysis. Fine noted that Capablanca was also an expert at bridge and better than most at tennis and even at baseball—he was a member of the Columbia University team. Yet this drive to win at everything coexisted with a diffident attitude that led many admirers to say he was lazy and wasted his talent.

According to a popular story, Capablanca learned chess while watching his father playing a game with a friend in their Havana home. Within a few days, the story goes, the boy was defeating his father and was bitten by the chess bug. He nourished the bug at the Havana Chess Club, the site of so many major matches. At the age of twelve he won his first title there as champion of Cuba. Young Capa defeated Juan Corzo in a twelve-game match and then "retired" from chess to devote his time to his studies.

In 1905 he came to New York to begin work for his engineering degree, where he spent many hours in lightning games at the Manhattan Chess Club. The chess clock was now a permanent part of the game, maligned by the older masters but still necessary. Yet the idea that the clock should be used to play very fast chess—five minutes a side for an entire game—was new. In the United States "rapids chess" became the training instrument for hundreds of masters and Capablanca was one of the first. This partly accounts for the resourceful tactical ability of American players and, of course, for the success of men such as Fine and Reshevsky when in deep time trouble.

Rapids chess taught Capablanca a different skill—how to avoid time trouble. He developed the trait of avoiding bad moves. Then he learned the more difficult lesson of finding good, sharp moves at the same fast rate. Years later, when he played a game at tournament speed—thirty-six moves in two hours or less—Capablanca would immediately recognize the natural moves and discard the others without having to consider them.

By 1908 Capa was breaking all records with the size and speed of his simultaneous exhibition play on tours throughout the country. He was being touted as a rival to the great Marshall and a match was arranged a year later in 1909. Like the Capablanca-Alekhine match eighteen years later everyone who followed the game closely expected the older man to finish off his young rival. But what an upset—8-1, Capablanca!

After the Marshall match Capa solidified his status in the United States by winning a few minor tournaments, while watching with envy the great tournaments 3,000 miles away.

Then, at twenty-three, he duplicated the feat of Pillsbury by winning his first major foreign tournament, San Sebastian, 1911. In the following decade his star rose swiftly and supporters busied themselves with organizing a world championship match with Lasker.

There were few reverses during this period. At St. Petersburg in 1914 he finished second, one-half point behind Lasker but a respectable three points ahead of Alekhine and way in front of Marshall and Tarrasch. But then the war intervened, suspending European competition from the minute the guns of August were heard during the closing rounds in Mannheim in 1914.

During this dormant period Capa busied himself with New York tournaments in which only Marshall was a rival. In an eight-year period Capablanca won 136 tournament, match, and exhibition games against masters and lost only 10. In his whole career he lost only thirty-five games.

Lasker was no longer interested in the title of world champion—a remarkable contrast with Alekhine's reign—and he offered to relinquish it. Capa naturally refused and a match was arranged for his hometown, Havana, in 1921. The young man won four games and drew fourteen before Lasker conceded the match and championship.

For the next six years he was Capa the Almost Unbeatable. He took the strong London, 1922, tournament with eleven wins and four draws ahead of a field that included Alekhine, Vidmar, Rubinstein, Bogolyubov, Reti, and Tartakover. More victories followed. But in the New York, 1924, tournament and a year later at Moscow he started off badly, conceding first to Lasker in New York and first and second to Bogolyubov and Lasker in Moscow.

In 1927 the New York organizers held a second great tournament and here Capa reestablished his reputation. The tournament committee refused to invite Lasker, claiming that he was guilty of unsportsmanlike behavior—those foul cigars, for example—and arranged a six-grandmaster marathon. Capablanca was in tremendous form and was so far ahead of the field that with five games left, he offered all his opponents draws in advance. Against Nimzovich Capa had to avoid strong moves because his opponent's mistakes were giving the world champion too much of an advantage. Capa had the tournament director pass his opponent a note advising him to make stronger moves. He finished 2½ points in front of Alekhine. Nevertheless, a match with Alekhine was inevitable, the fans believed.

Had Capa won that historic 1927 encounter, he might have remained champion until World War II. Lasker had retired, the young Russians were inexperienced, and neither Fine nor Reshevsky was ready until the late 1930s. Only Alekhine remained a threat and Capa would surely take his measure, his supporters believed. But Capablanca lost the first match game and conceded defeat thirty-three games later. Alekhine never allowed a return match.

In his remaining years Capa searched for the crushing tournament success that would force Alekhine into a rematch. But he was also busy with his work as a Cuban diplomatic officer. Between 1929 and 1935 he entered only two tournaments. His last major triumph was at Moscow, 1936, when he bested Botvinnik, the leader of a new generation, by half a point and Flohr by 3½ points. He also tied for first with Botvinnik later that year in Nottingham.

But two years later in Holland, at the tournament organized by Dutch radio station AVRO, he finished a dismal seventh in essentially the same field of supergrandmasters as at Nottingham. He was fifty years old and was prematurely suffering from angina pectoris, which took his life three years later.

In his later years Capa was often criticized for supercaution because of his aversion of all dangers. The result was many quick draws. Yet Capablanca was one of the best defensive players of all time. The following game, for example, is a case of brilliant reversal against Colle, whose monolithic attacking opening won so many victories in the 1920s.

Carlsbad, 1929

	COLLE	CAPABLANCA
1	**P-Q4**	**N-KB3**
2	**N-KB3**	**P-QN3**
3	**P-K3**	**B-N2**
4	**QN-Q2**	**P-K3**
5	**B-Q3**	**P-B4**

Capablanca understood the psychology of openings, although his contributions to theory are few. Edgar Colle of Belgium chose a simple system of development that worked well. He built a bridge of central pawns at Q4, QB3, and K3, posted an attacking bishop on Q3, and prepared for P-K4-5 as an assault wedge. The trouble with being so successful with this opening is that Colle became a prisoner of it. When an opponent, such as Capablanca here, chooses some other defense to 1 P-Q4, White should also alter his preparations. Black's choice is an ideal anti-Colle weapon.

6	**0-0**	**N-B3**
7	**P-B3**	. . .

White has problems finding good squares. He can't play P-K4 without admitting a great deal of queenside play to Black. On 7 P-QN3, B-K2; 8 PxP, PxP; 9 B-N2, 0-0; 10 P-B4, he has a good game, but Black also stands well with 10 . . . Q-B2, followed perhaps by . . . N-K1, . . . B-B3, and/or . . . P-B4.

7	. . .	**B-K2**
8	**P-K4**	**PxP!**

Now 9 PxP, N-QN5; 10 B-N1, B-R3, followed by . . . R-QB1 and . . . N-Q6, is very upsetting to a player who dreams of mate on KR7.

9	**NxP**	**0-0**
10	**Q-K2**	. . .

Colle's first mistake, aside from the choice of opening. Since Black can thoroughly frustrate White's attacking plans with . . . N-K4, Colle should have played 10 NxN, BxN and then 11 Q-K2.

10	. . .	N-K4
11	**B-B2**	**Q-B1!**
12	**P-KB4**	**B-R3**
13	**Q-Q1**	**N-B3!**

Naturally 13 . . . BxR loses material upon 14 PxN, but more pertinent is that 13 . . . N-Q6 is also an error because it facilitates White's attack after 14 R-B3, NxB; 15 RxN. Then P-K5 is coming fast.

14	**R-B3**	**P-N3!**

Another excellent move, which anticipates P-K5, R-R3, and Q-R5 while at the same time shortening the diagonal of White's attacking bishop. The weakening of KB6 and KR6 cannot be exploited until White's queen bishop emerges from the first rank. Now 15 NxN, QxN; 16 P-K5, B-B4ch and . . . N-N5 is bad.

15	**QN-N3**	**NxN**
16	**NxN**	**B-N2**
17	**Q-K2**	**B-B4**
18	**R-R3**	. . .

This has worked for Colle many times before, but here 18 K-R1 is preferable. Black penetrates in the center now as he uses the pin on the knight.

18	. . .	Q-B3!
19	P-K5	N-Q4
20	Q-B2	. . .

White discovers that he can't play the natural 20 B-K4 because of 20 . . . NxQBP! 20 B-K3 is also an attractive move, but 20 . . . BxN!; 21 PxB, QR-B1 puts him in a bad way and gives Black a treasured open file.

20	. . .	BxN
21	PxB	QR-B1
22	B-Q1	P-B3!

The question of who has the kingside attack might be legitimately asked. From now on every White move is difficult. 23 B-B3, for example, loses to 23 . . . QxBch, and 23 B-Q2 falls to the clever 23 . . . NxP!; 24 BxN, PxP; 25 B-B3 (25 PxP, RxB), P-K5; 26 B-K2, P-K6!

| 23 | Q-R4 | R-B2 |
| 24 | B-B3 | Q-B5! |

There is no longer a defense to the queen pawn. Black has conducted the counterattack very neatly.

25	**B-K3!**	**NxB**
26	**BxB**	**N-B4!**

Now 27 Q-B2, Q-B8ch! transposes into a won endgame.

27	**Q-K1**	**R-B2**
28	**B-K4**	**QxPch**

And Black took two quick pawns before White blundered into a pretty finish: 29 K-R1, PxP; 30 BxN, KPxB; 31 PxP, R-K2; 32 R-K3, QxNP; 33 P-K6, PxP; 34 RxP, K-B2!; White Resigns.

Sharp in exact defense, the little combinations, and the mastery of simple middlegames—that was enough for Capablanca usually. If it wasn't, there was always the ending. Whereas Capa rarely studied the openings, he spent many hours probing the depths of theoretical endgame positions. It is said he studied more than a thousand rook-and-pawn endings to attain the perfect technique. Only Fischer has been able to duplicate that kind of prolonged preparation. Here is one of many great Capablanca endings, versus Tartakover (Black), New York, 1924:

White has secured a strong positional advantage because of his greater space and superior minor piece. His liability is the weak queen bishop pawn. If rooks are traded off, Black's knight should be strong enough to hold against the bishop. But it is a different story with rooks on the board, as Tartakover learns. First White needs a file to call his own.

27	**P-R5!**	. . .

Here 27 . . . PxP loses a pawn to 28 R-R1, K-B1; 29 RxP. Black goes after the only White weakness.

27	. . .	**R-B3**
28	**PxP**	**PxP**
29	**R-R1**	**K-B1**
30	**R-R7**	**R-B3**
31	**P-N4!**	. . .

The first phase is over. White has a rook on the seventh rank and has weakened Black's king knight pawn. Before he forces a trade with R-Q7, Capa seeks to make his pawns as dangerous as possible.

31	. . .	**N-B5**
32	**P-N5**	**N-K6ch**

Plugging up the diagonal doesn't avail: 32 . . . N-Q7; 33 R-R6!, N-K5; 34 P-B4, or 33 . . . K-N2; 34 P-B5.

33	**K-B3**	**N-B4**

An amusing line is 33 . . . N-Q8; 34 R-R6, K-N2 (. . . RxP; 35 K-K2); 35 P-B5, NxP; 36 K-B4!, N-K5; 37 BxN, PxB; 38 P-B6ch!, and White wins the king-and-pawn ending: 38 . . . RxPch; 39 PxR, KxR; 40 KxP, K-R2; 41 K-Q5, K-N1; 42 K-B6!, P-KN4; 43 KxP, P-N5; 44 P-Q5.

34	**BxN**	**PxB**
35	**K-N3!!**	. . .

One of the finest moves ever made in a rook-and-pawn endgame. The rook will restrain Black's king. The White king will support the king knight pawn and threaten mate when it reaches KB6. Against these advantages Black's win of two pawns is meaningless. He is lost.

35	. . .	RxPch
36	K-R4	R-B6

The White king is advanced far enough to hide at KN6. For example, 36 . . . R-B8; 37 K-R5, K-N1; 38 R-Q7 is followed by K-N6 and K-B6 and the advance of the passed pawn.

37	P-N6	RxPch
38	K-N5	R-K5

It's a simple mate after 38 . . . RxP; 39 K-B6, K-N1; 40 R-Q7. The same goes for 38 . . . R-N5ch; 39 K-B6!

39	K-B6	K-N1
40	R-N7ch	K-R1
41	RxP	. . .

And White sweeps the board because of mate threats, the pregnant king knight pawn, and the rook on the seventh rank. The themes occur over and over in Capa's games. The finish here was simple: 41 . . . R-K1; 42 KxP, R-K5 (Black can't save the queen rook pawn by 42 . . . P-R3; 43 R-R7, P-N4; 44 P-R5, or the queen pawn after 42 . . . R-R1; 43 K-K6); 43 K-B6, R-B5ch; 44 K-K5, R-N5; 45 P-N7ch!, K-N1 (the king-and-pawn ending is quite easy); 46 RxP, R-KN8; 47 KxP, R-QB8; 48 K-Q6, and the queen pawn won in a few moves.

What is Capablanca's legacy? First, it was the mastery of technique, the ability to maintain an advantage, to cultivate it, and to push it home to victory. Few Americans had good technique before Capa, but virtually all the top-ranked masters that followed him did. We see this over and over again in Reshevsky, Fine, Evans, Kashdan, and of course Fischer. Second, he had the ability to anticipate danger and reduce it before it occurred. Capa could smell tactical dangers lurking several moves ahead and deactivate them before they were threats. Third, he was the great endgame player, the first on these shores to make its study a habit. He brought rook-and-pawn endgames to a science. A player with more energy than

Capa, such as Reshevsky or Fischer, would later turn this to great advantage.

The quintessential Capablanca game is hard to choose. Many of the examples we've given so far would suffice. Perhaps his greatest game, however, was atypical. Forced to defend right out of the opening, Capa has no chance for the initiative. He finds that exchanges do not help him and there are no simple positions to steer for. He has to fight his old opponent, Marshall, in a game of great complexity, a classic of active defense:

New York, 1918

	CAPABLANCA	MARSHALL
1	**P-K4**	**P-K4**
2	**N-KB3**	**N-QB3**
3	**B-N5**	**P-QR3**
4	**B-R4**	**N-B3**
5	**0-0**	**B-K2**
6	**R-K1**	**P-QN4**
7	**B-N3**	**0-0**
8	**P-B3**	**P-Q4!?**

This was the great surprise Marshall had waited almost a decade to play against his Cuban rival. In the previous four years Capa hadn't lost more than one tournament game. Here under tournament conditions he must find a refutation of a strong theoretical innovation.

9	**PxP**	**NxP**
10	**NxP**	**. . .**

If White were a lesser player he would have refused the dangers by playing 10 P-Q4, PxP; 11 NxP, with a rapid draw in sight. Capa has already made the most courageous decision of the game.

10	. . .	NxN
11	**RxN**	**N-B3**

Today we know that 11 . . . P-QB3, followed by 12 . . . B-Q3 and . . . Q-R5, is a resource with more long-range potential. But this was also Marshall's first tournament game with the countergambit, as well as Capablanca's. Black's choice is not illogical. He also plans . . . B-Q3 and brings his knight into position to play . . . N-N5.

12	**R-K1**	. . .

Even better is 12 P-Q4, so that 12 . . . B-Q3 can be met by Wolf's 13 R-K2!, N-N5; 14 P-KR3, Q-R5; 15 N-Q2, followed by bringing the knight to defense at KB3 or KB1. The rook squelches the attack by protecting the second rank, especially the king bishop pawn. This is considered the refutation of Marshall's 11 . . . N-B3.

12	. . .	**B-Q3**
13	**P-KR3**	**N-N5!?**

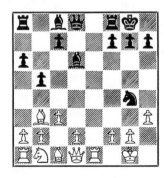

The correctness of this further sacrifice is still not established more than fifty-five years later. On 14 PxN, Q-R5; 15 Q-B3 (15 P-KN3, BxNP!), B-R7ch!; 16 K-B1, BxP; 17 Q-K4 (17 R-K4, B-B5!!), K-R1, followed by . . . P-KB4, Black has a lot of punch left. This is much better for Black than the line once thought crushing for him—15 . . . Q-R7ch; 16 K-B1, BxP; 17 QxB, Q-R8ch; 18 K-K2, QR-K1ch because of 19 B-K6!

14   **Q-B3!**   . . .

Stopping the attempt to transpose into the above line with 14 . . . B-R7ch; 15 K-B1, Q-R5. The play becomes very complex here.

14   . . .   **Q-R5**
15   **P-Q4!**   . . .

One of the misconceptions about Capablanca is that he was a calculating machine. The machine wouldn't waste any time on 15 QxR?, QxPch but might have been lured into 15 R-K8?!, B-N2!!; 16 RxRch, RxR; 17 QxN, R-K1!; 18 K-B1, Q-K2; 19 Q-Q1, Q-K5; 20 P-B3, Q-K4 and 21 . . . Q-R7 with strong threats.

But Capablanca avoided long calculations. Only when the alternative was a clearly inferior position would Capa waste his time looking ten moves ahead. Positional values determined most of his moves. He had the ability to "sense" the right move, unconsciously using his internalized positional judgment, without deep thought.

15   . . .   **NxP!**

Probably still in Marshall's pregame analysis. On 15 . . . P-KR4 Black threatens . . . B-N2, but White can escape after 16 N-Q2, B-N2; 17 N-K4, QR-K1; 18 B-N5!, or even after 16 B-K3, protecting KB2.

16   **R-K2!?**   . . .

The most difficult move in the game and one of the most difficult Capa ever made. On 16 QxN Black doesn't play 16 . . . B-N6 because of 17 QxPch! Instead, he wins with 16 . . . B-R7ch; 17 K-B1, B-N6 because now 18 QxPch?? is met by 18 . . . RxQch! Here again White could go in for 16 R-K8, but again Black has a brilliant response. This time it is 16 . . .

NxPch; 17 PxN, B-N2!!; 18 RxRch, RxR; 19 Q-K3, B-B5!, with a devastating attack.

Capa's choice is not a bad move. It takes the rook out of danger, gives protection to the second rank, and kicks the Black knight out. But there was a better move: 16 B-Q2!, threatening both 17 QxN and 17 R-K8! Subsequent analysis has shown that even with the best continuation of the attack, 16 . . . B-N2; 17 QxB!, N-Q6; 18 R-K2, Q-N6; 19 K-B1, Q-R7; 20 P-KN4!! White escapes and wins.

16 . . . **B-KN5**

This is the momentary lapse in Black's initiative that White has been waiting for. The move played looks forceful enough but is inferior to 16 . . . N-N5! Then 17 QxR allows a crushing attack with 17 . . . Q-N6; 18 PxN, Q-R7ch; 19 K-B2, BxP. 17 B-KB4 is also bad because of 17 . . . B-N2! The best try for White is either 17 R-K8, N-B3!; 18 RxRch, KxR; 19 N-Q2, or 17 N-Q2, N-B3; 18 N-B1 (but not 18 QxR, B-KN5; 19 N-B3, Q-N6; 20 QxRch, KxQ; 21 PxN, NxNP, which is very unclear).

17 **PxB** **B-R7ch**
18 **K-B1** **B-N6**

There was nothing in 18 . . . N-R8; 19 B-K3!, QR-K1; 20 B-B2!, QxBch (20 . . . NxB; 21 QxPch!); 21 QxQ, NxQ; 22 KxN. This line must have disillusioned Marshall, who might have suspected he had the edge. On 19 . . . N-N6ch; 20 K-K1, NxRch; 21 KxN, QR-K1; 22 N-Q2, White again wins. The fact that Black has nothing better than the discovered check at move 20 in this last line suggests that White's best move in the text position is 19 K-K1!, transposing. Capa's choice is good, and it must have pained Marshall to see how expertly the Cuban consolidates now.

19 **RxN** **Q-R8ch**
20 **K-K2** **BxR**

If he tries 20 . . . QxB, White has a choice between two winning methods: 21 QxB, QxPch; 22 K-Q3! (and not 22 N-Q2, QR-K1ch), QxR; 23 K-B2, P-N5; 24 P-N5!; or 21 R-B1!, QR-K1ch; 22 K-Q3 or 21 . . . QxPch; 22 N-Q2. White shuts the door on the attack here and steals the initiative.

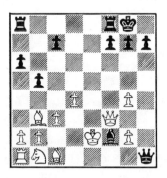

21	**B-Q2!**	**B-R5**
22	**Q-R3!**	**QR-K1ch**
23	**K-Q3**	**Q-B8ch**
24	**K-B2**	**B-B7**

This aggressive move actually makes things more troublesome for Black because of the pin-to-be. It is surprising how easily White unscrambles his queenside, where his material advantage is bottled up, ready to explode.

25	**Q-B3**	**Q-N8**

A nice line is 25 . . . R-K7 (bringing a new piece to the attack but also putting it en prise); 26 N-R3!, RxBch; 27 KxR, QxR; 28 QxB, QxPch; 29 N-B2, consolidating.

26	**B-Q5!**	**P-B4**
27	**PxP**	**BxP**

In another eight moves, believe it or not, White will announce a mate in six! This is a different kind of technique than what we've characterized as Capablanca's, but it is in keeping with the nature of the game.

| 28 | **P-QN4** | **B-Q3** |
| 29 | **P-R4!** | **P-QR4** |

The last try of a great swindler. The White rook was about to make its triumphant entrance anyway.

30	**RPxP**	**PxP**
31	**R-R6!**	**PxP**
32	**NxP**	**B-N5**
33	**P-N6**	**BxN**
34	**BxB**	**P-R3**
35	**P-N7**	**R-K6**

And White announced mate beginning with 36 BxPch!, RxB; 37 P-N8(Q)ch, R-K1; 38 QxR(8)ch. One of the great defensive games. This success of Capablanca's style had an effect on American chess that is still felt today.

The Capablanca School: Isaac Kashdan

Aside from Capablanca, who was after all born in Cuba, the first American of native birth to even venture across the Atlantic after Marshall was Isaac Kashdan of New York. Born in 1905 Kashdan was twenty-eight years younger than Marshall and surely would have beaten him had they met in a match. But this was 1932–33. The absence of money for something as frivolous as a U.S. chess championship was obvious during a period of the Depression when thousands of people had no money for decent clothing or housing.

Kashdan, a graduate of Stuyvesant High School and CCNY, was one of several new masters to come from New York during its heyday as the chess capital of the country. In contrast, by the early 1970s there were as many young masters developing in Chicago and Riverside, California, as in New York.

As the first member of the new generation, Kashdan had impressive credentials. He lead the U.S. Olympic team in four international team championships, scoring 13-2 at the Hague in 1928, 13-2 at Hamburg in 1930, 9-5 at Prague in 1931, and 9-4 at Folkstone in 1933. Kashdan's second-place finish behind Alekhine at the Pasadena International Tournament of 1932 was especially impressive. His lifetime record with Alekhine—six draws, one loss.

Kashdan had much in common with Capablanca and was known in Europe as "der kleine Capablanca," the little Capablanca. The opening was just a phase of the game to Kashdan, no more important than the middlegame. But to draw or win games you had to know how to play simple positions with advantages such as the two bishops and how to play the endings with Capa-like efficiency. One of Kashdan's weaknesses was his mania for preserving the two bishops. The following is a good example of Kashdan at work in a "Capablanca position."

INTERNATIONAL TEAM TOURNAMENT, Folkestone, 1933

	KASHDAN	MIKENAS (Latvia)
1	**P-K4**	**P-K4**
2	**N-KB3**	**N-KB3**
3	**NxP**	**P-Q3**
4	**N-KB3**	**NxP**
5	**Q-K2**	**Q-K2**
6	**P-Q3**	**N-KB3**
7	**B-N5**	**. . .**

Kashdan was usually content to have small advantages—the small initiative, control of open files, better bishops. He has to work to make something out of symmetry but his opponent, a sharp tactician who thrives on unbalanced situations, gives him ample opportunity. When he had the Black pieces, Kashdan would play here 7 . . . B-K3; 8 N-B3, P-KR3, aiming at getting the two bishops.

7	. . .	QxQch
8	BxQ	B-K2
9	N-B3	N-B3

There is not much danger to Black if he develops accurately. 9 . . . P-KR3 puts the question to White's bishop and is probably best.

10	N-N5	K-Q1

Knowing Kashdan, an opponent might have tried 10 . . . B-Q1 because White would never give up his bishop to wreck Black's pawns after 11 BxN. Now White could take a sizable edge in space with 11 0-0-0, but Kashdan wants to advance his queenside pawns, so he puts his king on the other side.

11	0-0	P-QR3
12	QN-Q4	NxN
13	NxN	P-B4?

Black has easy equality with 13 . . . N-Q4!; 14 B-Q2, B-B3. But because his opponent has presented him with so few problems in the opening, Mikenas is looking for more than a draw.

14	N-B3	B-K3
15	B-Q2!	. . .

The beginning of queenside ambitions. Besides threatening 16 N-N5, White intends P-QN3, P-B4, and P-Q4, with a mobile mass. Again, Black can still answer this with exact defense.

| 15 | . . . | **P-R3** |
| 16 | **P-QN3** | **K-Q2** |

The road to dynamic equality was 16 . . . R-QB1; 17 P-B4, P-Q4!, or 17 P-Q4, P-B5! Black gets squashed without open lines.

17	**P-Q4!**	**KR-QB1**
18	**P-B4**	**P-Q4**
19	**QPxP!**	**BxP**

Black is unpleasantly forced into this because 19 . . . PxP; 20 P-QN4, P-QN4; 21 PxP e.p. preserves an extra pawn after 21 . . . QR-N1; 22 B-K3, N-Q4; 23 BxP!, NxB; 24 BxBch, KxB; 25 KR-K1.

| 20 | **P-QN4** | **B-R2** |
| 21 | **P-B5** | . . . |

White has a tangible asset in his passed pawn and in the imprisoned Black pieces. Mikenas typically seeks a tactical solution.

21	. . .	**K-K2**
22	**N-Q4**	**B-N1**
23	**QR-B1**	**B-K4**
24	**B-QB3**	**B-B5**

Designed to irritate White and to avert 25 N-B5ch. Black has some tricky possibilities in mind. He can play . . . P-QR4 and open the file, or he can try . . . N-K5, or both.

25	**R-B2**	**N-K5**
26	**B-N2**	**P-QR4!**
27	**P-N3**	**B-K4**
28	**P-B3**	**PxP!?**

If the knight moves, Black could justifiably resign after White plays P-N5 and N-B5ch or P-B6. His next move threatens . . . RxB.

29	**NxB**	**RxP**
30	**PxN**	**RxB**

On 30 . . . BxB; 31 R-N1, PxN; 32 R(2)xB wins, as does 30 . . . PxN; 31 BxB, RxR; 32 B-Q6ch.

31	**RxR**	**BxR**

32	**PxP!**	. . .

The simplest and perhaps the only sure winning line. White surrenders his knight to retain a winning queen bishop pawn. Even in the bishop-of-opposite–color endgame, White scores with his pawns.

32	. . .	**PxN**
33	**P-Q6ch**	**K-K1**

33 . . . K-Q1 transposes after 34 R-B8ch, K-Q2; 35 R-B7ch.

34	**B-R5ch!**	**K-Q2**
35	**R-B7ch**	**K-B3**

Equally disappointing is 35 . . . K-Q1; 36 B-N4!, RxP; 37 BxP, K-K1; 38 P-Q7ch, or 36 . . . B-Q5ch; 37 K-N2, BxP; 38 BxP, BxP; 39 R-Q7ch. A very nice series of points for a "little" combination.

36	**B-B3ch!**	. . .

Now 36 . . . KxP loses to 37 R-B7ch! The rest is *kinderspiel*.

36	. . .	**K-N4**
37	**RxPch**	**K-B5**
38	**P-B6**	**Resigns**

During the early 1930s Kashdan was second only to Flohr of Czechoslovakia in the search for a rival to the world champion, Alekhine (assuming Capablanca would never be given a return match). At the great Alekhine tournament at Bled, 1961, Kashdan finished a strong fourth behind the champion, Bogolyubov, and Nimzovich. Kashdan also defeated Lajos Steiner in a match during this period.

Another impressive example of the Capablanca-like technique was this early endgame against Rellstab from the 1930 Stockholm tournament.

The position appears to favor White (Rellstab) because of his control of the open file and his greater freedom of piece action on the queenside. Black's fast move toward that side of the board is as surprising as it is instructive. First he stops N-N6.

15	. . .	N(4)-Q2!

And also threatening . . . P-QN4 and . . . B-N2, with a strong initiative. White now retreats so that he can meet 16 . . . P-QN4 with 17 N-B6.

16	N-QB3	N-N3
17	KR-Q1	B-Q2
18	N-B3	R(K)-Q1
19	N-K4	QR-B1

Compared with the diagram, Black has made enormous strides after White blocked the queen bishop file. White's rook strength has proven to be temporary and his apparent initiative is over. White actually has less than an equal game because his pieces are poorly placed. If 20 RxR, RxR; 21 K-B1, B-R5; 22 P-N3, B-B3, with a chance to exploit the hole on QB6.

20	NxNch?	PxN!
21	B-R6	N-R5!

This is even better. The Black knight must gain key outpost squares on the queenside while the White queen bishop is really offside on KR6. The following trades only maximize the strengths of Black's remaining minor pieces.

22	RxR	BxR!
23	RxRch	BxR
24	P-QN3	N-B6
25	N-Q2	B-Q2
26	P-QR3	P-QN4!

Black fixes the queen rook pawn and ensures the winning of it. If White had continued 27 P-QN4, Kashdan's plan was 27

. . . P-QR4; 28 PxP, BxP; 29 B-Q3, B-B2! and . . . B-Q3, winning the pawn.

The game continued 27 B-Q3, P-R4; 28 P-K4, B-K2; 29 N-B3 (29 B-K3, BxP; 30 B-Q4, B-N7; 31 BxBP, N-K7ch ensures the advance of the rook pawn, which is the story of the remainder of the game—making way for the pawn), BxP; 30 B-Q2, B-N7; 31 N-Q4, P-R5; 32 PxP (32 BxN, BxB; 33 NxNP?, BxN; 34 BxB, P-R6 queens), PxP; 33 N-B2, N-N8!; 34 B-N4, P-R6; 35 B-B4, B-R5; 36 N-K1, B-B6!; 37 N-Q3, B-B7!; 38 P-B3, P-R7; and White resigned.

5. RESHEVSKY, FINE, AND THE 1930S

♛ *Practically every player has a penchant for a certain kind of position which he is only too happy to attain, and a distaste for some other type or types which he would avoid at all costs . . . Reshevsky is the exception . . . To Reshevsky, boring positions simply do not exist.*

Max Euwe, Meet the Masters *(1940)*

Samuel Reshevsky

Suddenly it was 1936 and there were at least three future grandmasters deserving of Marshall's title. After several unavailing attempts to raise money for a match challenge, the National Chess Federation announced a major domestic tournament. All the new stars—Kashdan fresh from his European performances, Reuben Fine, the college champion who dominated New York's chess clubs, and Samuel Reshevsky, the prodigy grown up, among others—were invited. It was like New York 1857 all over again, and, in fact, it was the first U.S. championship tournament since the American congresses of the late nineteenth century. Who would raise the American banner in European events?

The first championship tournament since Mackenzie's days

was a cliffhanger. Reshevsky was an early favorite but drew his second round and then lost two games in a row. Fine's play was typically erratic—outplaying Kashdan in a clever endgame one day and then getting crushed by one of the lesser lights the next. Kashdan never got moving.

The battle turned out to be a battle between Reshevsky and Albert C. Simonson, a star of New York's Met League for many years. At twenty-two, Simonson was as young as anyone except Fine and was considered to be enormously talented. He earlier had represented the United States in the 1933 Olympiade at Folkestone, at the age of nineteen.

In the rounds following his poor start, Reshevsky put on one of those hustling spurts that would characterize his lifetime of tournament play. By round twelve he was even with Simonson. Then in the finale Simonson lost, while Reshevsky nosed ahead with a draw.

No Americans and very few foreigners have been as continuously successful as Samuel Reshevsky. He won the U.S. title in 1936 and again in 1969, and four times in the interim. In 1941 he won a match from Horowitz, $9\frac{1}{2}$-$6\frac{1}{2}$, and in 1970 he drew his three games with former world champion Vassily Smyslov as part of the USSR-world match. In between, Reshevsky defeated Kashdan, Najdorf, Benko, Lombardy, Donald Byrne, Bisguier, and Gligorich in matches and drew the infamous 1961 match with Bobby Fischer in actual games played. (The match was awarded to Reshevsky after a complex dispute over playing times.)

Despite one of the most successful and lengthy careers in the history of the game, Reshevsky is often criticized for the way he wins. Boring, sterile, and uncreative are a few of the words critics use to denigrate his style. "Reshevsky plays penny-pinching chess," said Larry Evans. He avoids the unclear positions and chooses the dull, Evans suggested. If he had a choice between playing a mate in five moves or defending against a mate in six, he would choose the latter. True, there are no young players who model their play after Reshevsky's, no "Der

Kleine Reshevsky." But Sammy's style is not easily understood.

Reuben Fine, who continually seemed to watch Reshevsky's successes from second place in tournaments, explained his rival's victories as the product of a will to win unmatched in grandmasterdom. There were other players with the talent, but they just didn't want to win as much as Sammy did. But the key was Reshevsky's tactical skill. He didn't care about the openings, as Euwe and Fine did. He wasn't a Botvinnik-like strategic genius, Fine added. And his endgame victories were more the result of hard work than talent, said Euwe. "He is above all a practical man . . . his games give the impression that he does not seek for absolutely the best move, but is content if he finds a good one," the former world champion added. But tactical skill was enough to make him one of the world's top ten players for more than thirty years.

One of the more common misconceptions about playing styles is the assumption that there are only two breeds of chessplayer—the tactical attacker and the positional defender. But Reshevsky is the tactical defender. And he can be a positional player who uses tricks as much as Frank Marshall did. The following is an example of the sharp defender's play.

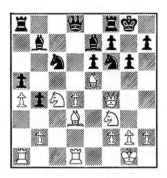

Reshevsky is Black against S. Landau, an imaginative attacker, at Kemeri, 1937. White's pieces appear excellently posted and he seems to have a certain advantage. For example, he intends 19 Q-R6, with threats of 20 N-N5 and 21 BxN. Black's game looks critical. If 18 . . . R-K1; 19 N-N5, or 18 . . . N-Q4; 19 Q-R6, Reshevsky is in trouble. Is 18 . . . K-N2 therefore forced?

18	. . .	**N-R4!**
19	**Q-K3**	. . .

White evades a clever trap: 19 Q-R6, NxB!; 20 PxN (20 N[4]xN, R-B1, and the attack dies), BxN!; 21 BxP (else . . . B-N4), BPxB!; 22 RxQ, QRxR; 23 PxB, N-B5, and Black wins because of the trapped White queen. If White stops the threatened 24 . . . B-N4 with 24 K-R1, Black still wins with 24 . . . R-B4; 25 R-KN1, R-Q5!, followed by . . . RxN or . . . R-R4.

19	. . .	**R-B1**
20	**QR-B1**	**NxB**
21	**PxN**	**B-B4!**

Another double-edged move. The bishop serves an important defensive function on K2, so why move it? And why force White to play his queen to R6? Tactically, the move works because if 22 BxP, BxQ; 23 RxQ, RxR.

22	**Q-R6**	**Q-K2**
23	**N-N5**	. . .

White has no good move in a position that still looks promising for him. The defensive 23 B-K2, which also threatens 24 N-N5, can be handled by 23 . . . BxN; 24 BxB, Q-R5, indirectly attacking the knight and directly threatening . . . BxPch.

Note that 23 NxP does not win a pawn: 23 . . . BxN; 24 PxB, Q-R2, with a commanding position. Reshevsky reasons that Black has a small edge after 23 N-Q6, KBxN; 24 PxB, RxR!; 25 QxR, Q-B3; 26 Q-K3, BxN; 27 QxB, QxQ; 28 PxQ, R-Q1.

23	. . .	**P-B3!**
24	**PxP**	. . .

Black has calculated that 24 BxP, PxB; 25 QxPch, Q-N2 is a dead end and that the more complex 24 . . . PxN; 25 BxN, BxPch; 26 K-R1, BxPch!; 27 KxB, Q-N2ch leads to mate.

24	. . .	**BxPch!**

Undoubtedly overlooked by Landau. On 25 K-R1, RxP, Black is a pawn ahead with an easy defense.

25	**KxB**	**QxPch**
26	**N-B3**	. . .

And king move would allow a quick mate. White's game fell apart quickly and after 26 . . . BxN; 27 PxB, QxBPch; 28 K-N1, R-B5!; 29 QxR (no better), NxQ; 30 B-B1, R-B4; 31 R-Q8ch, K-N2; 32 R-Q7ch, K-R3, White resigned.

Even as an eight-year-old prodigy, Reshevsky demonstrated his skill in tactics. His professional career is perhaps the longest of any major player of this century, if one includes his exhibitions at kindergarten age. Reshevsky was born November 26, 1911, in an obscure Polish town. He learned chess at three, could defeat most of the villagers at four, and was giving exhibitions at the ripe old age of six. Just before his ninth birthday Reshevsky's family brought him to New York for a series of American exhibitions. In one famous photograph the prodigy, who looks even younger, is dressed in a little sailor suit as he demolishes nineteen intensely concentrating cadets at West Point.

Reshevsky's career had to wait another eleven years, while he finished his studies and was graduated from college. His rise was moderate, compared with the meteoric spurts of Fine and Arthur Dake. (Dake was a young sailor from Oregon who walked into the Manhattan Chess Club one day in the early 1930s and astounded the club regulars with his unexpected skill.)

In Reshevsky's first international event, Margate, 1935, he confirmed his youthful promise by defeating Capablanca (see Appendix A, game 13). He finished there in first place and followed with the U.S. championship in 1936, third place in the great Nottingham tournament of 1936, a tie for first at Kemeri in 1937, and a victory at Hastings in 1937.

There followed a series of U.S. championships, which, Kashdan noticed, all followed the same pattern. First Reshevsky set a tough pace but then someone stayed up there in the tournament table with him. In 1936 it was Simonson, in 1938 and 1940 it was Fine, and in 1942, Kashdan himself. The last round was always crucial, and yet Reshevsky always finished first.

Along the tournament trail Reshevsky showed not only his tactical depth but also a positional understanding of great weight. The essence of Reshevsky's chess philosophy, Fine, his perceptive rival, said, was this: "Every position is an individual phenomenon and is to be treated as such, regardless of what the customary opinion about it may be."

This is a Reshevsky-Kashdan position from the Western championship of 1934. (The Western Chess Association merged with the American and National Chess Federations in 1939. The Western Opens, a series of powerful events beginning at the turn of the century, thus gave birth to the strongest of all

Swiss system events, the U.S. Open.) The year before in this tournament Reshevsky had been victimized by one of his worst traits. He smashed Fine in excellent fashion but finished second because he drew four other games.

Here, against Kashdan, White appears to have a small advantage and Reshevsky is bent on winning. The problem is how does White exploit his edge? Black is well protected on the kingside. He has a nice blockade square at Q4. Black cannot be easily tempted into . . . PxP because that gives White the queen bishop file. Meanwhile, Black has just attacked the queen pawn with 17 . . . N-N3, stopping a possible BxPch.

18	**BxN!!**	. . .

One of the last moves one would expect. But it is the only one to demonstrate a clear advantage. White prepares to defend his queen pawn by fianchettoeing his other bishop. Black will be forced into an exchange on his Q5 and this will give White an opportunity to exploit the outposts K5 and QB5. In the semiclosed position that follows, Black's two bishops—especially his king bishop—are no match for well-posted horses. Also note that 18 NxN, RPxN; 19 PxP, BxBP; 20 P-K4 doesn't work because of 20 . . . NxP!

18	. . .	**RPxB**
19	**P-QN3**	**PxP**
20	**PxP**	**N-Q4**

Black has an excellent game, it appears. But a closer inspection reveals that the two White knights will not be removed from their excellent posts without grave weakening, that, except for his blockading knight, Black has no effective pieces, and that Black's knight pawn is artificially isolated and weak.

21	**B-Q2**	**B-KB3**

Perhaps better is 21 . . . B-QB3-N4 to get rid of the knight.

22	**QR-B1**	**Q-K2**
23	**N-N2!**	. . .

Beginning a voyage to QB5. Black's game is headed downhill from here on. As played, he misses a good defensive try in 24 . . . BxN; 25 QxB, B-B3 and . . . B-N4. Another is 25 . . . RxR; 26 RxR, Q-Q2 and . . . Q-N4.

| 23 | . . . | **QR-B1** |
| 24 | **N-R4** | **B-N4** |

And Kashdan, realizing that his trusted bishops were not all they're cracked up to be, was faced with a certain loss of a pawn after 25 RxR, RxR; 26 N-B5, BxB; 27 QxB, N-B6; 28 R-K1, R-Q1; 29 Q-B4!, and, for example, 29 . . . N-Q4; 30 QxPch, or 29 . . . R-KB1; 30 N(K)-Q3. The pawn cost him the game at move 69.

The other Reshevsky trademark is coolness under fire. No one clings to survival so tenaciously as Reshevsky. And few play as well under pressure. In the last round of the Nottingham tournament all the leaders muffed opportunities. Usually it's the first round of a tournament that produces the blunders, but at Nottingham Flohr overlooked an elementary mating threat and drew with Tartakover, Capablanca overlooked several of Bogolyubov's good moves and ended up fighting for a draw, Fine almost threw away an easy win against Tylor until the Englishman counterblundered, and Euwe allowed the loss of a piece to Thomas, who incredibly overlooked it. Only Reshevsky remained cool and demolished Vidmar in twenty-six moves. As Tarrasch said of his longtime enemy, Lasker, he sometimes loses a game but never loses his head.

This comes through clearest in time trouble. Every Reshevsky game in this early period appeared inevitably headed for a scramble in which Sammy had less than a minute for his last dozen moves. Of fourteen games at AVRO,* he was in time

* The Dutch Broadcasting Company AVRO (Algemene Vereniging Radio Omroep) invited the eight strongest players of 1938 to a tournament. The purpose was to decide which deserved the opportunity to play Alekhine for the world championship. Although Paul Keres of Estonia won the super event on tie breaks ahead of Fine, the match between Keres and Alekhine never took place because of World War II.

trouble in twelve. Why does he take so much time in the late opening to find unspectacular moves?

The charge has often been made that Reshevsky, among others, including Viktor Korchnoi and Walter Browne, intentionally seeks time trouble. But the real reason for his early middlegame "thinks" between moves 12 and 18 is that he wants to familiarize himself with all the structural peculiarities of the position. By that stage in the game some of the tactical themes have already begun to suggest themselves. Strategic plans predict themselves. Thus, as Reshevsky told the English author Assiac, he has acquainted himself much better than his opponent with the middlegame's undercurrents. Then follows the final blitz of moves and Reshevsky's tactical skill carries him through.

One of the best demonstrations of this is from the 1948 world championship tournament, in which Reshevsky finished in a tie for third.

The Hague, 1948

	BOTVINNIK	RESHEVSKY
1	**P-Q4**	**N-KB3**
2	**P-QB4**	**P-K3**
3	**N-QB3**	**B-N5**
4	**P-K3**	**P-B4**
5	**P-QR3**	**BxNch**
6	**PxB**	**N-B3**
7	**B-Q3**	**0-0**
8	**N-K2**	**P-QN3**

Reshevsky was the first American player to understand how to play a closed position well. A corollary of this is that he was the first to appreciate the many possibilities of the knight. Here he stakes out the queenside and plans to win a pawn with . . . B-QR3, . . . N-QR4, and . . . R-QB1. At the same time Black must defend against a notorious kingside attack. During the previous decade White's attacking setup was rated superior to Black's defenses, and many brilliant wins were scored. Capablanca's excellent redeployment, which Black now begins, puts the position under a question mark.

| 9 | **P-K4** | **N-K1!** |

Black stops B-KN5, a pin that is very difficult to get out of because Black has already castled and has given up the bishop that usually defends from K2. The second purpose of . . . N-K1 is to provide an additional piece for the assault on the forward bishop pawn (. . . N-Q3). Finally, the move unblocks Black's king bishop pawn and prepares to meet P-KB4 with . . . P-KB4, locking up White's bishops.

10	**B-K3**	**P-Q3**
11	**0-0**	**N-R4**
12	**N-N3**	**B-R3**
13	**Q-K2**	**Q-Q2**
14	**P-B4**	**P-B4!!**

A very fine blockading move that seems outrageously weakening but is vital to Black's survival. Consider what happens if

Black doesn't act boldly: Bronstein-Najdorf, Budapest, 1950, diverted from the same opening with 8 . . . P-Q3; 9 P-K4, N-K1!; 10 0-0, P-QN3; 11 P-B4, B-R3?; 12 P-B5!, and White's initiative exploded because of his open lines and space edge on the kingside. The game was over shortly after 12 . . . P-K4; 13 P-B6!, K-R1 (13 . . . NxP; 14 B-N5); 14 P-Q5!, N-R4; 15 N-N3, PxP; 16 N-B5, B-B1; 17 Q-R5.

In the Botvinnik-Reshevsky position Black could also get mated with great ease if he does not stop P-KB5. For example, if 14 . . . Q-R5; 15 P-B5!, BxP; 16 PxKP, BxP (16 . . . PxKP; 17 RxRch, followed by R-B1ch and Q-B3); 17 B-QN5!, Q-N6; 18 P-Q5, B-B1; 19 BxN, RxB; 20 RxP!, KxR; 21 Q-R5ch and mate in a few moves.

<table>
<tr><td>15</td><td>**QR-K1**</td><td>. . .</td></tr>
</table>

Wrong rook as we'll see in a second. The idea of P-Q5 is better served by 15 KR-K1.

<table>
<tr><td>15</td><td>. . .</td><td>**P-N3!**</td></tr>
</table>

Black's last two moves look like horrible loosenings of his kingside, but having blocked the position with . . . P-B4, Black must support his bishop pawn. The move played also allows Black to answer 16 P-Q5 with 16 . . . N-N2.

<table>
<tr><td>16</td><td>**R-Q1**</td><td>**Q-KB2**</td></tr>
<tr><td>17</td><td>**P-K5**</td><td>. . .</td></tr>
</table>

Change of plans. White decides here to work against the other bishop pawn by threatening 18 KPxP, PxP (18 . . . NxQP; 19 PxP, N[3]xP; 20 PxP or B-KB2); 19 BxQP!, NxQP; 20 Q-K5.

<table>
<tr><td>17</td><td>. . .</td><td>**R-B1**</td></tr>
<tr><td>18</td><td>**KR-K1**</td><td>**QPxP**</td></tr>
<tr><td>19</td><td>**QPxKP**</td><td>. . .</td></tr>
</table>

This preserves the queen bishop pawn by keeping the bishop file closed. Yet it leaves Black with a won game positionally and a sure advantage in the ending. Once the pawns are fixed, Black usually finds his game very comfortable in the Nimzo-Indian. Worse than that from White's point of view is the logjam of his pieces in the center. He can't take advantage of the board's only open file until he moves the white-squared bishop. But this piece is the main defense of the forward bishop pawn. In the next stage Black maneuvers his knight against a new weakness, while White maneuvers his knight to the defense of the weak pawn.

19	. . .	N-KN2
20	N-B1	KR-Q1
21	B-KB2	N-R4
22	B-N3	. . .

An ugly move. But 22 P-N3 provokes Black into mating ambitions with 22 . . . B-N2, followed by . . . B-R1 and . . . Q-N2.

22	. . .	Q-K1!
23	N-K3	Q-R5
24	Q-R2	. . .

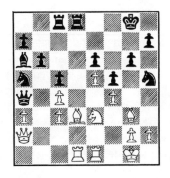

White just manages to hold onto his buttons. But it has taken Black more than twenty-three moves to achieve his advantage. To be exact, it has taken him two hours and twenty-six minutes, leaving him four minutes for the remaining seventeen moves. His winning plan is not completely clear, although trading queens and doubling rooks on the queen file seems indicated. Reshevsky's play under difficult time pressure is superb.

24	. . .	NxB
25	PxN	P-R4!

This completes the bind on the kingside that Black began with 14 . . . P-B4. Once P-N4 is stopped, Black need only worry about piece sacrifices on the kingside.

26	B-K2	K-B2
27	K-B2	Q-N6!

Black foresees a minor piece endgame in which his king marches to the queenside for an easy victory.

28	QxQ	NxQ
29	B-Q3	. . .

The threat was . . . N-Q7-K5ch. Black needs a small opening for his minor pieces.

29	. . .	K-K2
30	K-K2	N-R4
31	R-Q2	R-B2

Again White has found a traffic jam of pieces. To win, Black must have a winning avenue, and for this reason Botvinnik's next move has been harshly criticized. In truth, 32 R-KR1, R(2)-Q2; 33 R(2)-Q1 retains chances of blockading the position. In time pressure, Black would then have to watch for tricky chances of P-N4 opening up space for White's rooks and bishop. For example, on 33 . . . N-N6, threatening 34 . . . N-B8!, White responds with 34 P-N4!, RPxP; 35 R-R6!, RxB; 36 R-R7ch, drawing.

32	P-N4?	R(2)-Q2!

Not 32 . . . RPxP; 33 R-KR1, R-KB1; 34 R-R6, with great counterplay. Black now threatens to smash through by use of the queen file pin.

33	**PxBP**	**NPxP**
34	**R(1)-Q1**	**. . .**

The now-open knight file spells White's doom after 34 R(2)-Q1, K-B2; 35 R-KR1, K-N3; 36 KR-N1 (threatening P-N4), K-R3; 37 R-KR1, B-N2, and White is soon forced to lose material.

34	**. . .**	**P-R5**
35	**K-K1**	**N-N6**
36	**N-Q5ch**	**. . .**

A desperation sacrifice in a hopeless position. On 36 R-N2, RxB cracks through. Botvinnik's move, like his thirty-second, was intended to rattle his opponent, but he moved quickly and surely with the following: 36 . . . PxN; 37 BxP, NxR; 38 RxN, PxP!; 39 BxR, RxB; 40 R-KB2, K-K3; 41 R-B3, R-Q6, and after Botvinnik played 42 K-K2, he resigned.

By 1948, when he won this game, the only game Botvinnik lost before clinching the event, Reshevsky was a mature, experienced tournament pro. But his persistent problems continued to deny him the highest rungs on the championship ladder. A typical comment came from a 1948 tournament book: "His play showed the same weaknesses that have always characterized it: inaccurate openings and severe time pressure, both reflections of lack of preparation." Reshevsky has matured further in the past quarter century. His time pressure problems are less frequent and he prepares well for opening novelties in top tournaments. He still draws too many games against weaker players to consistently win first place in grandmaster tournaments.

As with most counterpunchers, Reshevsky has often fared better with Black than with White. This is something rare. Marshall's victories with the Black pieces, for example, usually were the result of poor play by an opponent. But Reshevsky has shown an American chess public how to win with Black by exploiting just mediocre play. Offer him an early draw and he might accept. But press Reshevsky hard and he lashes back.

Nottingham, 1936

	EMANUEL LASKER	RESHEVSKY
1	P-Q4	P-Q4
2	P-QB4	PxP
3	N-KB3	N-KB3
4	P-K3	. . .

Reshevsky prefers the simpler openings. With Black he often likes to maintain solid equality, with the defense in a Ruy Lopez. With 1 P-Q4, a Queens Gambit or Nimzo-Indian is usually sufficient for equality. With a knight on Q4 Reshevsky is content to play almost any middlegame.

4	. . .	P-K3
5	BxP	P-B4
6	N-B3	P-QR3
7	0-0	P-QN4
8	B-Q3	. . .

An unusual retreat but in keeping with Lasker's aversion to hackneyed moves. The Reshevsky-Vidmar game referred to earlier went (via transposition) 8 B-N3, B-N2; 9 Q-K2, N-B3? (. . . QN-Q2); 10 R-Q1, Q-N3; 11 P-Q5!, PxP; 12 P-K4!, with a marked advantage.

8	. . .	PxP!

Reshevsky was also the first American to fully understand what Nimzovich was talking about. The blockade of the isolated pawn, for example, is one subject Sammy has mastered. By 8 B-Q3 White has reduced control of Q5, so Black eagerly plays for a blockade. On 9 NxQP now we have a symmetrical position in which, if anything, Black's more active bishops confer the advantage on him.

9	PxP	B-N2
10	B-N5	B-K2
11	Q-K2	0-0
12	QR-Q1	QN-Q2
13	N-K5	N-Q4!

In this semiopen position it is very much in Black's interest to exchange off minor pieces. On 14 BxB, QxB; 15 QNxN, BxN; 16 B-K4, White concedes Black equality. Lasker chooses a tricky attacking line but misses the essential followup three moves later.

14	B-B1!?	KNxN

Creating the infamous Hanging Pawns, which will be surveyed by another blockading knight.

15	PxN	N-B3
16	P-QR4!	Q-Q4!?

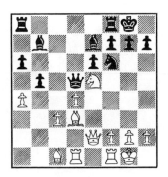

Reshevsky is most at home in counterattack—when called upon to defuse danger. Of course, he prefers the attack that mates in one move to the defense that escapes by one move. But everyone (almost) can attack. Few can defend as well as Reshevsky, and that is his margin of success.

Here White has offered a strong pawn sacrifice that would allow him to play P-QB4 and B-N2. The lost queen rook pawn is meaningless—that is, meaningless in the middlegame. Reshevsky's reply complicates the game, and although it is not as powerful as was thought during the game, its practical effect was powerful. Lasker now fumbles.

17	**N-B3?**	. . .

"A sorry retreat, but the seemingly aggressive 17 P-KB4 could be effectively answered by . . . P-N5!," Reshevsky wrote in his notes. But then 18 P-B4! puts Black in real trouble because 18 . . . QxPch; 19 B-K3, Q-B6; 20 BxPch! and 21 R-Q3 is too strong. If Black must retreat his queen, White stands very well.

17	. . .	**KR-B1!**

Black is in the driver's seat now that the kingside attack has collapsed. 18 PxP, PxP; 19 BxP, RxP threatens 20 . . . RxN; 21 PxR, Q-R4, with devastation.

18	**B-N2**	**N-K5**
19	**R-B1**	**N-N4!**

White has been victimized by Black's bluff and his otherwise very astute counterplay. Now 20 N-K1, PxP! and . . . P-R6 makes the meaningless pawn useful in the winning plan.

20	**PxP**	**PxP**
21	**BxP**	. . .

And here 21 N-K1 can be met by . . . R-R7 or by 21 . . . N-R6ch; 22 K-R1, N-B5.

21	. . .	**NxNch**
22	**PxN**	**Q-N4ch**

White surrenders. He loses the queen after 23 K-R1, Q-N5!

As was the case for so many others, World War II changed Reshevsky's life. After a very successful career as boy prodigy and young master, he returned to nonchess activities in the 1940s. During the next decade the cold war froze the highest levels of chess and prevented a true test of Reshevsky's talent against that of the younger Russian stars. Against Botvinnik, the world champion, in the 1954 United States–USSR radio match, Reshevsky won the minimatch 2½-1½. Reshevsky tournament victories included Buenos Aires in 1960 (tied with Korchnoi) and the 1969 U.S. championship, as well as good finishes at Dallas in 1957, Maribor and Sousse in 1967, and Netanya 1969. The mature Reshevsky played the openings better, got into time pressure less frequently, but developed a new flaw—blundering occasionally in the fifth hour of play, not necessarily because of shortness of time but because of fatigue.

This was partly the fault in Reshevsky's performance in the 1970 Interzonal at Palma de Mallorca—seventeenth in a field of twenty-four. But even then, thirty-four years after Notting-ham and his first U.S. championship, he was still capable of superb chess.

INTERZONAL, Palma de Mallorca, 1970

	RESHEVSKY	POLUGAYEVSKY
1	**P-Q4**	**N-KB3**
2	**P-QB4**	**P-B4**
3	**N-KB3**	**. . .**

Seeking the simplicity of an open center to the double-edged imbalance of 3 P-Q5.

3	**. . .**	**PxP**
4	**NxP**	**P-K3**
5	**N-QB3**	**B-N5**

Black's system is similar to the Paulsen Variation of the Sicilian (1 P-K4, P-QB4; 2 N-KB3, P-K3; 3 P-Q4, PxP; 4 NxP, P-QR3; 5 P-QB4, N-KB3; 6 N-QB3, B-N5) and gives Black no problems if he plays accurately. Polugayevsky also makes a wise psychological choice, as Reshevsky lost badly to Fischer in this line earlier in the tournament.

6   **N-N5**   . . .

Reshevsky-Fischer went 6 P-K3, N-K5!; 7 Q-B2, NxN; 8 PxN, B-K2; 9 B-K2 (9 B-Q3!), 0-0; 10 0-0, P-QR3; 11 P-KB4?, P-Q3; 12 P-KB5, PxP!, with advantage to Black. Black also equalizes easily against 6 N-B2, BxNch; 7 PxB, Q-R4; 8 Q-Q3, N-B3; 9 B-R3, P-Q4!, or 6 B-Q2, N-B3; 7 N-B2, B-K2.

6   . . .   **0-0?!**

Black makes the first of several small but cumulatively dangerous slips. He has a fine game immediately with 6 . . . P-Q4!; 7 B-B4, 0-0!; 8 P-K3 (8 N-B7?, N-R4), P-QR3; 9 P-QR3, B-R4; 10 N-Q6, N-B3; 11 B-N3, BxNch!, or 7 P-QR3, BxNch; 8 NxB, P-Q5!; 9 N-R2, 0-0; 10 P-K3, N-B3.

7   **P-QR3**   **BxNch**
8   **NxB**   **P-Q4**
9   **B-N5!**   . . .

Preserving some tension in the position and undermining the strength of . . . P-Q5.

9   . . .   **P-KR3**
10   **B-R4**   **P-KN4?**

A more serious error. Black can still obtain equal play with 10 . . . P-Q5; 11 N-K4, and then 11 . . . P-KN4; 12 NxNch, QxN; 13 B-N3, P-K4 or . . . N-B3.

11   **B-N3**   **P-Q5**
12   **N-N5**   . . .

Upset by White's failure to play the book line, 10 BxN, Black faces an uncertain middlegame. True, White will have to weaken himself with P-K3, but Reshevsky's king seems much safer considering the two bishops than Black's.

12   . . .   **N-B3**
13   **P-K3**   **PxP**

Paul Morphy.

(Courtesy of the John G. White Department of Folklore, Orientalia, and Chess, Cleveland Public Library.)

George Henry Mackenzie.

(Courtesy of the Collection of the John G. White Department of Folklore, Orientalia, and Chess, Cleveland Public Library.)

Sam Loyd.

son Whipps Showalter (*seated left*) and Solomon Lip-
tz (*seated right*) at the U.S. Chess Association's meet-
n St. Louis.

(Courtesy of the Collection of the John G. White Department of Folklore, Orientalia, and Chess, Cleveland Public Library.)

Harry Nelson Pillsbury.

match for the World Championship between Frank Mar-l (*left*) and Dr. Tarrasch (*right*).

(Courtesy of the Collection of the John G. White Department of Folklore, Orientalia, and Chess, Cleveland Public Library.)

José Capablanca playing thirty simultaneous games at the Imperial Chess Club, London, in 1911.

(Courtesy of the Collection of the John G. White Department of Folklore, Orientalia and Chess, Cleveland Public Library.)

Issac Kashdan.

Samuel Reshevsky, at age ten, playing twenty simultaneous games at the Hotel Breslin, New York, in 1922. He won eighteen and drew two.

(Courtesy of the Collection of the John G. White Department of Folklore, Orientalia, and Chess, Cleveland Public Library.)

Reuben Fine (*right*) and Herman Steiner (*left*).

(Photo by Nancy Roos, courtesy of Burt Hochberg.)

Arnold Denker as he appeared in a 1947 Camel cigarette ad.

Al Horowitz.

(Courtesy of *The New York Times*.)

(UPI photo.)

Herman Steiner and his wife during their honeymoon.

Arthur Bisguier.

(Photo by Burt Hoch

Robert Byrne at the 1972 U.S. Championship.

(Courtesy of Burt Hochberg.)

William Lombardy.

(Photo by Carol Hochber

Bobby Fischer.

Ken Rogoff.

(Photo by J. Politowski, courtesy of *Overboard*.)

(Courtesy of the U. S. Chess Federation.)

Andrew Soltis at the 1973 Chicago U. S. C. F. International.

(Courtesy of Burt Hochb

Greg de Fotis.

14	**PxP**	**P-K4**
15	**B-Q3**	**B-N5**

Reshevsky has made a career out of exploiting inaccurate attacking moves such as this. With 15 . . . N-KN5; 16 Q-K2, Q-N3, White has difficulties with this pawn because 17 P-K4? is a horrible positional move.

16	**Q-B2**	**P-K5**
17	**B-K2**	**Q-R4ch**
18	**K-B2!**	. . .

In the middlegame, Reshevsky correctly judges, Black has more problems with his pieces, especially the king.

18	. . .	**BxB**
19	**KxB**	**QR-B1?**

Cheapo! Will White miss 20 . . . QxN; 21 PxQ, N-Q5ch?

20	**N-Q6!**	**R-R1**
21	**QR-Q1**	**N-R4**
22	**B-K1**	**Q-N3**
23	**P-KN4!**	**N-B3**
24	**B-B3**	. . .

White has such a magnificent positional harmony that his game almost plays itself. The text leads to a forced win involving the sacrifice of the Exchange and a nice thirtieth move.

24	. . .	NxP
25	QxP	P-B4
26	Q-K6ch	K-R2
27	NxBP!	N(3)-K4
28	R-Q7ch!	. . .

And the attack—properly a counterattack—crashes home after 28 . . . NxR; 29 QxNch, K-N3; 30 P-KR4!! (the point of White's continuation—P-R5 mate is threatened and Black must occupy the R4 flight square), P-KR4; 31 N-K7ch, K-R3; 32 PxPch, KxP; 33 Q-Q5ch, Resigns. Yet another memorable survival.

Reuben Fine

Besides being one of the six strongest American chessplayers of all time and one of the supergrandmasters of the 1930s, Reuben Fine is remarkable in other ways.

First, Fine's career was as brief as Reshevsky's was long. His first European tournament was in 1935—at the age of twenty-one—and he in effect retired from international chess after his triumph in the great AVRO tournament in Holland three years later. Aside from occasional New York tournaments and the U.S. championship of 1944, Fine played no more serious chess after 1938. Like Morphy, whose career was even shorter, Fine retired at the height of his success.

Also, Fine was the first American to write. Morphy's brief fling at annotation was not impressive by modern standards. Marshall surely enjoyed illuminating the swindles in his own games but went no further. Aside from *My Chess Career* and a few other books aimed at novices, Capablanca left no literary heritage.

But Fine's contributions to the American chess library were

considerable. His *Basic Chess Endings* is a classic, still carried by grandmasters to tournaments as an essential part of their luggage. Fine's revision of *Modern Chess Openings* in 1939 and his later work, *Practical Chess Openings*, were two of the best-selling openings books ever printed. And there were others: *The Ideas Behind the Chess Openings*; *The Middle Game in Chess*; *Chess the Easy Way*; *The World's Great Chess Games*; and *Lessons from My Games*.

Writing books enabled Fine to become the first professional in America since Marshall gave up the tournament circuit in the 1920s. Capablanca had his sinecure in the diplomatic service, Reshevsky was an accountant, and Edward Lasker was an engineer. Kashdan had tried to make a living solely from chess but gave up shortly before Fine came to the fore.

Reuben Fine was born in New York City on October 11, 1914, and learned chess from an uncle when he was about eight years old. It remained one of several games he played, with no special emphasis until just before high school graduation, when he joined the Marshall Chess Club. At that point, Fine later wrote, "the real passion for chess began and lasted some eight years." He was not yet fifteen when the chess bug bit.

At first Fine was a tactician. He was fond of saying later that he never opened a chess book until he was a master. But his mastery developed from playing for hours a day, several days a week through his late teens. By 1932 Fine was champion of the Marshall club and dazzled opponents with a sharp tactical skill honed on thousands of skittles games. The same year Fine won the Western Open, then the strongest annual event in the United States.

Like Reshevsky, Fine could attack but excelled at fighting defense. Unlike Reshevsky, Fine prepared his openings and only got into bad time trouble after a very complex middle-game. The following is the lightning counterattack from a brief match with Carlos Torre in Mexico during 1934.

Black (Fine) has just played 16 . . . P-B5! to keep White from getting his knight to Q4 after QPxP. White's pieces are not particularly active, and Black has a nice queenside initiative because of his passed bishop pawn and his potential for dominating the queen knight file.

There is a right way and a wrong way for White to react to 16 . . . P-B5! The right way is to counter with 17 P-QN3, forcing a liquidation of the advanced pawn and opening White's side of the dangerous file. Black is still better, of course. But Torre, once an attacker of terrifying reputation, chooses the wrong way.

	17	**P-KN4?**	**P-B3!**

Black chooses to open up the same side of the board on which his opponent has the greater power. It is this very policy that White has avoided by not playing 17 P-QN3. The policy is not always successful but is the hallmark of a dynamic defender. Best now for White is 18 PxP so that 18 . . . NxP can be met by 19 N-K5.

	18	**R-KB2**	PxP
	19	**BPxP**	. . .

The alternative, 19 QPxP, gives White the blockade square at Q4 but allows the clever 19 . . . P-Q5!! that Fine had prepared. The idea is to capitalize on the newly open long diagonal leading to the White king. On 20 NxP (or 20 BxP, RxP; 21 B-B3, Q-B2 and . . . B-N2), B-N2ch; 21 N-B3, Black wins with 21 . . . NxP!; 22 B-Q2, Q-Q4; 23 N-N6, QxNch! So White might try 21 K-N1, B-R5; 22 R-B1, because 22 R-Q2, Q-Q4 is disaster. But even then Black continues 22 . . . Q-Q4; 23 KN-B3, Q-K5! and either . . . NxKP or . . . RxP next move.

19	. . .	**B-N2**
20	**Q-B2**	**B-QB3**
21	**N-B3**	**N-B4!!**

Another lure to tempt the opening of the long diagonal. On 22 PxN, P-Q5; 23 BxP, RxN; 24 RxR, BxNch; 25 K-N1, R-Q1, Black should win. Fine's last move is not just a pretty tease. It's effect is felt in two moves.

22	**R(1)-B1**	**N-Q6**
23	**R-N2**	**NxKP!!**

Even if Torre hadn't cooperated by putting an unprotected rook on KB1, Black could have won by doubling rooks on the king bishop file. The diagonal is opened by force now.

24	**PxN**	**P-Q5**
25	**N-K4**	**PxB**

On 25 BxP Black would win the Exchange with 25 . . . RxN. Now White is hopeless and resigned after 26 K-N1, Q-Q4!; 27 N-B3, Q-Q6!; 28 QxQ, PxQ; 29 R-N3, P-K7.

In 1934 the Depression was in its fifth year, but this didn't seem to affect American chess. The year before, *Chess Review* became the first permanent national chess magazine under the editorship of Kashdan and later under I. A. "Al" Horowitz. "It is significant," the new magazine said in its first issue, "that the revival of chess interest dates with the commencement of the depression." After the wild spending of the 1920s, the magazine said, "People look about for some saner, more economical method of spending their leisure."

Reuben Fine looked about in 1934 and found the job market very poor for a young man of twenty. He decided to play chess for a living "temporarily." After his Mexican tour, Fine performed well on the U.S. team at the Warsaw International Team Tournament in 1935 and followed up with a tie for second and third place at an event in Lodz, Poland. But his real introduction to international play began at Zandvoort, Holland, in 1936. Fine finished first ahead of a strong field of masters that included Euwe, Gruenfeld, and Bogolyubov. From there on it was nearly two years of continuous chess—as Euwe's second in the return match with Alekhine, as victor in a match with Gideon Stahlberg of Sweden, and as the touring master playing in tournaments and giving exhibitions in the Soviet Union. Fine spent much of the time in Holland and married a Hollander.

As suggested earlier, Fine prefers to study the openings to being surprised over the board. Consequently, he chooses sharp opening plans with many tactical chances that confer advantage on the alert player. In the following game Fine confronts the leader of the new Soviet School.

Nottingham, 1936

BOTVINNIK   FINE

1   **N-KB3**   **P-Q4**
2   **P-B4**   **PxP!?**

And why not? Why should Black play a complicated but constricted position with pawns at Q4, K3, and QB3 when he can transpose into a freer Queen's Gambit Accepted in which Black has good central control. On 3 P-K3, for example, the second player can try 3 . . . N-QB3; 4 BxP, P-K4, or 3 . . . P-QN4!?; 4 P-QR4, P-QB3; 5 PxP, PxP; 6 P-QN3, P-QR4; 7 PxP, P-N5! Or, as Fine played successfully against Keres at Zandvoort,

3 . . . P-QB4; 4 BxP, N-KB3; 5 0-0, P-QR3; 6 P-QN3, P-K3;
7 B-N2, N-B3; 8 P-QR4, B-K2; 9 N-K5, N-QR4!

3	**N-R3**	**P-QB4**
4	**NxP**	**N-QB3**

Black has the makings of a reversed Maroczy bind with . . .
P-B3 and . . . P-K4. At Semmering a year after this game
Keres played the simplifying 5 QN-K5 to thwart this and the
game was drawn quickly.

5	**P-QN3**	**P-B3!**
6	**B-N2**	**P-K4**
7	**P-N3**	**KN-K2**
8	**B-N2**	**N-Q4?!**

This was correctly criticized by Alekhine for allowing White's
freeing plan of N-KR4 and P-B4. The game becomes very
sharp here and Black has his difficulties. Better is 8 . . . N-B4,
anticipating White's plan.

9	**0-0**	**B-K2**
10	**N-R4!**	**0-0**
11	**Q-N1!**	. . .

Two very nice moves give Botvinnik the early pull. His first
threat is 12 B-K4, P-KN3; 13 BxNP, with a smashing attack.

11	. . .	**R-B2**
12	**N-B5**	**B-K3**
13	**P-B4**	**PxP**

Black would love to maintain the strong point at K4 for
another few moves so that he can go on the counterattack with
. . . N-Q5! But he hasn't that much time.

14	**PxP**	. . .

| 14 | . . . | **N-N3!** |

The first difficult decision for Black. Now 15 NxN, QxN; 16 NxBch, RxN; 17 P-K3, or 16 K-R1 is sufficient for a slight edge, but White deserves more. Botvinnik discovers another good idea, which prevents the intended 15 . . . NxN; 16 PxN, BxP because of 17 N-K3!—for example, 17 . . . BxKP; 18 R-B2, QxP; 19 N-B1!

15	**B-K4!**	**BxQN!**
16	**PxB**	**NxP**
17	**B-QB3**	. . .

Of course, 17 NxBch, RxN; 18 BxPch, K-B1 leaves Black high and dry with an initiative in the center, as White's most productive minor pieces are traded off. Black could try to consolidate with 17 . . . B-B1, but Fine has a superior resource, characteristically a counterattack, which puts the onus back on White.

17	. . .	**N-Q5!**
18	**NxN**	**PxN**
19	**BxPch**	**K-B1**
20	**B-N4**	**P-Q6!**

Another shot, threatening . . . Q-N3ch. White must exchange his queen bishop as a result, and this takes away a defender of the queen pawn. Fine has squirmed into a position that cannot be lost for him.

21	BxBch	RxB
22	QxQP	QxQ
23	PxQ	N-N3

There is no demonstrable advantage to either side in this position despite the extra White pawn or the superior Black pieces. To maintain his material, White must defend. After 24 B-K4, R-Q1; 25 QR-B1, N-Q4; 26 P-QR3, R(K)-Q2; 27 K-N2, P-QN3; 28 K-B3, Black found equilibrium with 28 . . . N-B2!; 29 K-K3, N-R3; 30 R-QB3, N-B4, and the game was soon drawn.

The second Botvinnik game pits Fine against the Russian's favorite variation of the French. Botvinnik errs early in the opening and Fine puts on a typical power play with his heavy pieces. The White rooks, like the beasts of burden they symbolize, steadily push everything out of their path.

AVRO, 1938

FINE   BOTVINNIK

1	P-K4	P-K3
2	P-Q4	P-Q4
3	N-QB3	B-N5

Named after Simon Winawer, naturally enough a Russian master of the nineteenth century, this variation was molded by Botvinnik into one of the terrors of the 1930s and 1940s. Perhaps Fine has a prepared variation.

4	P-K5	P-QB4
5	PxP	. . .

And this is it. When Euwe asked Fine in 1936 to help him prepare for the return Alekhine match a year later, the

American immediately began to research the former champion's style. Inevitably this forced Fine to review his own opening repertoire and ask himself what he would do against the French or how he would play against Alekhine's Dutch. In doing so Fine toughened up his own openings, adding ideas that he might never have developed if he was on his own on the tournament circuit. After all, why did he need to prepare opening innovations in the United States?

Fine's choice here often leads to a sacrifice of a pawn because Black easily regains the bishop pawn and then assaults the king pawn. The variation involves a number of tricky gambit possibilities, which, as expected, turn out to be difficult for the Russian to handle under tournament conditions.

Against Flohr in the same event Fine revealed how extensively prepared he was by springing another odd sideline: 5 B-Q2, N-K2; 6 N-B3. He was rewarded again when the Czech played 6 . . . N-B4? (instead of 6 . . . QN-B3); 7 PxP!, BxP; 8 B-Q3, N-R5; 9 0-0, N-B3; 10 R-K1, P-KR3 (10 . . . 0-0 allows the ancient sacrifice, 11 BxPch!); 11 N-R4!, B-B1; 12 R-QB1, B-Q2; 13 NxN, QxN; 14 P-QB4!, with a big advantage.

5	. . .	N-K2
6	N-B3	QN-B3
7	B-Q3	P-Q5

This sharpens the tension and helps Fine along. 6 . . . Q-B2 might have been better than 6 . . . QN-B3 because 7 B-KB4, N-N3; 8 B-N3, QxBP looks good for him. As played, Black should play the nonrisky 7 . . . N-N3 which watches the king pawn and obstructs a kingside attack.

8	P-QR3	B-R4
9	P-QN4	. . .

Here begins the kind of pawn sacrifice that Fine must have considered in advance.

9	. . .	NxNP
10	PxN	BxP
11	B-N5ch	. . .

The trouble with this move is 11 . . . B-Q2!, with a succession of equalizing trades: 12 QxP, BxNch; 13 QxB, BxB. A better line was 11 0-0!, BxN; 12 R-N1, with excellent attacking chances for White. He can play N-N5-K4 and use his two fine bishops.

| 11 | . . . | N-B3? |

Botvinnik makes one of his rare opening inaccuracies and Fine methodically crushes him from this move forward. It is astonishing how powerful White's initiative is.

12	BxNch!	PxB
13	R-R4!	BxNch
14	B-Q2	P-B3?!
15	0-0	0-0
16	BxB	PxB

Black cannot hold such a pawn without active pieces. Moreover, Botvinnik's bishop is the sickly child of the French Defense—too sheltered by its own pawns. Best of all, from White's view of the board, is the outpost square Q6. As Nimzovich said, this outpost is satisfactory for a knight but even better for a rook.

17	**Q-K1**	**P-QR4**
18	**QxP**	**B-R3**
19	**KR-R1**	**B-N4**
20	**R-Q4!**	. . .

The rook pawn can be captured at will. White wants to keep his queen on the board to maintain tension. Now he aims at occupying Q6 and driving the bishop back into oblivion with P-QB4.

20	. . .	**Q-K2**
21	**R-Q6**	**P-R5**

There is no sturdier defense. 21 . . . KR-Q1 is met by the steady 22 Q-Q4 or 22 R-K1. Black is totally without counterplay.

22	**Q-K3**	**R-R2**
23	**N-Q2!**	. . .

The winning move. After P-QB4 Black loses more space and the bind is absolute. Desperation follows.

23	. . .	**P-R6**
24	**P-QB4**	**B-R5**
25	**PxP**	**QxP**
26	**RxRP**	. . .

In terms of maneuvering space, Black is surprisingly worse off without his extra pawn than with it. He must lose the king pawn whenever Fine decides to go for it. White has a better theme on the open files.

26	. . .	R-K1
27	P-R4	R(2)-R1
28	N-B3	Q-N7
29	N-K5	Q-N8ch
30	K-R2	Q-B4
31	Q-KN3	Resigns!

Black is faced with R-KB3-B7 and R-Q7. His bishop can't move without dropping the bishop pawn. His queen rook must protect the bishop. The other pieces have no future. A high-powered performance from a sharp opening—typical Fine.

AVRO, the tournament sponsored by the Dutch radio station, Algemene Vereniging Radio Omroep, was the last great tournament before World War II. By tying with Keres for first place Fine had established himself as one of the half dozen best players in the world. Keres, who had better tie-breaking points than Fine, was unofficially named a challenger to Alekhine. The world champion, meanwhile, was preparing to accept a match challenge from Flohr when the war interceded.

Once again a great war suspended international chess activity, this time for six years. For Fine this meant a return to America and his studies, an end to his foreign chess career, and the beginning of a new profession—as a psychiatrist. Fine's "The Psychology of the Chess Player" was a highly acclaimed professional paper on the game of chess and an analysis of some of its leading players. One of Fine's conclusions was that professional players—Alekhine, Steinitz, and Morphy—tended to be less stable mentally than grandmasters who had other pursuits—Lasker, Euwe and Botvinnik.

The 1940s was a period of mixed interest for Fine, who became a member of the older generation in contrast with the young postwar masters. Fine continued to write books and play an occasional tournament. He also set something of a record in 1945 by simultaneously playing four blindfold games against master-level players at ten seconds a move. One of his losing opponents was Robert Byrne, age fifteen.

Despite these feats Fine failed at one thing—winning the U.S. championship. We'll see how he failed in 1944 when Denker won. The closest he came was second place, a half point behind Reshevsky in 1940. A careless loss to A. Kupchik sealed his chances for tournament victory. The 1944 U.S. championship was Fine's last. More and more a professional psychiatrist, Fine's remaining tournaments were the 1948 and 1951 New York Internationals. In the former Fine was again the master of the prewar period, but in the second he had to settle for a creditable fourth place.

But Fine left the national chess scene a class above the lesser masters of his day. In the following encounter, another defensive and tactical gem, he takes on a leader of the postwar juniors, George Kramer.

New York, 1948

	KRAMER	FINE
1	**N-KB3**	**P-Q4**
2	**P-B4**	**PxP**

As creative as Fine was in the opening, none of his ideas retained his name. Perhaps this should be remembered as the Fine Variation.

3	**P-K4!?**	. . .

Highly risky in a positional sense because White leaves a gaping hole at his Q4. If he can neutralize this with a timely P-Q4, he has a strong game in the center.

3	. . .	P-QB4
4	BxP	N-QB3
5	P-QN4	. . .

Without this, Black obtains a slight advantage by fianchettoeing his king bishop and expanding on the queenside with . . . P-QR3 and . . . P-QN4. White has planned a sort of delayed Wing Gambit, a poor relative of the Sicilian Variation. On 5 . . . NxP; 6 P-Q4, White threatens 7 N-K5, with chances.

5	. . .	P-K3!
6	P-N5	. . .

It was more important to Black to maintain Q5 control. On 6 PxP, BxP Black is already better with 7 B-N2, N-B3 or even 7 . . . BxPch. Now he regroups thematically.

6	. . .	QN-K2!
7	N-B3	N-KB3
8	0-0	N-N3

White still has problems on the black squares and the risky attempt at correcting that (9 P-Q4, PxP; 10 NxP, B-N5) is best. If Kramer was interested in the pawn sacrifice at move 5 he should be consistent and go into 9 P-Q4. Now he becomes disoriented on the queenside.

9	P-Q3	B-K2

White's next and last few moves, though useful, do not conform to any coherent middlegame plan. (Page Capablanca!) But Black's moves have more purpose. He gets K4 for one of his knights and he prepares . . . P-B4 for a kingside attack. At first this appears artificial, and White's plan for P-QR5 looks more natural. Fine sees that superior control of the center makes his plan the better one.

10	P-KR3	0-0
11	P-QR4	K-R1
12	R-K1	N-Q2

13	**Q-N3**	**P-N3**
14	**B-K3**	**B-N2**
15	**P-R5**	**PxP!**

No doubt the last move White had counted on.

White had threatened 16 P-R6, B-B1; 17 P-Q4, and 18 P-Q5, with a massive edge in space. White could have prepared P-Q4 with subtler means than this queenside diversion, which would have been better. Fine's resource is not uncommon for him. Pawn structure is only one of five or six middlegame premiums, all of which are inferior to active pieces. In Nimzovich's phrase, 15 . . . PxP! is an ugly move, but watch how it draws White's attention completely to the queenside.

16	**R-R2**	**B-Q3!**
17	**KR-R1**	**B-B2**
18	**N-K2**	**. . .**

18 P-Q4 is playable but clearly in Black's favor: 18 . . . PxP; 19 BxQP, QN-K4!; 20 NxN, NxN; 21 BxN?, BxB; 22 RxP, Q-Q5, for instance, with command of the black diagonals. Also excellent for Fine is 19 NxP, N-B4; 20 Q-B2, N-B5. White cannot eliminate the problem of weak black squares but should not surrender them.

18	. . .	Q-K2
19	**B-Q2**	**N-N3**
20	**BxRP**	**P-B4!**

Only the two lonesome knights protect White's kingside, while a queen, a rook, two bishops, and a knight are potential attackers. The apparent win of a pawn—21 BxKP, PxP; 22 PxP—doesn't work after 22 . . . BxP, and neither does 21 PxP, RxP; 22 BxP because of 22 . . . P-B5!; 23 BxP, RxN!; 24 PxR, N-R5, with mating threats of . . . Q-N4ch and . . . NxPch. Finally, White rejects 21 N-Q2, Q-Q3; 22 P-N3, P-B5! as equally unpleasant.

21	**BxN**	**BxB**
22	**N-N3**	. . .

Again there is a virulent attack on 22 PxP, RxP; 23 BxP, P-B5!; 24 QxP, RxN!; 25 PxR, N-K4!

22	. . .	**N-B5**

Black keeps the king pawn protected and retains the trumps such as doubling rooks on the queen file. His advantage is great.

23	**R-N1**	**PxP**
24	**PxP**	**QR-Q1**
25	**Q-K3**	**Q-B3**
26	**K-R2**	**P-N4!**

Fine wouldn't dare do this if he didn't have such control of the black squares. He intends . . . P-KR4 and . . . P-N5, with a quick mate.

27	**P-K5**	**Q-N2**
28	**R-KR1**	. . .

Kramer overlooks a hammerblow in a losing position. After 28 N-K1, P-KR4; 29 P-B3, P-N5, an invasion on the king bishop or king knight file cannot be avoided for long.

28	. . .	NxNP!
29	**KxN**	**RxN**
Resigns		

Arnold Denker

After twice finishing second to Reshevsky in U.S. championships and one third place result, Fine must have eagerly awaited the 1944 national competition: Reshevsky was not going to play. It was clear that the winner would need a very heavy plus when the tournament began at the Park Central Hotel in New York City. Aside from Fine, thirty-year-old Arnold Denker, Horowitz, Steiner, and A. S. Pinkus, the wartime tournament was missing several strong players.

In the seventh round Fine drew black against Denker in what became the deciding game. Denker eventually won nine games in a row and topped the field with a score of 15½-1½—his margin of victory over Fine being the following critical game.

U.S. CHAMPIONSHIP, New York, 1944

	DENKER	FINE
1	**P-Q4**	**N-KB3**
2	**P-QB4**	**P-K3**
3	**N-QB3**	**B-N5**
4	**P-K3**	**P-QN3**

This move disappeared from tournament chess sometime after this game but reappeared some twenty years later because, in Fischer's words, everything else had been analyzed to death. One idea of 4 . . . P-QN3 is to meet 5 KN-K2 with 5 . . . B-R3, putting immediate pressure on White's pawns.

5	**B-Q3**	**B-N2**
6	**N-B3**	**N-K5!?**
7	**0-0!**	. . .

In another famous game of the period Denker offered A. S. Pinkus a pawn in the opening. The gambit appeared dubious and Pinkus wrote on his scoresheet, "Show me," as he accepted it. When Pinkus was away from the board, Denker added to his scoresheet, "I will." He did.

With 7 0-0! White offers a pawn in two ways, neither of which is very comfortable for Black. On 7 . . . BxN; 8 PxB, NxQBP; 9 Q-B2, Black saves his piece with 9 . . . BxN; 10 PxB, Q-N4ch; 11 K-R1, Q-KR4, intending perpetual check. But White's attack is strong after 12 R-KN1!, QxBPch; 13 R-N2, P-KB4; 14 B-N2!. Also on 7 . . . BxN; 8 PxB, P-KB4, White is very well situated after 9 P-Q5!, N-B4; 10 B-R3!

7	. . .	**NxN**
8	**PxN**	**BxP**

Fine is, of course, playing for a win. But Denker has been given the kind of position Fine handles well—tactical, tricky, and sharp.

9	**R-N1**	**B-R4**

9 . . . 0-0 is out of the question because of 10 Q-B2, but 9 . . . N-B3!? is an attractive idea. Black will transfer the knight

to the kingside for defense. In 1969 Fischer wrote that White then has nothing for the pawn, and in Gligorich-Larsen in Lugano a year later Black in fact won. But he was very lucky, considering his position after 10 R-N3, B-R4; 11 P-K4, N-K2; 12 P-Q5, N-N3; 13 N-Q4, Q-K2; 14 B-B2, B-N5; 15 N-N5, 0-0?; 16 Q-R5.

10	**B-R3**	**P-Q3**
11	**P-B5!**	. . .

An easy move for an attacking player of Denker's skill. The move is a preparation for PxQP and the advance of the king pawn.

11	. . .	**0-0**
12	**PxQP**	**PxP**
13	**P-K4**	**R-K1**
14	**P-K5**	**PxP**
15	**NxP**	. . .

The position has become quite fluid because of the pawn exchanges, and for this reason combinations create themselves. For example, 15 . . . N-B3 allows the perennial 16 BxPch!, KxB; 17 Q-R5ch, K-N1; 18 QxPch and 19 R-N3. Nor does

15 . . . P-KR3; 16 Q-R5!, Q-B3; 17 NxP, QxN; 18 B-N6 work for Black.

15   . . .   Q-N4?!

A losing move, although Fine's suggested 15 . . . P-N3 also runs into problems after 16 B-N5!, Q-Q4; 17 P-B3, B-B3; 18 N-N4, Q-Q1; 19 P-Q5!, BxB; 20 RxB, P-QR3; 21 PxP!, QxQ (if 21 . . . PxR; 22 Q-R1!!); 22 N-B6ch, K-R1; 23 RxQ, RxP; 24 R-Q8ch, K-N2; 25 B-N2, RxN; 26 R(5)-Q5 and wins. Perhaps Black can hold with moves such as 17 . . . N-B3; 18 N-N4, K-N2, but it seems doubtful.

16   **P-N3**   **P-N3**

On 16 . . . N-B3 the nicest winning line is 17 NxP!, KxN; 18 R-N5!, Q-B3 (18 . . . NxP; 19 RxQ, N-B6ch; 20 K-N2, NxRch; 21 P-B3 is insufficient); 19 Q-R5ch, P-N3; 20 QxRPch, Q-N2; 21 BxPch, K-B3; 22 Q-R4ch. Now Black loses because of the absence of the queen on the queenside.

17   **Q-R4!**   **Q-Q1**
18   **KR-B1**   **P-QN4**

Desperation. Denker would have loved to play 18 . . . N-R3; 19 QxB!, PxQ; 20 RxB, QxP; 21 B-N2, Q-Q4; 22 BxN, or 20 . . . N-N5; 21 BxN, PxB; 22 NxBP.

19   **BxQNP**   **Q-Q4**
20   **P-B3**   **B-N3**
21   **R-B5!**   . . .

A great shot that leads to a crushing position after 21 . . . QxRP (best); 22 BxR, QxRch; 23 R-B1, Q-B4; 24 BxPch, K-N2; 25 B-B8ch!

21   . . .   **BxR?**
22   **BxB**   **R-KB1**

23	**B-B4!**	**B-B3**
24	**BxQ**	**BxQ**
25	**BxQR**	**Resigns**

A strong player throughout the 1930s and 1940s, this was Denker's best achievement. He retained the U.S. title in a match challenge by Steiner two years later, 6-4, but retired from tournament chess (except for an occasional U.S. championship) until the early 1970s, when at the age of fifty-six he again competed in European events.

Denker's lightning attacks were greatly feared during his heyday, but he was never able to make the transition to topflight international chess. At the annual Christmas tournament at Hastings in the winter of 1945, Denker finished third in a tie with Euwe and Steiner. Later in the first great postwar tournament, Groningen, 1946, he finished a disappointing tenth.

I. A. Horowitz

I. A. "Al" Horowitz was, next to the titans Fine and Reshevsky, the most familiar figure in American chess during the 1930s and 1940s. Under his editorship *Chess Review* became the most successful chess magazine in American history. Through his nationwide exhibition tours Horowitz made friends from Georgia to Oregon. Like Denker, Horowitz was awarded the title of international master by FIDE in 1950. On the U.S. teams in the Olympiades of 1931, 1935, 1937, and 1950, Al was an ambitious and valuable member.

Although never a U.S. champion, Horowitz scored a number of successes, including three U.S. Open titles. In 1941 he lost a very hardfought match with Reshevsky, 0-3 with 13 draws. One of the games lasted until nearly 4 a.m. Horowitz's proudest moment was defeating Soviet grandmaster Salo Flohr (formerly of Czechoslovakia) in the only bright spot of the 1945 United States–USSR radio match.

Horowitz, who died in early 1973 after retiring as chess columnist of the *New York Times*, was a snappy attacker in the style of Marshall and Pillsbury. The following is one of his unheralded victories from the forerunner of modern U.S. championship tournaments.

SECOND ROSENWALD TOURNAMENT, New York, 1955

	RESHEVSKY	HOROWITZ
1	**P-Q4**	**N-KB3**
2	**P-QB4**	**P-B4**
3	**P-Q5**	**P-K4**
4	**N-QB3**	**P-Q3**
5	**P-K4**	**P-KN3**

The so-called Czech Benoni, with 5 . . . B-K2, flourished for a while in the 1960s. Black gets a cramped game in either case and White has the rare opportunity to play on both sides of the board.

6	**B-Q3**	**B-N2**
7	**KN-K2**	**0-0**
8	**P-KR3**	**N-R3**
9	**B-N5**	**N-B2**
10	**Q-Q2**	**Q-K1!**

A good idea that gets the knight out of the pin so that it can be transferred to more useful queenside vistas. The queen move also prepares . . . P-QN4, which is Black's main avenue of counterplay.

11	**P-KN4!**	**P-QR3**
12	**N-N3**	**P-QN4**
13	**P-N3**	**R-N1**
14	**P-B3**	**N-Q2**

Black has been denied . . . P-KB4, which usually frees his kingside, but he has chances on the other wing. If White continues the attack, he would have the interesting sacrifice 15 P-KR4, P-B3!; 16 B-K3, R-B2; 17 P-R5, P-N4; 18 N-B5, B-B1; 19 BxNP!? Reshevsky chooses a more solid approach of neutralizing the queenside.

15	K-B2	N-N3
16	QR-QN1	B-Q2
17	P-KR4	P-B3
18	B-K3	R-B2!
19	P-QR3	B-KB1
20	N-R2	B-K2
21	P-R5	P-N4
22	N-B5!?	. . .

Black, of course, must remove this knight and grant White the two bishops and white-square domination. But in the closed position these are not such great advantages. This decision, a major one, could be postponed until after 22 KR-QB1!, followed by P-QN4!

22	. . .	BxN
23	KPxN	P-K5!

An excellent sacrifice, which only a master would realize is forced. Given time for KR-QB1 and P-N4, Black is squashed.

Note here that on 24 BxKP Black plays 24 . . . N-Q2 and
. . . N-K4, as in the game, but not 24 . . . PxP; 25 P-N4!, with
a large advantage.

24	PxKP	N-Q2
25	B-K2	B-Q1
26	N-B3	N-K4
27	P-N4?!	BPxP
28	RxP	P-R4!

Black now gains a fighting initiative on the queenside. Perhaps when Reshevsky played 27 P-N4, he had intended here
to continue with the Exchange sacrifice 29 RxP, NxR; 30 PxN.
In that case Black stands well after 30 . . . B-N3; 31 BxB, RxB
because 32 N-R4? allows 32 . . . RxP!; 33 BxR, QxB; 34
N-B3, Q-B4ch; 35 K-N3, QxRP, with strong play.

29	R-N3	P-N5
30	PxP	PxP
31	Q-B2	N-R3
32	N-N5	R-Q2
33	R-R1	N-B4!

Offering another pawn.

On 34 RxP!, B-N3!; 35 R-R3, R-R1, or 35 R-KN1, R-R1,
Black has good tactical chances for his sacrifice pawns. Note

that 34 . . . B-N3! threatens to win with 35 . . . N(B)-Q6ch; 36 BxN, NxPch; 37 K-B3, NxB; 38 Q-B3, NxKBP!; 39 PxN, Q-K6ch.

	34	NxP?	. . .

Missing the tactical point that Horowitz had prepared. Who would believe that Black will be threatening the queen rook and the queen in two moves?

34	. . .	NxNPch!!
35	KBxN	Q-K4

Watch out for 36 . . . Q-R7ch! The text wins by force.

36	R-QB1	NxR
37	QxN	QxN?

A slip that turns it into a game again. Black wins fairly smoothly after 37 . . . Q-R7ch; 38 K-B3, RxN!; 39 P-B5, R-R3, followed by . . . R-R6.

38	P-B5	Q-K4
39	P-Q6ch	K-B1
40	Q-K6?	. . .

And this returns the favor. With 40 P-B6!, RxP; 41 P-B7, R-B1!, White is still alive in a position where Black's rooks appear much more dangerous than the White bishops.

40	. . .	Q-R7ch
41	K-B3	R-R2
42	P-Q7	B-K2
43	P-B6	R(1)-R1!

And now White wouldn't dare give up the only piece that stops . . . Q-B5ch and protects his third rank. Reshevsky played 44 P-B7, and the game was decided by 44 . . . RxP; 45 RxR, QxR; 46 P-R6, Q-Q3; 47 Q-B4, QxP; 48 B-R5, B-Q3; 49 K-N4, R-B1; 50 Q-Q5, Q-K2; 51 B-Q4, R-Q1; 52 K-R3, B-K4!; 53 B-B5, RxQ; 54 BxQch, KxB; 55 PxR, P-N6; 56 B-B3, K-Q3; 57 Resigns.

Herman Steiner

Although he was U.S. champion only a quarter century ago, many new players today have never heard of Herman Steiner. Humphrey Bogart knew him, however, as did dozens of others who frequented his Hollywood chess studio. And during the 1940s Steiner established a reputation as a stubborn defender and apostle of common sense. This kind of player doesn't give away games and is always a top scorer.

Steiner was born on April 15, 1905, in the small Austro-Hungarian town of Dunaiskoi Stredi and emigrated to America at the age of sixteen. For many years he lived in Astoria, Queens, just across the East River from Manhattan. A good-natured person with a prominent moustache, Steiner first gained attention in the chess community by winning the New York State championship in 1929. Two years later in a Los Angeles event he drew with Capablanca when very few nongrandmasters were doing that. He remained on the West Coast and organized a prestigious club in Los Angeles.

Though he played on three of the U.S. Olympic teams, Steiner's string of successes didn't begin until the 1942 U.S. Open, in which he tied for first with Abe Yanofsky of Canada. Four years later Steiner took first in the Open and then two years later won the U.S. championship in South Fallsburg, New York. The biggest applause in the disappointing 1945 United States–USSR radio match was reserved for Steiner, who had a plus score.

Steiner was resourceful but not inspired. His successes came from diligent persistence and hard work at the board. He was never a match for Reshevsky or Fine. Four years after winning the championship he decisively lost a match with young Larry Evans, who had won the 1951 U.S. championship tournament. Denker had narrowly defeated Steiner 6-4 in 1946.

But Steiner could excel by keeping a level head over a long game or a long tournament. He won the South Fallsburg event in the final round by squeezing out a point when his rival Kashdan was only drawing. In the following game, Steiner outlasts a worthy opponent in the interzonal of 1952.

Saltsjoebaden, 1952

	GOLOMBEK	STEINER
1	P-Q4	P-Q4
2	P-QB4	P-K3
3	P-KN3	P-QB3
4	N-KB3	B-Q3
5	QN-Q2	P-KB4
6	B-N2	N-Q2
7	0-0	Q-B3!?

An entertaining diversion from the usual 7 . . . KN-B3, 8 . . . 0-0, and 9 . . . Q-K1. Black foresees a direct attacking game with . . . P-KR4-5 or . . . P-KN4-5.

8	P-N3	. . .

Black's originality requires a more exact reply, such as 8 R-K1! On 8 . . . N-R3 Black cannot play . . . P-KR4. And on 8 . . . N-K2 White plays the surprise 9 P-K4!, BPxP; 10 RxP!, PxR; 11 NxP, with advantage.

8	. . .	N-K2
9	B-N2	P-KR4
10	P-K3	. . .

Too late to try 10 P-KR4 because of 10 . . . P-B5! Black has the makings of a very solid attack.

10	. . .	P-R5!
11	NxP	P-KN4
12	N(4)-B3	P-N5

Now 13 N-K1 invites destruction with 13 . . . Q-R3; 14 P-KR4, BxP!; 15 PxB, QxPch; 16 K-R2, N-KN3; 17 N-B2, NxP!

13	**N-R4**	**Q-R3**

With the obvious intention of 14 . . . N-KN3.

14	**R-K1**	**N-B3**
15	**N-B1**	**B-Q2**
16	**Q-B1**	**R-R2**
17	**B-QR3!**	**B-B2!**
18	**Q-B2**	**N-N3**
19	**NxN**	**QxN**
20	**P-B4**	**. . .**

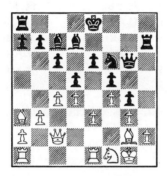

Black was intending . . . Q-R4 and . . . N-K5-N4-B6ch, with a strong attack. It is typical of Steiner that he has really risked very little in his assault. His position is still rock-solid, although, as usual in the Stonewall, a bit rigid. He wants to castle long now and double rooks on the file he has half opened.

20	**. . .**	**PxP e.p.**
21	**BxP**	**0-0-0**
22	**R-K2**	**QR-R1**
23	**R-B1**	**B-K1**
24	**P-QN4**	**N-K5**
25	**P-N5?**	**. . .**

White shouldn't force the game when he can prepare with 25 B-QN2 and 26 P-QR4. In the following heavy piece endgame, White is very weak on the white squares, a fact Steiner exploits very exactly.

25	. . .	PxNP
26	PxQP	PxP
27	BxN	BPxB
28	Q-B5	Q-QR3!

With . . . P-N5 on tap. Black now mobilizes his majority and runs over both sides of the board.

29	R-KB2	K-N1
30	R-B8	RxR
31	QxR	Q-K3
32	Q-QB5	P-R4!
33	Q-B2	P-N5
34	B-N2	B-N4
35	P-QR3	B-Q6

And Black realized his attacking potential after 36 Q-Q2, B-Q3; 37 PxP, PxP; 38 Q-N2, Q-R3!; 39 Q-KB2, R-R1; 40 R-K1, R-KB1; 41 Q-N2, P-N6; 42 B-B1, R-B1; 43 Q-KB2, R-B7; and White resigned in the face of . . . P-N7, . . . BxN, and . . . RxQ.

In addition to his tournament skill Steiner demonstrated his devotion to the game by being a U.S. Chess Federation (USCF) vice president and chess columnist of the *Los Angeles Times*. He died on November 25, 1955.

6. THE POSTWAR GENERATION:
The 1950s and Fischer

♛ *A chess traveler, browsing around in the United States, gains the conviction that a tremendous process of growth is in the making . . . "Beat the Russians" is the battle cry one hears from East to West.*

Max Euwe, after his American tour in 1955

Mayor Fiorello La Guardia stepped to the front of the ballroom of the Henry Hudson Hotel in New York and pushed a pawn to Q4. Nearly 5,000 miles away in the auditorium of the Central House of Art Workers in Moscow, Ambassador Averell Harriman made the same move from the Black side of the board. It was 10 A.M. in New York (6 P.M. in Moscow), September 1, 1945. And the object of 700 pairs of eyes in New York and more than 2,000 in the Moscow hall was the first moves of a transatlantic radio chess match between the two major victors of the war just drawing to a close, the United States and the Soviet Union.

The Radio Match, as it came to be known, attracted worldwide attention on two levels. First, it was the initial sports event between major nations since 1939. It was also the first time the new nation of Lenin and Stalin had competed in international competition in any field. It was assumed, by a world tired of war, to be the first cultural exchange between the two powers whose duty it was to preserve the peace.

On another level, the level of chess rivalry, the Radio Match loomed as the "match of the century." Just how good were the Soviet players? The West knew only of Mikhail Botvinnik, whose first-place tie with Capablanca at Nottingham, 1936, and third-place finish at the AVRO two years later established him as one of several worthy challengers to Alekhine's world championship. Americans also had heard of Salo Flohr of Czechoslovakia, Andre Lillienthal of Hungary, and Paul Keres of Estonia, each of whom took Russian citizenship before or during the turbulent period of war. They had heard of how 700,000 players took part in one national tournament, the Trade Union Championship of 1936. There were reports of the ambitious chess program launched by the Soviet government in thousands of local clubs and Houses of Young Pioneers.

The American team members and organizers conceded that in numbers the Soviets were far ahead. "Russia has at least 100 players who rank as masters," Kenneth Harkness, a prominent USCF figure and *Chess Review* editor, said. "In a larger contest they would probably beat us," he said. "But we believe our top ten men are equal to their top ten."

The Americans, after all, had swamped the opposition in four prewar Olympiades, Prague in 1931, Folkestone in 1933, Warsaw in 1935, and Stockholm in 1937. The United States hadn't lost a match in fifteen years. This was still an American team stocked with Fine, Reshevsky, Denker, Horowitz, Kashdan, Steiner, and several others. Certainly, American supporters felt, they could hold a team of youngsters that included Vassily Smyslov, twenty-four, David Bronstein, twenty-one, and Isaac Boleslavsky, twenty-six.

The answer was provided quickly when the first board game (Denker-Botvinnik) ended in twenty-five moves: 1 P-Q4, P-Q4; 2 P-QB4, P-K3; 3 N-QB3, P-QB3; 4 N-B3, N-B3; 5 B-N5, PxP; 6 P-K4, P-N4; 7 P-K5, P-KR3; 8 B-R4, P-N4; 9

NxKNP, PxN; 10 BxNP, QN-Q2; 11 PxN?!, B-QN2; 12 B-K2, Q-N3; 13 0-0, 0-0-0; 14 P-QR4, P-N5; 15 N-K4, P-B4; 16 Q-N1 (experts at both ends of the wireless thought White stood better here), Q-B2; 17 N-N3, PxP; 18 BxP, Q-B3; 19 P-B3, P-Q6!; 20 Q-B1, B-B4ch; 21 K-R1, Q-Q3; 22 Q-B4, RxPch!; 23 KxR, R-R1ch; 24 Q-R4, RxQch; 25 BxR, Q-B5; Resigns.

The Radio Match told thousands of fans that after years of isolation the Russians had returned to international chess, and with a vengeance. The United States would have to develop a new generation of masters to challenge them for world superiority. And, in fact, there was a new generation.

In the decade that followed the Radio Match, the United States exploded with young chess talent. As usual, most of the new stars came from the New York area. (From 1921 to 1957 no non–New York City college had won the U.S. intercollegiate team championship.) The roster included Larry Evans and Arthur Bisguier, the U.S. Junior cochampions of 1949; the Byrne brothers, Donald and Robert; James Sherwin; Edmar Mednis; William Lombardy; and, of course, Bobby Fischer. The list could also include Anthony Saidy, George Kramer, Arthur Feuerstein, Walter Shipman, and Charles Kalme. Clearly, this was the strongest single generation of talent the country has ever seen.

Leaving Fischer aside for a second—he is in a category all his own—it's very difficult to characterize the postwar generation. How could one link together the play of a technician like Evans, a classicist like Bisguier, a Nimzovichian tactician like Robert Byrne, and a master like Lombardy, who, one of his colleagues once complained, does "nothing but improve his position?"

Evans, for example, is a masterful defender with a technique not quite as simple and free as Capablanca nor as stodgy as Reshevsky. Born on March 22, 1932, Evans developed as a player during a period in which chess became much sharper. In the Sicilian Defense, Black was willing to accept a backward queen pawn in order to obtain dynamic play. In the King's

Indian, Black's cramped-looking setup was discovered to hold great strategic and tactical power. It was these lessons that Evans adapted in taking the U.S. championship away from favored Reshevsky in 1951. Evans also won the title in 1962 and 1968, when Fischer did not participate.

Perhaps Evans' most spectacular victory came in another United States–USSR match in 1954. The United States lost, 12-20 (and a year later by 25-7); but Evans scored 2½-1½ against Mark Taimanov, and Donald Byrne took three points from Yuri Auerbach.

MATCH, New York, 1954

	TAIMANOV	EVANS
1	P-QB4	N-KB3
2	N-KB3	P-KN3
3	N-B3	B-N2
4	P-K4	0-0
5	P-Q4	P-Q3
6	B-K2	P-K4
7	0-0	N-B3
8	P-Q5	. . .

White's choice of the so-called Classical System was very popular during the early 1950s, before the Samisch Variation came to the fore. White gets a fast-breaking queenside after 8 P-Q5 because of the ease with which he plays P-QN4 in preparation for P-QB5. Black must prepare for . . . P-KB4 and possibly for . . . P-B5 and . . . P-KN4-5.

8	. . .	N-K2
9	N-K1	N-Q2

The knight restrains P-QB5 here, although it may also be useful at K1, where it protects Q3 and QB2. White's position is fertile with ideas. Instead of 9 N-K1, Taimanov tried 9 B-Q2 against Fischer in their 1971 candidates' match and after 9 . . . N-K1; 10 R-B1, P-KB4; 11 Q-N3, P-N3; 12 PxP, PxP; 13 N-KN5, N-KB3; 14 P-B4! obtained a strong game that he eventually lost (game three).

White may also try 9 N-Q2, intending 9 . . . N-Q2; 10 P-QN4, P-KB4; 11 P-B3, N-KB3; 12 P-B5, P-B5; 13 N-B4, with a more aggressive attack than Taimanov now obtains on the queenside. Better for Black is 9 . . . P-B4!; 10 R-N1, N-K1; 11 P-QN4, P-N3, after which the White knight is misplaced. Taimanov will put it on Q3 to support P-B5.

10	**N-Q3**	**P-KB4**
11	**P-B3**	. . .

This was discredited by the current game and one between Najdorf and Gligorich from Mar del Plata, 1953, because Black's attack just rolls on. Evans tried 11 PxP in the first match game with Taimanov, and after 11 . . . PxP; 12 P-B4, P-K5; 13 N-B2, N-KB3; 14 B-K3, K-R1; 15 K-R1, R-KN1; 16 R-KN1, P-B4; 17 P-KR3, N-N3; 18 P-KN4, PxP; 19 PxP, N-R4!?, White could have gotten an edge with 20 Q-Q2! but lost after 20 PxN, Q-R5ch; 21 K-N2, NxPch!; 22 K-B1, B-R6ch. Actually, Black need not fix his pawns with 12 . . . P-K5 because with 12 . . . N-KN3; 13 PxP?!, N(2)xP; 14 N-B4, NxN; 15 BxN, N-N3; 16 B-K3, B-Q2; 17 Q-Q2, Q-R5!, he has very active play.

Considered best for White is 11 B-Q2, N-KB3; 12 P-B3, P-B5; 13 P-B5, P-KN4; 14 R-B1, with good chances on the bishop file.

11	. . .	**P-B5!**

Beginning a ready-made attack with P-KN4 and . . . R-B3-N3 in support of . . . P-N5. Black doesn't remove his knight from Q2 until P-QB5 can no longer be stopped.

12	**B-Q2**	**P-KN4**
13	**R-B1**	**R-B3**
14	**P-B5!**	. . .

An excellent pawn sacrifice similar to the more familiar offers on the kingside. Black's QB2 becomes a key target.

14	. . .	NxBP
15	NxN	PxN
16	N-R4	. . .

Premature was 16 N-N5 because of 16 . . . P-B3! (not 16 . . . P-QR3; 17 N-R3, P-N3; 18 P-QN4!); 17 PxP, NxP and . . . N-Q5, if need be.

16	. . .	P-N3
17	P-QN4!	PxP
18	BxNP	. . .

White has excellent compensation in his pressure along the bishop file and in the weak white squares in Black's camp. Now Black's advanced kingside pawns look foolish and his rook appears out of place.

18	. . .	B-B1!

Hoping to forestall P-Q6 and to blockade with the bishop on Q3 at some time. White could now continue with 19 Q-N3 (not 19 N-B3, P-QR3; 20 P-Q6, PxP; 21 N-Q5, NxN; 22 QxNch, B-K3) and 20 KR-Q1. Eventually one of Black's weaklings—on QB2, K4, or KN4—must give way. But Taimanov plays for the quick knockout.

19	**RxP?!?**	**. . .**

19	**. . .**	**N-B4!!**

A great answer that contains no less than three winning threats: 19 . . . QxR, 19 . . . N-K6, and 19 . . . BxB. White had assumed that play would continue 19 . . . QxR; 20 P-Q6, Q-N2; 21 PxN, BxP; 22 BxB, QxB; 23 Q-Q5ch, or 20 . . . Q-Q2; 21 PxN, B-KN2; 22 Q-Q5ch!. Now he realizes that 19 . . . N-B4 wins material because on 20 RxB, RxR; 21 BxB, Black has the *zwichenzug* 21 . . . N-K6, attacking his queen.

20	**BxB**	**QxR**
21	**B-R3**	**N-K6**
22	**Q-B1**	**Q-KN2!**

Another fine move. Evans realizes that he has great difficulty consolidating his materially won game after 22 . . . Q-Q2; 23 N-B3, NxR; 24 QxN. Instead, he plays for . . . P-N5-6, which must win because White has no defensible position on the kingside and his queenside initiative is much too slow without the missing queen rook.

23	**R-B2**	**B-Q2**
24	**N-B3**	**P-N5**
25	**B-N2**	**P-N6**
26	**PxP**	**QxP!**

Again he could win the Exchange with 26 . . . PxP, but that would give White counterplay. Black threatens 26 . . . R-R3, with mate to follow.

27	**B-B1**	**R-QB1**
28	**Q-K1**	**P-N4**

The point being a threat of 29 . . . P-N5; 30 N-Q1, R-KR3; 31 R-K2, NxB; 32 QxN, B-N4!. As it happens, White compresses his pieces more tightly around the king, who quickly suffocates from support.

29	**N-K2**	**Q-R5**
30	**P-N3**	**PxP**
31	**NxP**	**NxB!**

White loses immediately to any of the four recaptures of the knight (for example, 32 RxN, R-B7, or 32 QxN, QxNch!; 33 R-N2, QxRch; 34 KxQ, R-B7ch). The game ended with 32 N-B5, R-N3ch; 33 KxN, Q-R8ch; 34 K-K2, R-B7ch; 35 K-Q1, QxQch; 36 KxQ, R-N8ch; Resigns.

On the other side of the stylistic spectrum from Evans is the man who succeeded him as U.S. champion in 1954, Arthur Bisguier. Bisguier, born October 8, 1929, also won the U.S. Open three times during this period (1950, 1956, and 1959). Like Evans, whose first international result was at Hastings at Christmas of 1949, Bisguier also got his foreign debut in England. At Southsea in 1950 he gained a first place (tie with Tartakover) and won the international master title.

Whereas Evans is steady and positional, Bisguier is a classical attacker with very erratic results. He nearly became the first player to win the U.S. championship from Fischer (1962–63) and then finished eighth a year later against essentially the same players. Bisguier's weakness is often trying to be too original. When a game becomes hackneyed, he loses interest. On the other hand, Evans is often unsettled in original positions.

In 1954 a new series of annual events, the Lessing J. Rosenwald tournaments, began. After the first three, two of them won very easily by Reshevsky, who continued to dominate the younger masters, the Rosenwald was combined with the U.S. championship, which since 1948 had been held every three years. The following game is from the first tournament of the series, Bisguier crushes Reshevsky, who had not lost to an American since 1951, when a surprise defeat by Ariel Mengarini cost him the U.S. championship.

FIRST ROSENWALD TOURNAMENT,
New York, 1954

	BISGUIER	RESHEVSKY
1	**P-Q4**	**N-KB3**
2	**P-QB4**	**P-KN3**
3	**N-QB3**	**B-N2**
4	**P-K4**	**P-Q3**
5	**B-N5**	**. . .**

This was Bisguier's favorite for many years, although it is usually named after Auerbach, who played it in connection with B-K2. Bisguier prefers B-Q3 and P-KB4.

5	**. . .**	**P-KR3!**

An important finesse that diverts the queen bishop onto another diagonal so that it cannot return to Q2 or combine with Q-Q2 to play B-R6. By comparison, 5 . . . 0-0; 6 B-Q3, P-B4; 7 P-Q5, P-K3; 8 PxP!?, PxP; 9 KN-K2, N-B3; 10 0-0, P-KR3; 11 B-Q2, P-K4; 12 N-Q5, N-Q5; 13 N(2)xN, BPxN; 14 P-B4, with an excellent game.

6	**B-R4**	**0-0**

There is no rush to castle. Black establishes a fine game with 6 . . . P-B4!; 7 P-Q5, Q-R4 (now 8 B-Q2 is impossible); 8

B-Q3, NxKP!; 9 BxN, BxNch; 10 PxB, QxPch; 11 K-B1, P-KN4; 12 B-N3, P-B4; 13 R-B1! (13 N-K2 was first played by Bisguier against Peretz at Utrecht in 1961 but was punished in Stein-Geller, USSR, 1966, by 13 . . . Q-B3; 14 B-B2, P-B5; 15 P-KR4, R-B1!, with a strong attack), Q-N7!; 14 R-B2, Q-B3; 15 P-KR4, PxB; 16 Q-R5ch, K-Q1; 17 PxP, Q-R8ch; 18 K-K2, Q-Q5. The point of 13 . . . Q-N7! is to draw the rook off the first rank.

7   **P-B4!**   **P-B4!**

White now has a favorable position that is more active than the normal lines of the Four Pawns Attack because his bishop is already on KN5.

8   **P-Q5**   **P-QR3?**

There are two much more dynamic deas: 8 . . . Q-R4!; 9 Q-Q2, P-QN4, and 8 . . . P-QN4!; 9 PxP, P-R3; 10 PxP, Q-R4; 11 Q-Q2, NxRP; 12 N-B3, N-QN5. The opening was relatively new, and Reshevsky, a new convert to the King's Indian, shows his unfamiliarity.

9   **N-B3**   . . .

Not 9 P-QR4? because then 9 . . . Q-R4; 10 Q-Q2, P-QN4 is excellent for Black. Reshevsky mistakenly assumed that he could equalize once he got . . . P-QN4 in.

9   . . .   **P-QN4**
10   **B-Q3**   . . .

And here Black would have a terrific initiative on 10 PxP, PxP; 11 BxN (11 BxP, NxKP), BxB; 12 BxP, BxNch; 13 PxB, Q-R4, followed by . . . B-R3. After 10 B-Q3 Black must bid for counterplay with . . . PxP and . . . QN-Q2-N3.

His next move is an astonishing error—a "criminal" move, as the Europeans put it—because he shuts off his queenside chances on the knight file in the hope that in the distant future he will play . . . P-QR4-5 and open a file.

10	. . .	P-N5?
11	N-K2	B-N5
12	0-0	QN-Q2
13	Q-Q2	Q-B2
14	QR-K1	. . .

White has a beautiful position. In the center he owns the lion's share of territory and his preponderance of pawns there makes P-K5 a dangerous threat. Black minimizes that danger with . . . B-N5xN, but this also weakens him on the white squares.

14	. . .	QR-K1
15	P-KR3	BxN
16	RxB	P-K3

Black's worries increase after this move because his queen pawn becomes weak (17 PxP, PxP is met by 18 B-QB2 and 19 R-Q1) and because his kingside white squares are exploitable. But Black has no active plan to avoid P-K5 otherwise.

17	**PxP**	**RxP**
18	**N-N3!**	. . .

The threat here is 19 P-K5, PxP; 20 P-B5!, which blasts open the kingside defenses. Inferior would be 19 P-B5, R-K4, allowing a blockade.

18	. . .	**N-R2!**

A good defensive idea: If 19 P-K5, Black gets a good game with 19 . . . P-N4!

19	**N-B1**	**QN-B3?**

After this Black's game must try to survive on tactical resources alone. He needs a knight to control K4. For this reason 19 . . . KN-B3 is better, for example, 20 P-K5, PxP; 21 P-B5, PxP; 22 BxP, R-Q3, and Black is holding. Another good idea is 19 . . . R(3)-K1 to anticipate P-B5.

20	**P-B5!**	**R-K2**
21	**PxP**	**PxP**
22	**P-K5!**	. . .

This thematic break points up the absence of Black's knight from Q2. By exchanging his king pawn for Black's knight pawn, White begins an attack on the kingside files.

22	. . .	**RxP**
23	**RxR**	**PxR**
24	**BxP**	**P-K5!**

Reshevsky seizes his opportunity for centralization. On 24 . . . R-Q1; 25 Q-QB2, Black is virtually lost. Now 25 BxP could be played because on 25 . . . NxB; 26 Q-Q5ch, R-B2, White regains his piece. However, his queen knight pawn is loose and Black can maintain material equality.

25	**R-KN3!**	**Q-K4**
26	**N-K3!**	. . .

The threat of N-B5 frightens Black away from 26 . . . Q-Q5!, which he must have thought lost to 27 QxQ, PxQ; 28 N-B5. But then 28 . . . P-Q6!; 29 BxNch, NxB; 30 RxBch (or 30 NxB, P-Q7!), K-R1 gives Black good chances for a Marshall-like swindle in the ending. White would answer 26 . . . Q-Q5! with 27 Q-K1!, but this move is not as good as the one in the game.

26	. . .	Q-B5?!
27	Q-K1	N-N4?

The fourth strike (8 . . . P-QR3?, 10 . . . P-N5?, 19 . . . QN-B3?). A nice winning line follows 27 . . . QxB: 28 BxNch, K-R1 (else RxBch); 29 N-B5, Q-B5 (not 29 . . . Q-R4; 30 B-N6); 30 NxB, R-B2; 31 N-K6, Q-K4; 32 B-N6, R-K2; 33 N-Q8!, Q-Q5ch; 34 Q-K3, QxN; 35 QxPch, N-R2; 36 BxN, RxB; 37 Q-K6!, as pointed out by Kmoch. As bad as Black's position is, it may still be held by 27 . . . R-Q1; 28 N-B5, N-N4.

28	RxN!	PxR
29	B-N3	. . .

The queen is delightfully caught by White's minor pieces. The game went on with 29 . . . N-R4; 30 BxQ, NxB; 31 B-B5, B-Q5; 32 B-N4, N-Q6; 33 Q-K2, R-B7; 34 QxR, NxQ; 35 KxN, P-R4; 36 B-B5, but Black could have saved himself the time. Reshevsky, who had scored six points out of seven up to this round, was unexpectedly stopped by Bisguier, who had only three points but who won his last three games.

While Evans was attending Stuyvesant High School in Manhattan and Bisguier was at Bronx High School of Science, Robert and Donald Byrne were graduating from Brooklyn Technical High School. This brotherly rivalry occasioned some of the most interesting games ever played in Manhattan Chess Club junior championships. On one day, Robert would beat Donald: 1 P-K4, P-K4; 2 P-KB4, P-Q4; 3 PxQP, P-K5; 4 B-N5ch, B-Q2? (4 . . . P-QB3); 5 Q-K2!, P-KB4; 6 N-KB3, B-Q3; 7 P-Q4, N-K2; 8 N-N5!, NxP?; 9 NxKP!, BxP!? (so that if 10 N-B5ch, then Q-K2 holds the material even); 10 QN-B3!!, KBxB (10 . . . QBxB; 11 QxBch, P-B3; 12 QxP, PxN; 13 BxB!, NxB; 14 0-0!); 11 N-B5ch!, N-K6 (11 . . . Q-K2; 12 NxN, or 11 . . . N-K2; 12 N-K6); 12 RxB, Q-R5ch; 13 P-N3, QxQP; 14 NxB, NxN; 15 R-Q1!, Resigns.

And on a following day Donald would beat Robert: 1 P-Q4, P-Q4; 2 P-QB4, P-K3; 3 N-QB3, N-KB3; 4 B-N5, B-K2; 5 PxP, PxP; 6 N-B3, 0-0; 7 P-K3, QN-Q2; 8 B-Q3, R-K1; 9 0-0, P-B3; 10 Q-B2, N-B1; 11 QR-N1, N-K5; 12 B-KB4!?, P-KB4; 13 N-K5, N-K3; 14 P-KN4!, NxB; 15 PxN, B-Q3; 16 P-B3, NxN; 17 PxN, R-B1; 18 PxP, Q-R5; 19 K-R1, QxP; 20 P-B6!, Q-R3? (20 . . . BxN; 21 BxPch, K-R1; 22 PxB, PxP; 23 PxP, QxP[3] may hold); 21 BxPch!, K-R1?; 22 PxPch, QxP; 23 N-N6ch, Resigns.

Both Byrnes pursued careers as college teachers, although the older Robert (born April 20, 1928) turned to chess professionally in the late 1960s. It was at that point that Robert began to improve considerably, although he had become an international master in 1952, the year of his heroic efforts for the U.S. team in the Olympiade at Helsinki. Byrne's style, which had been a mixture of Nimzovichian strategy and excellent tactical skill, turned more aggressive during the 1960s. His play in winning the 1972 U.S. championship and in his most impressive qualifying score at the 1973 Leningrad Interzonal showed the influence of another master, one Robert J. Fischer. Byrne also won the U.S. Open three times during this era (1960, 1963, and 1968); the following victory was one of his best results.

U.S. OPEN, Chicago, 1963

	R. BYRNE	GLIGORICH
1	P-Q4	N-KB3
2	P-QB4	P-KN3
3	P-KN3	B-N2
4	B-N2	0-0
5	N-QB3	P-Q3
6	N-B3	P-B4
7	0-0	N-B3
8	PxP!?	. . .

The advantage of this step toward symmetry is that White, as usual, has the slight initiative conferred by the first move. He can attack Black's bishop pawn quickly and pose problems for his opponent's development (especially for the queen bishop). White also has opportunities to seize the queen file or to weaken Black's kingside with B-KR6xB.

8	. . .	PxP
9	B-K3	Q-R4

Maintaining symmetry with 9 . . . B-K3; 10 BxP, BxP?!; 11 N-Q4!, NxN; 12 BxN, B-QR3; 13 P-QN4! is not enough, although Black can improve with 10 . . . Q-R4; 11 B-QR3, KR-Q1; 12 N-Q2!. Then Black gets a bad ending with 12 . . . BxP; 13 NxB, RxQ; 14 NxQ, RxQR; 15 RxR, NxN; 16 BxKP, but he can sharpen the position with 12 . . . N-KN5!?; 13 N-Q5, N(5)-K4; 14 P-B4, NxP!?; 15 NxN, Q-N4; 16 N(4)-K3, B-Q5.

| | 10 | **B-Q2** | . . . |

An interesting finesse that tries to exploit the Black queen position. If Black retreats her majesty, White will play Q-B1 and R-Q1, followed by N-Q5 or B-KR6. Byrne also tried 10 N-Q5 against Evans in the 1962 U.S. championship and gained the upper hand with 10 . . . P-K3; 11 B-Q2, Q-Q1; 12 N-B3, Q-K2; 13 Q-B1. (Black maneuvered into a draw later on with a rook sacrifice that secured perpetual check.) But 10 N-Q5, B-B4; 11 B-Q2, Q-Q1 transposes into the game.

10	. . .	**B-B4**
11	**N-Q5**	**Q-Q1**
12	**N-R4!**	. . .

Black's bishop has problems here, which would be solved by the inexact 12 B-B3, B-K5!. Now if 12 . . . B-K3, White rolls up the pawn center with 13 P-K4 and P-B4.

12	. . .	**B-N5**
13	**P-KR3**	**B-Q2**
14	**B-QB3**	**Q-B1?**

Gligorich later improved with 14 . . . P-K4! (not 14 . . . P-K3??; 15 NxNch, costing a piece). After 15 P-K3, R-K1, Black can get an excellent game quickly, as in Bukic-Gligorich, Belgrade, 1969, which went 16 Q-Q2? (16 N-KB3!), NxN; 17 PxN, N-Q5!; 18 P-QN4, N-N4; 19 P-K4, NxB; 20 QxN, PxP; 21 QxNP, P-QN4!

15	**K-R2**	**R-Q1**
16	**P-B4**	**B-K1**
17	**P-K4**	**NxN**

Black cannot drive off the knight (17 . . . P-K3; 18 BxN), so he must exchange it off with the resulting pawn center working to White's initiative. Black's uncovered bishop pawn is the next target.

| 18 | **BPxN** | **N-Q5** |
| 19 | **R-B1!** | **P-K3?** |

This only induces White to advance. More solid was 19 . . . P-N3; 20 P-K5, N-N4, as 21 P-Q6, PxP is a good sacrifice for Black.

20	**P-K5!**	**N-N4**
21	**B-N4!**	**P-N3**
22	**P-Q6**	**B-QB3**

Black's queenside is the subject of a fine and original minority attack: 22 . . . R-N1; 23 P-R4!, N-Q5; 24 B-QB3, N-B3; 25 P-QN4!. Although Black appears to have a horrible game positionally, White still needs a winning plan. Black's last move allows Byrne to show off his tactical skill with a clever four-move combination that devastates Black's position.

| 23 | **BxP!!** | **BxB** |

Of course, 23 . . . PxB is met by 24 RxP, regaining the piece.

24   **BxP!**   **Q-N2**

What makes this combination so impressive is the number of chances for Black to sacrifice his queen that had to be considered. For example, 24 . . . QxR; 25 QxQ, KR-QB1 is met by 26 P-Q7!!, RxQ; 27 RxR, B-N2; 28 P-Q8(Q)ch, with an easy ending win.

More significant is 24 . . . BxR; 25 RxQ, KRxR, and now (a) 26 QxB, NxP!; 27 PxN, PxB, with chances; (b) 26 P-Q7, PxB; 27 PxR(Q)ch, RxQ; 28 QxB, R-B7ch, with a difficult ending ahead in which White may not be able to win; and (c) 26 B-R5!, threatening P-Q7 and QxB, and P-QR4 should win according to Kmoch.

25   **BxR**   **BxR**
26   **B-K7!**   . . .

The main point: Black's queen bishop, a problem piece throughout the opening, is once again in trouble. White must win the trapped bishop and keep an extra pawn on top of his positional hegemony.

26   . . .   **NxP**
27   **PxN**   **B-N4**
28   **R-B7**   **Q-N1**

On 28 . . . Q-N3 White would play 29 Q-B2, covering KB2 and intending 30 R-B8ch. In the following mop-up there is one high point left. After 29 P-R4, B-K1; 30 Q-B2, Q-N5 (hoping for 31 P-Q7, QxB; 32 R-B8, QxP; 33 RxR, in which Black's bishops offer some hope); 31 P-N3, P-N4; 32 N-N2, PxP; 33 NxP, B-Q5; 34 R-B4, Q-N3; 35 Q-Q1!, B-K4, White transferred his pieces quickly to the weak kingside.

36   **N-Q3!**   **B-N2**
37   **N-B5!**   **B-QB3**

38	**P-Q7**	**B-Q4**
39	**R-KN4!**	. . .

Threatening 40 RxBch, followed by a quick mate.

39	. . .	**P-B4**
40	**B-B6!**	. . .

And White forced an easy win, as Black would be mated in two moves if the rook is captured. Byrne notes that on 40 . . . QxN; 41 RxBch, K-B1, he would not have won the queen with 42 B-K7ch but would have played the superior 42 B-Q4: 42 . . . Q-Q3; 43 Q-R5, P-K4; 44 QxRP and mates, or 42 . . . Q-B3; 43 Q-Q2, P-K4; 44 BxP, P-QR4; 45 RxP. The game actually ended with 40 . . . K-B2; 41 RxBch!, KxB; 42 Q-Q4ch, P-K4; 43 QxB, KxR; 44 QxR, Resigns.

The youngest of the four "new generation" grandmasters was William Lombardy (born December 4, 1937). In the late 1950s there was some doubt as to which of the teenage champions was better: Lombardy or Fischer. After all, Lombardy had some impressive credentials too. He won the world junior championship in Toronto in 1957 with a shocking score of 11-0. Three years later he led the United States to victory in the Student Olympiade in Leningrad by taking twelve points out of thirteen games on first board. And on the two occasions he met world champion Botvinnik, Lombardy had drawn twice with more than ease.

Lombardy studied psychology at City College of New York but had decided before the Leningrad success on a different career: He entered a Jesuit seminary in the fall of 1960. A wise counselor, Lombardy was Fischer's second during the latter's world championship match with Spassky in 1972.

Lombardy's style can be irritatingly slow: he just solidifies a closed position and keeps improving it until it bursts with potential energy. On the Black side of the board, he can turn to sharp tactical play when pressed. His most famous win illustrates this well.

STUDENT OLYMPIADE, Leningrad, 1960

	SPASSKY	LOMBARDY
1	**P-K4**	**P-QB4**
2	**N-KB3**	**P-Q3**
3	**P-Q4**	**PxP**
4	**NxP**	**N-KB3**
5	**N-QB3**	**P-QR3**
6	**B-KN5**	**QN-Q2**

This sophisticated line has almost disappeared from international play, although this game was played during its heyday. Black does not commit his pawns so that he may play . . . P-K4 or . . . P-KN3 at a later stage. On 7 P-B4 Black gets a good game with 7 . . . P-KR3; 8 BxN, NxB, or 8 B-R4, Q-N3; 9 R-QN1, P-K4!. And 7 Q-B3, P-KR3; 8 B-K3?, P-K4! already give Black a slight edge.

7	**B-QB4**	**Q-R4**

Almost a necessity for Black because 7 . . . P-K3; 8 0-0, B-K2 allows 9 BxKP, and 7 . . . P-KN3; 8 Q-K2!, B-N2; 9 0-0-0 gives White a good attacking position in either case.

8	**Q-Q2**	**P-K3**
9	**0-0**	**. . .**

A controversial question in the early 1960s was whether White should castle queenside or kingside. In recent years the question has been answered by several successes, beginning with 9 0-0-0, P-N4; 10 B-N3, B-N2; 11 KR-K1: 11 . . . 0-0-0; 12 P-B3!, P-R3; 13 B-R4, P-N4; 14 B-B2!, N-K4; 15 K-N1, K-N1; 16 P-QR4!, or 11 . . . P-N5?; 12 N-Q5, PxN; 13 PxPch, K-Q1; 14 N-B6ch, or 11 . . . N-B4; 12 P-K5!, PxP; 13 BxP!, PxB; 14 NxKP, QN-Q2; 15 BxN, NxB; 16 RxP.

Spassky's choice here has it's advantages. Now 9 . . . P-QN4 is met by 10 B-Q5!, PxB; 11 N-B6 and 12 PxP, with a murderous attack on the king file. (9 0-0-0, P-QN4; 10 B-Q5 is met by 10 . . . P-N5!)

| 9 | . . . | **B-K2** |

More aggressive is 9 . . . P-R3; 10 B-R4, B-K2, which threatens 11 . . . NxKP. Then 11 QR-Q1, N-K4; 12 B-QN3, P-KN4! offers Black excellent play by securing K4 for Black's knight. Dubious, however, is 9 . . . P-KR3; 10 B-R4, P-KN4; 11 B-KN3, N-R4 because of 12 BxKP!, PxB; 13 NxP, NxB; 14 BPxN!, N-K4; 15 RxBch!, RxR; 16 QxQP, R-B3 (so far following Tal-Petrosian, Candidates Tournament, 1959); 17 Q-B7!!

| 10 | **P-QR3?** | . . . |

A small but significant positional error that negates White's impetus from the first move. After 10 QR-Q1, N-B4; 11 KR-K1, B-Q2; 12 P-QR3! is a useful move (Tal-Polugayevsky, USSR, 1959) because 12 . . . KNxP; 13 NxN, QxQ; 14 BxQ, NxN; 15 RxN, P-Q4; 16 BxQP, PxB; 17 R-K2, K-B1; 18 B-N4! favors White.

| 10 | . . . | **P-R3!** |

Now 11 B-R4, NxP! wins a pawn. White must retreat and, more important, concede the two bishops. One of the features of such modern openings is that the slightest inexactitude can land even White in a bad position very quickly.

| 11 | **B-K3** | **N-K4** |
| 12 | **B-R2** | **Q-B2!** |

Wisely observing that 12 . . . P-QN4 is met by 13 P-B4, N(4)-N5; 14 N-B6, with advantage. Now if White stops 13 . . . N(4)-N5 with 13 P-R3, he allows 13 . . . N-B5.

| 13 | **Q-K2** | **P-QN4** |
| 14 | **P-B4** | . . . |

There was no avoiding the loss of the two bishops if White wants to maintain an aggressive game. If he plays 14 P-R3 (stopping 14 . . . N-B5 via 15 N[4]xNP!, PxN; 16 NxP), Black continues 14 . . . R-QN1.

14	. . .	N(4)-N5
15	**P-R3**	**NxB**
16	**QxN**	**0-0!**

Black anticipates 17 P-K5, PxP; 18 PxP, N-Q2; 19 RxP?!, RxR; 20 BxP, QxP; 21 BxRch, KxB; 22 Q-B3ch, N-B3; 23 QxR, QxNch, as Lombardy pointed out.

17	**QR-K1**	. . .

So that is what White now prepares for. He cannot play 17 K-R1, getting his king conveniently out of the way, because that costs valuable tempo: 17 . . . B-N2; 18 P-B5, P-K4; 19 N(4)-K2, P-QR4!, with strong queenside chances.

17	. . .	**P-K4!**

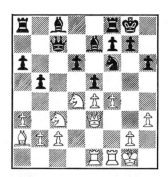

Although this concedes good white squares, such as Q4 and KB4, it is timely because Black can follow up with . . . P-Q4, threatening to win the queen with . . . B-QB4.

18	**N-B5**	**BxN**
19	**PxB**	**P-Q4**
20	**QxP?**	. . .

Perhaps influenced by the team situation, Spassky avoids the inferior ending that would follow 20 K-R1, P-Q5; 21 QxKP, QxQ; 22 PxQ, PxN; 23 PxN, BxBP. White could hold such an ending but has absolutely no winning chances.

20	. . .	B-Q3!
21	Q-K2	BxRP!

After this White's position becomes difficult. Although it seems that all that has happened is the exchange of Black's king pawn for White's rook pawn, there is more. Black has made . . . P-N5 inevitable and thus has secured good central play for himself. If he gets control of the king file and plays . . . N-K5 he will have a tremendous position. Note that 22 NxQP, Q-B4ch; 23 K-R1, BxP favors Black's outside passed pawns.

22	N-Q1	QR-K1
23	Q-B3?	. . .

A final error. Black gets only a pawn (but a good pawn) after 23 Q-Q2, RxR; 24 RxR, B-B4ch; 25 K-R1, N-K5; 26 QxP!, N-N6ch; 27 K-R2, QxP; 28 Q-K5, QxQ; 29 RxQ, B-Q3!. Now Lombardy wins a piece.

23	. . .	B-B4ch
24	K-R1	RxR
25	RxR	Q-R4!
26	N-B3	P-N5!

Evading the last trap: 26 . . . P-Q5; 27 R-R1!, PxN?; 28 BxPch.

27	NxQP	QxB
28	NxNch	PxN
29	Q-B6	Q-B5!
	Resigns	

With all of this said—and with a lot more that could be mentioned about Donald Byrne, Sherwin, Mednis, and Saidy, as well as the foreign grandmasters, Rossolimo, Benko, Browne, and Kavalek, who became part of our national chess scene—it is admittedly difficult to draw conclusions. Each of the postwar grandmasters took something from previous generations. Evans extended the Reshevsky technique to modern openings, Bisguier revived the Pillsbury spirit, Byrne and Lombardy adapted Fine's tactical fighting play. Each in their own way sought to unbalance positions and thereby create winning chances. "When evenly matched opponents play 'correctly,' " Emanuel Lasker had said, "the games seldom have any content and frequently end in draws." Avoiding the draw without doing injury to your position is perhaps the major theme of postwar international chess. In this respect the new American generation brought new ideas.

In a more specific vein, the postwar generation seemed to realize in their games a creative theory of survival. In European tournaments as far back as Steinitz, players tended to lose interest once their bid for the perfect game was ruined by an inexactitude. A bad position was bad in itself but also provoked a depressed mental attitude. Reti commented on this when he suggested that the difference between the incurable romantic Rudolf Charousek and the "efficient" Pillsbury was the latter's more hardheaded approach to the game.

Max Pavey was one member of this generation who suggested that it really took a lot to lose a game of chess. Pavey was a senior master and also a top bridge player who died at the age of thirty-nine in 1957. Pavey's lesson was that getting a bad position out of the opening was not a terminal disease. Americans should expect to have inferior openings because they are separated by 3,000 miles of water from the center of opening-theory development. But one error was not enough to lose a game. Sometimes even several mistakes would still leave one with a defensible position.

Or, as Larry Evans put it in *Chessworld* while explaining his theory of the second resource, "No matter how bad your position, if it's not totally lost, you will arrive at a point during the game where you will be presented with an opportunity to win or draw if you take advantage of it. I never give up in an inferior position. . . . The Europeans get the worst of it. The Americans have a more iconoclastic approach to the game. They have no respect for anybody and always expect a blunder from their opponent."

The will to survive is amply described by Evans in his game with Mednis from the 1969 U.S. championship. After obtaining a poor position on the Black side of a Sicilian Defense (1 P-K4, P-QB4; 2 N-KB3, P-Q3; 3 P-Q4, PxP; 4 NxP, N-KB3; 5 N-QB3, P-QR3; 6 B-K2, P-K3; 7 0-0, B-K2; 8 P-B4, 0-0; 9 B-K3, N-B3; 10 Q-K1, NxN; 11 BxN, P-QN4; 12 P-QR3, B-N2; 13 B-Q3, N-Q2; 14 Q-N3, P-B3?; 15 P-B5!, P-K4; 16 B-K3, N-B4!?; 17 Q-R4, NxB; 18 PxN), he found himself faced with the threat of R-B3 and R-R3.

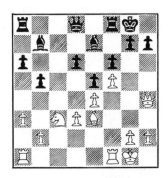

Whenever Black plays . . . P-KR3, White may certainly sacrifice his bishop to rip open the pawn protection. Evans correctly assays the attacking power of White's armada and plays as follows:

18	. . .	**R-B2!**
19	**R-B3**	**K-R1**
20	**R-R3**	**Q-KN1!**

Now White cannot bring new power immediately to the scene. For example, any knight move is met by a subsequent . . . P-Q4. So White aims at central action.

21	**R-Q1**	**B-KB1**
22	**Q-R5**	**R-Q1**
23	**P-Q4**	**R(2)-Q2**
24	**P-Q5!**	**R-B1**
25	**N-N1!**	. . .

With a very ingenious threat of bringing the knight to KN6 via Q2, KB3, and KR4.

25	. . .	**R-B7**
26	**N-Q2**	**B-B1**
27	**N-B3**	. . .

Things are beginning to look difficult. For instance, 27 . . . RxP; 28 N-R4, P-R3 is met simply by 29 N-N6ch, K-R2; 30 NxBch, QxN; 31 Q-N6ch, K-R1; 32 BxP. Now Evans must find an intricate bid for counterplay, which just does hold.

| 27 | . . . | **P-N3!** |
| 28 | **PxP** | **R-KN2!** |

White can still go ahead and win another pawn but his real trump in the coming ending will be control of the bishop file. Note that White must seek a queen trade to defuse Black's quick-brewing kingside counterattack.

29	**QxPch!**	**RxQ**
30	**RxRch**	**QxR**
31	**PxQ**	**RxP**
32	**R-QB1**	. . .

The initiative White obtained in late opening has not let up. Black's problem bishop still provides losing chances for Evans.

32	. . .	**B-N5**
33	**N-R4**	**KxP**
34	**P-R3**	**R-K7!**
35	**R-B7ch**	**K-N1**

36	**PxB**	**RxB**
37	**N-N6**	**RxKP!**

As Kmoch pointed out, Black is still in trouble if he preserves his bishop: 37 . . . B-R3; 38 N-K7ch, K-R1; 39 N-B5, R-K8ch; 40 K-B2, B-Q7; 41 NxP, P-N5; 42 PxP, BxP; 43 R-B4. After Evans' piece sacrifice the game entered a delicate situation with 38 R-B8, K-B2; 39 NxB, R-Q5; 40 P-N5, PxP; 41 N-K6, RxP; 42 NxPch. With Black's king active and his center pawn mobile, Mednis did not think he could preserve his own pawns and winning chances. The game was agreed drawn and Evans and the theory had been vindicated once more.

Robert J. Fischer: The Complete Champion

The proliferation of chess talent during the postwar era was not confined to the United States. It may be argued that the top players of today are no better than Morphy, Steinitz, and Lasker. But it must be conceded that there are *more* strong players today.

In the 1920s and 1930s one could assemble all the really great players of the day in one tournament—New York in 1924, Nottingham in 1936, AVRO in 1938. To do that in the 1960s or 1970s might require two events of the same size. In 1973, in fact, FIDE held two interzonal tournaments—one in Leningrad and the other in Petropolis, Brazil. Few of the eighteen players in either event were outclassed. Yet there were at least three supergrandmasters—Fischer, Spassky, and Petrosian—who did not participate. Qualitatively, it is debatable, but quantitatively chess has grown considerably.

Yet one player dominates chess today as no one since the eras of Morphy and Steinitz. With more than eighty-eight grandmasters as of 1973, and many more who will deserve the title in coming years, it is still safe to say that Bobby Fischer is head and shoulders above the competition. Many, including Fischer himself, would say he is the greatest to play chess. In the early 1970s it's hard to disagree. There are at least four reasons for Fischer's supremacy.

Profound Opening Preparation For most of his career Fischer concentrated on only three openings—the Ruy Lopez when he had White, the Najdorf Sicilian with Black against 1 P-K4, and the King's Indian against 1 P-Q4. Yet his mark on opening theory and practice is already deep. Who, for example, ever played the Exchange Variation of the Ruy Lopez (1 P-K4, P-K4; 2 N-KB3, N-QB3; 3 B-N5, P-QR3; 4 BxN, QPxB; 5 0-0!) before Fischer unleashed it at the 1966 Havana Olympiade? Who besides Bronstein experimented with the Poisoned Pawn Variation of the Najdorf after so many victories for White? Who revived the popularity of the old attacking variation of the Caro Kann: 1 P-K4, P-QB3; 2 P-Q4, P-Q4; 3 PxP, PxP; 4 B-Q3, N-QB3; 5 P-QB3? Who championed 6 B-QB4 against the Najdorf when every other grandmaster preferred 6 B-KN5, B-K2 or 6 P-B4?

Consider the following game.

STOCKHOLM INTERZONAL, 1962

	BILEK	FISCHER
1	**P-K4**	**P-QB4**
2	**N-KB3**	**P-Q3**
3	**P-Q4**	**PxP**
4	**NxP**	**N-KB3**
5	**N-QB3**	**P-QR3**
6	**B-KN5**	**P-K3**
7	**P-B4**	**Q-N3!!**

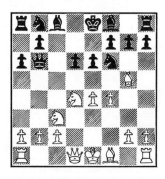

This move isn't quite as good as two exclamation points would warrant. But consider how surprising it is that a less well-developed player can begin foraging for pawns on the seventh move. Already the game is sharpened. White may sidestep the sacrifice with 8 N-N3, B-K2; 9 Q-B3, QN-Q2; 10 B-Q3, Q-B2, but he has then transposed into a normal variation in which his N-N3 puts a knight offsides.

8	**Q-Q2**	**QxP**
9	**R-QN1**	. . .

In the eleventh Spassky-Fischer world championship match game, Spassky played 9 N-N3, Q-R6; 10 BxN, PxB; 11 B-K2, P-KR4; 12 0-0, N-B3; 13 K-R1, B-Q2 against Fischer and then played the shocking 14 N-N1!, which succeeded more than it deserved. This lends credence to a common Russian complaint about Fischer's play. Even Spassky, one of the gentlest Fischer critics, commented after their 1970 meeting at Siegen, West Germany, which Spassky won, "He studies everything. It means that during the game, in the fight, he is not very creative. This is the weakness of Bobby. He plays too stereotyped, too practical, too 'American' style." The implication here is that a creative master like Spassky would find over-the-board such dazzling moves as 14 N-N1 (which won after 14 . . . Q-N5?!; 15 Q-K3!, P-Q4?!; 16 PxP, N-K2; 17 P-B4, N-B4; 18 Q-Q3, P-R5?; 19 B-N4! Spassky-Fischer, 11th game, 1972), but a "practical" player like Fischer would not. Recalling Reti's comments about Capablanca and Pillsbury, it's not a new criticism.

9	. . .	**Q-R6**
10	**P-K5**	. . .

This was popular as the Poisoned Pawn was first played in Keres-Fuderer, Goteborg interzonal, 1955, which went 10 . . . KN-Q2?; 11 P-B5!, NxP; 12 PxP, PxP; 13 B-K2!, QN-B3; 14 NxN, PxN; 15 N-K4, with a violent attack. White won after 15 . . . P-Q4; 16 0-0, Q-R5?; 17 B-R5ch!, K-Q2; 18 RxB!, Resigns.

10	. . .	**PxP**
11	**PxP**	**KN-Q2**
12	**B-QB4**	**B-K2**

Later Fischer tried 12 . . . B-N5, and after 13 R-N3, Q-R4; 14 0-0, 0-0, Tringov, the Bulgarian grandmaster, played 15 NxP?, PxN; 16 BxPch, K-R1; 17 RxRch, BxR; 18 Q-B4 in Havana, 1965. This had all been analyzed in *Archives* with the continuation running 18 . . . QxKP. Instead, after 18 . . . N-QB3!; 19 Q-B7, Q-B4ch; 20 K-R1, N-B3!; 21 BxB, NxP; 22 Q-K6, N(4)-N5, White had to resign. Even better is 12 . . . Q-R4!, which Fischer played against Mazzoni at Monaco in 1967.

13	**BxKP!**	. . .

And this was played by Andreas Duckstein, an Austrian master, in a surprise upset of former world champion Euwe four years before. White obtains a tricky attack after 13 . . . PxB; 14 NxP, BxB; 15 N-B7ch, K-Q1; 16 QxBch, KxN; 17 N-Q5ch, K-B3; 18 P-K6 (18 N-K7ch draws). Also note that 13 . . . BxB runs into another strong attack with 14 BxPch!, KxB; 15 0-0ch.

13	. . .	**0-0**
14	**0-0**	**BxB!**

Improving on Euwe's 14 . . . PxB; 15 NxP, N-QB3; 16 N-Q5!, B-B4ch; 17 K-R1, N(3)xP; 18 NxR, BxN; 19 N-B7, R-N1; 20 N-K6, N-KN3; 21 Q-Q5, K-R1; 22 Q-Q4!, which left him with a lost game.

| 15 | **QxB** | **P-R3!** |

As pointed out by Kmoch after the Euwe game, this is best. Awful is 15 . . . QxN; 16 RxBP!, RxR; 17 Q-Q8ch, N-B1; 18 BxRch, or 15 . . . Q-B4; 16 RxBP, QxNch; 17 K-R1, RxR; 18 Q-Q8ch.

| 16 | **Q-R4?** | . . . |

An error that Fischer had assumed was White's best. A year later in *Shakmatny Bulletin* a convincing argument was made by Soviet analysts that 16 Q-R5! gets White the better game: 16 . . . PxB (16 . . . QxN; 17 RxP!, QxNch; 18 K-R1); 17 NxP, RxRch; 18 RxR, Q-K2; 19 Q-B5, N-N3; 20 Q-B8ch, QxQ; 21 RxQch, K-R2; 22 N-B7!

| 16 | . . . | **QxN!** |

Kmoch mentioned 16 . . . PxB and 16 . . . NxP; 17 BxB, QxN; 18 BxP, R-R2, but not this third capture. Black now holds his extra piece with precise, albeit daring, defense.

| 17 | **RxBP!** | **RxR** |
| 18 | **Q-Q8ch** | **N-B1** |

Now 19 BxB, N-B3!; 20 NxN, QxN ends the attack, as does anything that allows 19 . . . BxB.

19	**BxRch**	**KxB**
20	**R-B1ch**	**K-N3**

Forced but quite safe. Examine how Black's kingside pawns and his bishop cover all the dangerous kingside checking squares. Bilek was running short of time at this point.

21	**RxN**	**B-Q2!**

A great move that cuts lines of communication between White's attacking and defending pieces. Here, 22 R-B6ch would force a perpetual check if Black did not play 22 . . . K-R2!

22	**N-B3**	**Q-K6ch**
23	**K-R1**	**Q-B8ch**
24	**N-N1**	**QxP!**

The helplessness of White's position is illustrated by another pawn capture by the queen. Best here is 25 Q-K7, Q-B5; 26 R-B3!, threatening 27 R-N3, although Black can defend with 27 . . . K-R2.

25	**R-N8**	**Q-B7**

This stops White's last dangerous idea of 26 Q-B6ch. Bilek's flag was on the tilt.

26	**R-B8**	**QxRP**
27	**R-B3**	**K-R2!**

And now Black is ready to develop his queenside with 28 . . . Q-N1, 29 . . . B-B3, and 30 . . . N-Q2, but there is an anticlimax: White oversteps the time limit and forfeits. But that's not all. While White was spending two and a half hours in a variation considered strongly to favor White, Fischer had taken less than seven minutes for the first 23 moves! It was almost all prepared in advance.

Fischer, of course, is not faultless in the opening. We recall how in his sixth match game with Petrosian in 1971 White erred with 1 N-KB3, P-QB4; 2 P-QN3, P-Q4; 3 B-N2?, allowing Fischer (Black) to build a powerful center with 3 . . . P-B3!; 4 P-B4, P-Q5; 5 P-Q3, P-K4. What has been overlooked is that just twelve months before at the Palma interzonal Fischer played 1 P-QN3, P-Q4; 2 B-N2, P-QB4; 3 N-KB3? against Henrique Mecking and was rewarded when Black played 3 . . . N-QB3?

During the 1972 world championship match the American champion surprised many fans with his broadened opening repertoire. Actually, considering Fischer's relentless pursuit for new ideas, one should expect him to be prepared in many openings even if he doesn't play them regularly.

For example, in 1965 Fischer was invited to play in the Fourth Capablanca Memorial in Havana. The U.S. State Department, however, would not allow travel to what it regarded as an unfriendly neighbor. Instead, Fischer arranged to play the match by teletype. He sat in the back room of the Marshall Chess Club while his moves were relayed to an unseen opponent 1,500 miles away at the Havana Libre hotel. (This, by the way, was Fischer's return to chess after an absence of nearly two years.)

All went well until Fischer played Viktor Ciocaltea of Rumania. Ciocaltea's first move, 1 P-Q4, was played on the Marshall club board by a FIDE judge. Fischer replied with his usual 1 . . . N-KB3. Then came the remarkable reply, 2 P-K5!? There was considerable consternation on West 10th Street as the officials realized that White's first move had been 1 P-K4 and not 1 P-Q4. Could Fischer take his move back? Could the error in transmission be explained? It didn't matter because Fischer waved aside the fears by playing 2 . . . N-Q4. He was willing to play Alekhine's Defense, an opening he had never played before in tournament chess and was not to play again for five years. But he was sufficiently prepared to hold Ciocaltea to a draw in an unfamiliar opening.

One of Fischer's strengths is the ability to overcome his

weaknesses. In the 1959 candidates' tournament he obtained a bad position several times on the White side of the Caro-Kann. But by the time he returned to the world championship cycle at the 1962 interzonal, Fischer was armed with ideas in the placid Caro-Kann that enabled him to outplay unmercifully such experts in the opening's nuances as Gideon Barcza and Lajos Portisch.

Excellent Endgame Technique   The ending was once a Fischer problem, as it is with most young players. But he studied thousands of endings until he mastered them better than the leading grandmasters. The following is a Fischer endgame against Tal (Black) from the 1962 Curaçao candidates' tournament after 1 P-K4, P-QB4; 2 N-KB3, N-QB3; 3 P-Q4, PxP; 4 NxP, P-K4; 5 N-N5, P-QR3; 6 N-Q6ch, BxN; 7 QxB, Q-B3; 8 Q-Q1, Q-N3; 9 N-B3, KN-K2; 10 P-KR4, P-KR4; 11 B-KN5, P-Q4; 12 BxN, P-Q5!; 13 B-KN5!, PxN; 14 PxP, QxPch; 15 B-K2, P-B3; 16 B-K3, B-N5; 17 Q-Q3!, QxQ; 18 PxQ, BxB; 19 KxB, 0-0-0; 20 QR-Q1, N-K2!; 21 P-Q4, N-Q4; 22 R-QB1, KR-K1; 23 KR-Q1, P-B4.

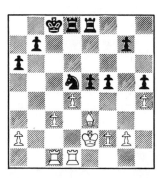

After several exchanges the chances are approximately even. White retains the advantage of bishop over knight from the seventh move, but his pawns are sufficiently weakened to compensate Black. What follows is an intricate series of ideas by

White to improve his chances and to reach a favorable ending, even though he is temporarily a pawn behind, in which Black's kingside pawns are weak. How this is accomplished is the ultimate in endgame instruction.

24   **B-N5!**   **R-Q2**

White wants to liquidate the mobile Black center pawns. After 24 . . . PxPch; 25 K-B3, Tal must transpose into the game continuation.

25   **PxP!**   **RxPch**
26   **K-B3**   **R-K5**
27   **R-Q3**   **R-QB5**
28   **R(1)-Q1!**   **. . .**

Utilizing the pin on the queen file made possible by his twenty-fourth move, Fischer prepares for the paralyzing 28 . . . R-B4; 29 P-B4, N-N3; 30 B-K3, RxR; 31 RxR, R-B3; 32 P-B5, after which the kingside pawns are fertile reaping grounds.

28   **. . .**   **RxBP**
29   **RxR**   **NxR**
30   **R-QB1**   **R-QB2**

Forced: the alternative is 30 . . . R-Q6ch; 31 K-B4, P-KN3; 32 B-B6.

31   **B-B4**   **R-B3**
32   **B-K5!**   **. . .**

This is the kind of optimum ending situation White has been seeking. His bishop cuts defenses on both sides of the board and prepares for the advance of the king to KN5. Note now that 32 . . . NxP loses exquisitely to 33 RxRch, PxR; 34 BxP, P-B4; 35 K-B4, P-B5; 36 KxP, P-B6; 37 P-N4!, followed by the advance of the outside passed pawn, or more mundanely by 34 . . . K-Q2; 35 K-B4, K-K3; 36 K-N5, P-R4; 37 KxRP, P-R5; 38 K-N6, with the same idea.

32   . . .   N-Q4!

Now 33 RxRch, PxR; 34 BxP, K-Q2 keeps White from entering the kingside via KB4. He must therefore keep rooks on the board until an avenue is created (for example, after the removal of the knight).

33   **R-Q1**   **N-B3?**

This error appears minor but leaves Black very few drawing chances afterward. Black can maintain the knight position with 33 . . . R-B4; 34 BxP, K-Q2; or can seek a simple rook ending with the more involved 33 . . . K-Q2!; 34 RxNch, K-K3; 35 R-R5, P-QN3.

34   **K-B4**   **P-KN3**

Black wants to avoid this move which burns all black-squared bridges on the kingside. Yet 34 . . . R-B7; 35 B-Q4, as pointed out by Soviet master Christyakov, will lose all three kingside pawns for Black!

35   **P-B3!**   **N-Q2**
36   **B-Q6**   **R-B7**
37   **P-N3**   **R-K7**

The advantage of bishop over knight in an open endgame position will be revealed after 37 . . . RxP; 38 K-N5, P-N4; 39 KxP, P-R4; 40 KxRP, P-N5; 41 K-N5, R-R7; 42 R-QR1. The simple fact is that White's pawns advance but Black's can't. This is what Fischer could only sense—he couldn't calculate it all out because it was still three moves to adjournment. It is this endgame sense, not calculating ability, that distinguishes the competent endgame players from the great.

38   **K-N5**   **R-K3**
39   **B-B4**   **N-B1**
40   **R-Q6!**   **P-R4!**

Black cannot allow the trade of rooks on White's terms: 40 . . . RxR; 41 BxR, N-K3ch; 42 KxP, P-N4; 43 KxBP, followed by P-N4. He sets a little trap in allowing 41 RxR?, NxRch; 42 KxP, NxBch; 43 PxN, P-N4, after which Black has the chances. White can draw then with 44 KxBP, P-N5; 45 K-K4, P-R5; 46 K-Q4, K-Q2; 47 K-B4.

| | 41 | **K-R6!** | **R-K7** |

Otherwise 42 K-N7!. Black now hopes for 42 K-N7, N-K3ch; 43 KxP, NxBch, with drawing chances.

| | 42 | **R-Q2** | **R-K2** |
| | 43 | **B-Q6** | . . . |

This sealed move confines the rook to Black's second rank. This is the final hemming-in process which leads to a beautiful two-stage *zugzwang*.

| | 43 | . . . | **R-R2ch** |
| | 44 | **K-N5** | **R-KB2** |

A charming variation worked out in home analysis would go 44 . . . N-Q2; 45 KxP, R-R1; 46 K-N7, R-K1; 47 K-B7!. If the rook goes back to R1 White plays 48 R-B2ch, K-Q1?; 49 B-K7 mate! On any move to a black square on the king file White plays 48 R-B2ch, K-Q1; 49 B-B7ch, with a bishop discovery capturing the rook.

| | 45 | **R-QN2!** | . . . |

Zugzwang no. 1: Black runs out of useful tempi after 45 . . .
P-R5; 46 P-R3. One pawn must fall. After sixteen moves White
regains his sacrificed pawn.

45	. . .	P-B5
46	BxP	R-B4ch
47	K-R6	P-QN4
48	B-Q6	P-N5
49	P-N4	RxP
50	P-N5!	. . .

White must end up with two connected kingside pawns after
this excellent plan. The rest of the game was fairly simple except
for the final position: 50 . . . N-K3; 51 KxP, R-Q6; 52 B-K5,
R-K6; 53 K-B5, N-B1; 54 R-N2!, R-B6ch; 55 B-B4, K-Q2;
56 P-N6, N-K3; 57 P-N7!, RxBch; 58 K-K5, R-B1; 59
PxR(Q), NxQ; 60 K-Q5, P-R5 (60 . . . N-K3; 61 R-KB2!
wins the king rook pawn); 61 R-N7ch, K-K1; 62 K-Q6, P-N6;
63 P-R3!, Resigns. This is *zugzwang* no. 2. Black must lose
both queenside pawns since he cannot move anything else.
Altogether a classic ending. Nine years later Fischer won a remarkably similar ending against Taimanov, with the major
difference being that Black's weak pawns were on the queenside and White's bishop was on white squares.

Capablanca's Middlegame Play Improved   Fischer, like another prodigy, Capablanca, made chess look simple again. The
clear, clean use of open files, the ability to make the most out
of a small advantage, and the ability to move quickly are all
part of the Capablanca legacy. This last aspect is not part of
chess theory per se but is an invaluable asset to a grandmaster.
Consider this situation from the 1959–60 U.S. championship.
Robert Byrne with White has obtained a very strong position
with 1 P-Q4, N-KB3; 2 P-QB4, P-K3; 3 N-QB3, P-Q4; 4
PxP, NxP; 5 N-B3, P-QB4; 6 P-K3, N-QB3; 7 B-B4, NxN; 8
PxN, B-K2; 9 0-0, 0-0; 10 Q-K2, P-QN3; 11 R-Q1, Q-B2; 12
P-K4, B-N2; 13 B-K3, QR-B1; 14 B-Q3, PxP; 15 PxP, B-R6?!;
16 P-K5!, N-N5; 17 N-N5, P-KR3; 18 B-R7ch!, K-R1; 19

Q-R5, N-Q4; 20 B-Q3, Q-K2; 21 N-R7!, NxB; 22 PxN, KR-Q1; 23 R-KB1.

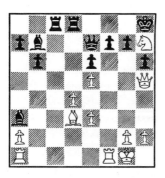

Black has chronic weaknesses throughout his kingside and cannot repair them without tactics. The next few moves reflect skill on the part of both players.

| 23 | . . . | **R-Q2** |
| 24 | **P-R4!** | **R-B6!** |

The point is that White's bishop has no good retreat, and on 25 QR-Q1 Black chops it off.

| 25 | **N-N5!** | **RxB!** |
| 26 | **RxP** | **R-Q7** |

Now Fischer threatens 27 . . . RxPch; 28 K-B1, RxN! If 27 RxQ, RxPch; 28 K-B1, RxR, Black stands well—for example, 29 R-K1, R-R7.

| 27 | **P-K4!** | . . . |

A great response, which closes the long diagonal. If Black tries to defend with 27 . . . Q-K1 now, he is mated by 28 Q-N6! And 27 . . . BxP loses to 28 RxQ, RxPch; 29 K-B1, RxR; 30 NxB.

| 27 | . . . | **QxR** |
| 28 | **NxQch** | **RxN** |

Certainly no better was 28 . . . K-N1; 29 NxPch, PxN; 30 Q-K8ch.

> 29   **QxR**   **BxP**

White surely has a won game if he can consolidate against the bishops and rook. But Byrne's ingenious attack has been expensive. He's taken all but five minutes of his two and a half hours. Fischer has nearly an hour left. With more time, Byrne might have worked out a defense with 30 QxKP!, B-N7; 31 R-K1, BxPch; 32 K-R2, RxPch; 33 K-R3, or 31 . . . BxNP; 32 R-Q1!. But he doesn't have the time.

> 30   **R-K1?**   **RxPch**
> 31   **K-B1**   **B-Q4!**
> 32   **R-K2**   **R-N5**

Objectively, 32 . . . RxR is best, seeking an ending in which White's pawns are blockaded by bishops. Without any pawns on the board the two bishops can stand off the queen.

But there is something more important here. Although Fischer says that he plays "the board," not "the man," the temptation to play an objectively weaker move is great here. By keeping rooks on the board, Black forces White to worry about his king's defenses. There are many chances for perpetual check and some chances even to win. The key is the clock.

> 33   **R-QB2**   **K-R2**
> 34   **P-R5**   **R-N4!**

The threat is the "cheapo" 35 . . . R-B4ch, which Byrne, of course, saw. The real problem is how to play for a win. Byrne miscalculates here and believes he can find a safe harbor for his king. He realizes that 35 R-B2 is dangerous for him. In fact, it loses to 35 . . . B-B5ch; 36 K-K1, B-N5ch; 37 K-Q1, B-Q6!; 38 R-B1, R-N7!; 39 QxRP, R-N7!, as Kmoch discovered.

But White has winning chances with 35 QxRP!, trying to

obtain a passed rook pawn. Byrne didn't realize his king was safer where it was.

35	**K-K2?!**	**R-N7ch**
36	**K-Q3?**	**R-N6ch**
37	**K-K2**	**R-N7ch**
38	**K-K3?**	**R-N6ch**
39	**K-B2**	**R-N4**

Once again threatening . . . R-B4ch. But the difference here is that 40 QxRP hangs the rook to 40 . . . R-N7ch.

40	**K-K2**	**. . .**

Now that time control has been reached, Byrne sat back and was ready to adjourn. On close inspection he would have realized that 40 . . . R-N7ch; 41 K-B1! is the right move so that he can play 42 QxRP. On 41 . . . RxR, of course, he has 42 Q-N6ch. White should have played K-B1 on the thirty-sixth or thirty-eighth moves, however, because now:

40	**. . .**	**R-N7ch**

As Fischer inspected his scoresheet and wrote down this move, he claimed a draw because the position has occurred for the third time. Not luck alone.

Fischer always played well in positions in which exact piece play conferred clear advantages on one player either through the exploitation of open files or simply by "getting there faster." In the Sicilian Defense or Ruy Lopez this kind of play always does well. In the French and Caro-Kann, White's plan is not so simple. In these openings Fischer at first experienced considerable difficulty when he faced top grandmasters.

In the following, Fischer's seventh game against Petrosian in their 1971 candidates' match, the Capablanca imprint is clear.

MATCH, Buenos Aires, 1971

	FISCHER	PETROSIAN
1	**P-K4**	**P-QB4**
2	**N-KB3**	**P-K3**
3	**P-Q4**	**PxP**
4	**NxP**	**P-QR3**

The former Armenian champion had used this twice against Spassky during their return title match, with mixed results.

5	**B-Q3**	**N-QB3**
6	**NxN**	**NPxN**
7	**0-0**	**P-Q4**
8	**P-QB4!**	**. . .**

Spassky had played 8 N-Q2, N-B3; 9 Q-K2, B-K2; 10 P-QN3, 0-0; 11 B-N2 and obtained a slightly better game after 11 . . . P-QR4; 12 P-KB4!, P-N3; 13 QR-Q1, N-Q2; 14 P-B4, although 14 P-B5! was better. Fischer was naturally prepared for this line. He follows an old game between Russian grandmasters Auerbach and Taimanov that left Black too opened up to enjoy his slightly superior center.

8	**. . .**	**N-B3**
9	**BPxP**	**BPxP**
10	**PxP**	**PxP?**

That earlier game continued 10 . . . NxP; 11 B-K4!, B-K2; 12 N-B3, B-N2; 13 Q-R4ch, Q-Q2 (13 . . . K-B1; 14 R-Q1 ties Black up); 14 QxQch and 15 R-Q1, winning a pawn. The text was condemned by Soviet analysts during postmortems of the Spassky-Petrosian match. The major alternative, which Petrosian later said was best, is 10 . . . QxP, although it is not clear where he will put the queen after 11 N-B3—for example, 11 . . . Q-B3; 12 B-B2!, threatening 13 B-R4, or 11 . . . Q-N2; 12 B-KN5, intending BxN and B-K4.

11	**N-B3**	**B-K2**
12	**Q-R4ch!**	. . .

After 10 . . . PxP Fischer thought for twenty minutes, a fairly long "think" for him, and decided upon this discom-bobulating check. After 12 . . . B-Q2 White can occupy the Q4 square with his most powerful piece, but he has better in 13 Q-B2!, 0-0; 14 B-KN5, attacking two pawns. On 13 . . . P-Q5; 14 N-K4, or 13 . . . B-K3; 14 B-KN5, P-R3; 15 BxN, BxB; 16 Q-R4ch!, Black keeps his material but has a terrible game.

12	. . .	**Q-Q2?!**
13	**R-K1!**	. . .

Like the great Cuban master, Fischer avoids the complex (13 B-QN5, PxB; 14 QxR, 0-0; 15 Q-R5, P-Q5!?; 16 NxP, B-N2, with attacking chances) when he can enter a vastly superior ending. Black has serious problems after the queens depart because of his isolated pawns and lack of control of open lines, such as the king file.

13	. . .	**QxQ**
14	**NxQ**	**B-K3**
15	**B-K3**	**0-0**

Black cannot protect such holes as his QB4 for long: 15 . . . N-Q2; 16 P-B4!, P-N3; 17 B-Q4 and 18 QR-B1. Now White secures the square for a knight.

	16	**B-QB5**	**KR-K1**

More aggressive play is offered by 16 . . . BxB; 17 NxB, KR-N1!; 18 P-QN3, P-QR4; 19 NxB, PxN; 20 RxP, P-R5.

	17	**BxB**	**RxB**
	18	**P-QN4!**	**. . .**

Another thematic move, which is superior to the more natural 18 QR-B1, P-QR4; 19 R-B5, R-N2; 20 P-QN3, B-Q2; 21 N-B3, P-R5.

	18	**. . .**	**K-B1**

Or 18 . . . R-N2; 19 P-QR3, P-QR4; 20 P-N5, N-Q2; 21 QR-B1, with a vast superiority.

	19	**N-B5**	**B-B1**
	20	**P-B3**	**R(2)-R2?**

Petrosian often plays such moves in pawn-blocked middlegame positions. He can't get away with it here. The idea is probably to prepare for 21 . . . R-N1 or 21 . . . N-K1. He should hope for 20 . . . RxRch; 21 RxR, N-Q2; 22 NxNch (better 22 N-N3! and K-B2-K3-Q4!), BxN; 23 R-QB1, B-N4!

Now with a few very simple shots Fischer converts Black's merely inferior situation into a virtually paralyzed one.

21	**R-K5!**	. . .

Stops 21 . . . N-K1, which would have been followed by 22 . . . N-B2, protecting Black's two weak pawns.

21	. . .	**B-Q2**
22	**NxBch!**	. . .

Although this completely ties Black up and was awarded two exclamation points by Petrosian and Suetin, it wasn't even considered at all by the grandmaster spectators in the Buenos Aires press room. Robert Byrne reported that Miguel Najdorf thought the move was weak. If White wanted to stop 22 . . . B-N4, he said, Fischer should play 22 P-QR4.

22	. . .	**RxN**
23	**R-QB1**	**R-Q3**

Else 24 R-B6, P-QR4; 25 PxP! is too strong. The threat was 24 BxQRP!

24	**R-B7**	**N-Q2**
25	**R-K2**	**P-N3**

White threatened 26 B-B5, forcing the knight to move. If the knight allows R(2)-K7, Black can resign. Note how White has continued to trade one small advantage for a larger one since the early opening.

26	**K-B2**	**P-KR4**
27	**P-B4**	**P-R5**

This last error puts the pawn on a square on which it can't be protected. After 28 K-B3 Black must totally eliminate his second-rank defenses to prevent 29 K-N4. The problem for Black was finding a move. On 27 . . . R-K1; 28 RxRch, KxR; 29 R-R7 and K-K3-Q4-B5, Black is helpless.

28	**K-B3**	**P-B4**
29	**K-K3!**	**P-Q5ch**
30	**K-Q2**	**N-N3**

White would have continued 31 B-B4!, followed by K-Q3 and R-K6 if Black continued to pass. Or 30 . . . K-B2; 31 B-B4ch, K-B3; 32 K-Q3, and Black can only move his queen rook.

31	R(2)-K7	N-Q4
32	R-B7ch	K-K1
33	R-QN7	NxNP
34	B-B4!	Resigns

As has often been said, "Fischer plays best without an opponent." That is, he is in total command when his opponent presents no major source of counterplay to distract him from his own plans. Here Petrosian has done very little distracting and must resign in face of R-KR7 and R-R8 mate—for example, 34 . . . R-QB1; 35 R-KR7, R-KB3; 36 R-R8ch, R-B1; 37 B-B7ch.

Superior Mental Attitude So far we've pointed out the similarities between Fischer and Capablanca. Perhaps the most important difference is psychological. Capablanca was often lazy, was a slow starter in tournaments because he wasn't mentally primed for winning it, and lost enthusiasm in later years, perhaps because of his inability to secure a return title match with Alekhine.

Fischer, on the other hand, is the essence of a tough chess mind. He doesn't concede an inch. When their game was adjourned at the 1970 Siegen Olympiade, Vlastimil Hort of Czechoslovakia said, "I don't know who is better, Bobby, but I offer you a draw." Fischer replied "I don't know who is better either, but I have an extra pawn." The game continued another twenty moves before Fischer conceded the draw.

After eleven rounds at the 1970 interzonal at Palma de Mallorca, Fischer led by a half point and seemed certain of being one of the six qualifiers for the later candidates' matches. Ewfim Geller, rated the sixth best player in the world then, offered Fischer, who had Black, a draw after seven moves. The position was symmetrical, and one could remember a dozen grandmaster games that drifted into deadly drawish positions even when both sides were trying for a win. Fischer relaxed and softly laughed, Geller laughed too. Then Fischer said something, Geller's face reddened, and the game went on.

On the twentieth move Fischer entered a long, difficult ending a pawn ahead. After the first adjournment Geller had succeeded in trading off all but two of Fischer's pawns, while each player retained two rooks. The second time control passed. Geller relaxed. And then on the sixty-sixth move he made a gross error, thinking that two moves later if Fischer advanced his last pawn he could play PxPch. But Geller's White pawn was pinned by a rook. After this hallucination— Geller thought his king could capture the rook four squares away !—he made another blunder on the seventy-first move and resigned on the seventy-second.

Fischer then proceeded to win nine of his last eleven games, including the last six in a row. At the 1962 interzonal in Stockholm Alexander Kotov, the Russian grandmaster, reported that Fischer asked him how many points he had scored in his 1952 interzonal victory in the Swedish capital. "You are seeking one more rival," Kotov said as he recalled it was 16½ points. "Then I must have 18½," Bobby replied. "I shall have." He scored 17½ — 2½ points ahead of his nearest rival.

One senses this determination to win every game, to destroy absolutely an opponent's self-confidence, in his tournaments and matches. Fischer embarrassed Taimanov and Bent Larsen by 6-0 shutout scores before meeting Petrosian. After he took a 4½-2½ lead against the Armenian, one might have expected quiet draws to clinch the match. But the following was the eighth game.

MATCH, Buenos Aires, 1971

	PETROSIAN	FISCHER
1	**P-Q4**	**N-KB3**
2	**P-QB4**	**P-K3**
3	**N-KB3**	**P-Q4**

Fischer always enters the Queen's Gambit Declined this way so he can avoid the fixed pawn structure of the Exchange Variation.

4	**N-B3**	. . .

Against 3 N-QB3, P-Q4; 4 PxP, Fischer plays 4 . . . NxP; 5 P-K4, NxN; 6 PxN, P-QB4; 7 N-B3, PxP; 8 PxP. Against Spassky (ninth match game, 1972) he introduced the innovation 8 . . . N-B3; 9 B-QB4, P-QN4!?. An older Fischer game (against Berliner, Western Open, 1963) went 8 . . . B-N5ch; 9 B-Q2, BxBch; 10 QxB, 0-0; 11 B-Q3 (better 11 B-QB4), P-QN3; 12 0-0, B-N2; 13 KR-Q1, N-B3; 14 Q-N2, Q-B3; 15 QR-B1, KR-Q1; 16 B-N5, QR-B1; 17 N-K5?, NxN; 18 PxN, Q-B5!; 19 R(B)xR, RxR; 20 Q-Q4. Here Fischer played 20 . . . P-KN4!! (shades of Paulsen-Morphy!); 21 P-B3, P-N5; 22 B-K2, PxP; 23 PxP, K-R1; 24 K-R1, B-R3!; 25 Q-B2, BxB; 26 QxB, QxP(4), and won.

4	. . .	**P-B4**
5	**P-K3**	**N-B3**
6	**P-QR3**	**N-K5!?**

A surprise for Petrosian and the onlookers. White intended 7 QPxP, BxP; 8 P-QN4 and 9 B-N2. Black could play 6 . . . P-QR3 with almost certain equality because he can always play . . . QPxP and . . . P-QN4 himself. The text, typical Fischer, seeks to unbalance the chances.

7	**Q-B2**	. . .

There was nothing to speak of for White after 7 B-Q3, NxN; 8 PxN, QPxP; 9 BxBP, B-K2; 10 0-0, 0-0; 11 Q-K2, B-Q2, although 11 P-K4! is better. After 7 Q-B2, NxN we have a Petrosian-Korchnoi game from a previous candidates' match that year, which went 8 QxN, BPxP; 9 NxP, NxN; 10 QxN, PxP; 11 QxQch, KxQ; 12 BxP, B-Q2; 13 B-Q2, R-B1, with a quick draw. Two points down, Petrosian must play for more.

7	. . .	NxN
8	PxN!	B-K2
9	B-N2	0-0
10	B-Q3	P-KR3
11	0-0	N-R4!

White threatened to gain excellent play for his bishops with 12 BPxP, KPxP; 13 P-B4, BPxP; 14 NxP, NxN; 15 BxN, B-B3?; 16 BxB, QxB; 17 PxP.

12	N-Q2?	. . .

Everyone hated this move, including Petrosian, who suggested 12 BPxP, KPxP; 13 Q-K2, B-B3; 14 N-K5 in the postmortem analysis. The point of 13 Q-K2 is to provide a bishop retreat on the attacking diagonal after . . . P-B5. Note that 12 BPxP, P-B5? would not work because of 13 B-R7ch, K-R1; 14 PxP, P-KN3; 15 BxP!, PxB; 16 N-K5.

12	. . .	QPxP
13	NxP	NxN
14	BxN	P-QN3

Black stands very well. On the temporary sacrifice, 15 P-Q5, PxP; 16 QR-Q1, Black gets excellent compensation with 16 . . . PxB!; 17 RxQ, RxR. Also, 15 Q-K4, R-N1; 16 B-Q3 is handled by 16 . . . P-B4!; 17 Q-B4, B-Q3; 18 Q-B3, B-N2; 19 Q-K2, P-K4, as suggested by Robert Byrne.

15	**P-K4**	**B-N2**
16	**Q-K2**	**R-B1**

Black threatens 17 . . . PxP; 18 PxP, BxKP. Here Petrosian begins to vacillate. He wants to attack with P-KB4-5 but also wants his bishop to control Q5. On 17 B-Q3, B-KB3; 18 P-K5, B-K2, both sides have good diagonals for their white-squared bishops. Black is in good shape after 19 P-KB4, P-B4; 20 PxP e.p., RxP; 21 B-B4, B-Q4!

17	**B-N3?!**	**P-QN4!**

Black is now ready for . . . Q-N3 and a queenside initiative. He can still hold the kingside easily, but Fischer aims for the terrain that grants him winning chances. White must attack.

18	**P-KB4!**	**Q-N3**
19	**K-R1?**	. . .

In *64* Korchnoi questioned this. The assumption in the Buenos Aires press room was that 19 P-B5, the natural continuation, would be met by 19 . . . PxQP; 20 PxQP, P-K4, but the Leningrader offers 21 K-R1!, PxP; 22 P-K5, with excellent attacking chances in view of P-K6 and P-B6. Instead, Black would play 19 . . . P-B5; 20 B-B2, P-K4; 21 KR-Q1, KR-Q1, but Korchnoi said White was all right with Q-B2 and B-B1-K3.

19	. . .	PxP
20	**PxP**	**P-N5!**

There is no doubt that Black stands better after this. He threatens 21 . . . B-R3 in addition to . . . PxP. Inevitably, he dominates the queenside files and pressures the suddenly weak White center. After all his quiet preparations for the attack one would expect Petrosian to continue it as he does. Best, however, was defense, beginning with 21 PxP, BxNP; 22 R-B3, B-B6; 23 RxB.

21	**PxP**	**BxNP**
22	**P-Q5**	**B-B6**
23	**BxB**	**RxB**
24	**B-B2**	. . .

24 B-R2, conceding a terrible game, was better than this futile bid for complications.

24	. . .	**PxP**
25	**P-K5**	**R-K6**
26	**Q-Q2**	**P-Q5**

The diagonal is opened for Black's good bishop: 27 KR-N1, Q-B3; 28 RxP, P-Q6!; 29 R-KN1, R-K7; 30 QxP, QxPch!

27	**QR-N1**	**Q-R3**
28	**R-B2**	. . .

On 28 QxP Black should have a simple endgame win with either 28 . . . BxPch; 29 KxB, R-K7ch; 30 R-B2, Q-B3ch, or 28 . . . Q-K7; 29 R-N1, QxB; 30 QxR, BxPch. White's king is too exposed to offer resistance in a heavy piece ending.

28	. . .	**R-Q1**
29	**K-N1**	**B-K5**
30	**BxB**	**RxB**
31	**P-R3**	**P-Q6**
32	**R-N3**	**Q-B5**
33	**R-N2**	**R(1)-Q5!**

Applying force to the weakest White point. Now P-KN3 is mandatory, after which White's second rank has no pawn protection. Very instructive technique.

34	P-N3	R-Q4
35	K-R2	R-N4
36	R-R2	R-N8

With a murderous threat of 37 . . . R(5)-K8. The quickest answer to 37 RxP is 37 . . . R-K7!; 38 RxR, PxR; 39 Q-Q8ch, K-R2; 40 R-R8, R-R8ch!, followed by mate.

37	P-N4	R-K7!
38	RxR	PxR
39	QxP	QxPch
40	K-N2	R-N6!

And here White resigned in face of 41 Q-KB2, Q-K5ch, and then: (a) 42 K-N1, R-N8ch; 43 K-R2, Q-R8ch; 44 K-N3, R-N8ch; 45 K-B4, R-KB8 or 45 K-R4, P-N4ch and mates; and (b) 42 K-R2, R-KB6!; 43 Q-KN2, Q-B5ch; 44 K-N1, R-KN6 or 44 K-R1, R-B8ch.

A tough mind at work. As Fischer explained to friends, "If you sit down at the board thinking your opponent is better than you, what's the point of playing?"

There are many other aspects of Fischer's play that we could discuss in depth if this book were of unlimited space. We could mention his thorough research of old chess books. In 1963 Fischer wrote a series of analytical articles for *Chess Life* and chose to comment on the little-known match between Steinitz and Dubois played 101 years earlier. We could mention the Fischer attack in the Dragon Variation of the Sicilian Defense, which has revolutionized one of the oldest opening systems. We could mention Fischer's incredible score in U.S. championship tournaments: 11-0 in 1963–64 and 61-3 with 26 draws overall in eight tournaments, for an 82 percent average. One could go on and on.

So much has been written about Bobby in the last few years that it would belabor the obvious to recall the familiar facts. Suffice it to say that Robert James Fischer was born March 9, 1943, and first learned the moves at the age of six, two years later than Capablanca and Reshevsky but two years earlier than Morphy and ten years earlier than Pillsbury.

But whereas Capablanca, Reshevsky, and Morphy temporarily retired from the game in their early teens, Fischer pursued his new interest with a passion. He played regularly at the old Brooklyn Chess Club—he lived in Brooklyn until the early 1960s—and searched for every bit of chess literature he could devour. As world champion, Fischer looked back and recalled that he used to play twelve hours a day in summer. Naturally, with only schoolwork to compete for his time, Bobby progressed quickly.

In 1955 he tied for third in the Brooklyn club championship. A year later he became the youngest U.S. junior champion. In 1957 he won the U.S. Open, and in January 1958, at the ripe old age of fourteen, Bobby Fischer won the U.S. championship. A number of events, some good and some bad, occurred during these years, but they were all forgotten after Fischer began his international career. Only his super-brilliant victory over Donald Byrne, the struggle hailed by Hans Kmoch as the "Game of the Century," in the disappointing 1956 Rosenwald tournament is remembered.

The Bobby Fischer that burst onto the international tournament circuit with a debut at Portoroz in 1958 was simply a younger, cockier version of the Fischer of today. In the final round it was obvious that Tal, Gligorich, and Petrosian would graduate to the candidates' tournament the following year. But Benko with 12 points, Fischer and Bronstein with 11½, and Olafsson of Iceland, Szabo of Hungary, and Pachman of Czechoslovakia with 11 were still fighting for the three remaining berths.

The final round couldn't have been better scheduled by a dramatist: Gligorich had White against Fischer, while Olafsson played the low-ranked De Grieff of Colombia, Szabo had the wily Panno of Argentina, Pachman played the other Argentine, Sanguinetti, and Benko met Neikirch of Bulgaria. Bobby clearly had the toughest opponent, especially as Gligorich had nothing to lose.

Benko, needing only a draw, split the point in record time and automatically became a grandmaster. Pachman, the great opening theoretician, didn't get enough from his first-move advantage and had to settle for a draw in twenty-eight moves. He was eliminated. But here was Fischer playing one of the most aggressive openings with the Black pieces against the Yugoslav Gligorich. Bobby chose the infamous Argentine Variation of the Najdorf Sicilian (1 P-K4, P-QB4; 2 N-KB3, P-Q3; 3 P-Q4, PxP; 4 NxP, N-KB3; 5 N-QB3, P-QR3; 6 B-N5, P-K3; 7 P-B4, B-K2; 8 Q-B3, P-R3; 9 B-R4, P-KN4!?; 10 PxP, KN-Q2?!), with which three Russians had defeated three Argentines in the previous interzonal.

"Gliga" played the dangerous sacrifice discovered by the Russians (11 NxP!, PxN; 12 B-N5!), and Fischer was immediately on the defensive. One slip would cost him years of work. But he defended accurately, and after three and a half hours, Gligorich offered a draw. Now for the surprise: Fischer turned it down! With one shake of a hand he could enter one of the closest guarded memberships in the world, the grandmaster club. But he refused. And now it was the Yugoslav's turn to sweat as Fischer traded off pieces and began to use his extra knight against his opponent. And now came the great reversal: Fischer offered a draw which Gliga immediately seized.

Such calmness and resolute attitude from a fourteen-year-old. There is a similar story of how the great Akiba Rubinstein won his first major tournament, Carlsbad in 1929, by refusing a draw against Heinrich Wolf, outplaying him into a virtually won position and then offering a draw to secure first. "With Wolf I make a draw when I want to—not when *he* wants to," Rubinstein explained.

Fischer's international career could be divided into three periods.

1958–60: "How good is Bobby Fischer?" During these years Bobby could handle most of the international stars but was two steps short of holding his own against the very best. At the 1959 candidates' tournament in Yugoslavia Tal unmercifully trounced him 4-0, while Petrosian took three points out of four from the young American. At Portoroz Fischer had an impressive 12-8 score but only took 1½ points out of five games against the other qualifiers. And then there was the disastrous 8½-10½ result at Buenos Aires in 1960.

1961–69: "You're all Russians to me!" Beginning with his strong second-place finish behind Tal at the Alekhine Memorial at Bled in 1961, Bobby demonstrated he was no longer a pushover for the elite of world chess. After crushing Tal and Geller, Fischer announced he would beat all four Russians in the tournament. To this the avuncular Paul Keres remarked that it couldn't happen. "To date you have beaten a Ukrainian and a Latvian. That leaves me, an Estonian, and Petrosian, an Armenian." Fischer replied, "Never mind what states you come from, you're all Russian to me!" As it turned out only Keres escaped with a draw.

Despite two prolonged absences from competition during this period, Fischer mounted a series of very impressive results. He took first places at Monaco in 1967, Skopje in 1967, Netanya in 1968, and Vinkovci in 1968, as well as close seconds at Havana in 1965 and Santa Monica in 1966. Perhaps the greatest disappointment for his many supporters, including many secret admirers in Eastern Europe, was his withdrawal from the 1967 interzonal in Sousse, Tunisia, after taking 9½ points in his first eleven games.

1970 on: "I am the best player in the world, of course." No one has ever put together a string of successes as Fischer did between his reemergence in April 1970 and his world championship match victory in August 1972. Not only did he win three very strong tournaments—Zagreb in 1970, Buenos Aires in 1970, and the Palma de Mallorca interzonal in 1970—but he scored an incredible 81.6 percent against an opposition largely composed of grandmasters. He also trounced Petrosian, 3-1, in the USSR-world match of 1970. And most of all was his streak of twenty straight victories—no petty draws included—beginning at the end of Palma and stretching into his final candidates' match with Petrosian. This was comparable to a football team going unbeaten, untied, and unscored upon through an entire season. Almost as an anticlimax, Fischer mauled his old nemesis, Boris Spassky, 12½-8½, in the match for the title in Reykjavik.

What about the future for Robert James Fischer? More than a year after Iceland, Fischer had not emerged from yet another miniretirement from the game. To be sure, he still studies chess. Somewhere between his afternoon tennis matches in the California sun and his early morning bowling sorties, Fischer keeps in shape.

A change in the ground rules for future title competition may keep Bobby on the chess throne for longer than anyone since Lasker's twenty-seven-year reign. FIDE agreed in 1971 to require that the winner of future championship matches be the player who wins six games. Fischer had complained that a player who gets out to a bad start—such as losing the first two games as he did against Spassky in 1972—would be at the mercy of a foe who simply drew the rest of his games. Instead of continuing the best-of-twenty-four-games format that had been in force since the war, FIDE altered the rules.

How this affects the future is plain to anyone who has sat down opposite the former prodigy from Brooklyn. You might hold him to a draw. You might take advantage of an occasional overanxious error. But you aren't going to beat Fischer six times. After all, in the ninety-three games between 1970 and the world championship, Fischer had only lost six games, and one of them was the forfeiture of the second match game in Reykjavik.

7. AFTER REYKJAVIK:

The Post-Fischer Generation

♛ *I never thought I'd see the day when chess would be all over the front pages here, but confined only to one paragraph in* Pravda. *I guess that's my fault.*

Bobby Fischer, at a reception at New York's City Hall, September 22, 1972

Like New York in 1857, Hastings in 1895, and New York in 1924, Fischer's resounding victory at Reykjavik in 1972 marked a watershed in American chess. Not since the "Morphy excitement" was there the explosion of interest in the game that followed the Iceland match. It's been estimated that more chess sets were sold at Christmas of 1972 in the United States than in the previous five years. At least three new syndicated chess columns began to appear in dailies. In New York, where there had always been a well-established wealth of places to play no fewer than nine new clubs opened within three month's of the match's end.

Even as Fischer was making his surge to the title from 1970 to 1972, a new wave of players was already on the scene—the post-Fischer generation. For the first time, a new group of young masters was spread across the country: Ken Rogoff from

Rochester; Andrew Soltis, Sal Matera, and Bernard Zuckerman from New York City; William Martz, Greg DeFotis, Richard Verber, Craig Chellstorp, and Andrew Karklins from the Chicago chess hub; and James Tarjan, Larry Christiansen, Kim Commons, George Kane, and John Grefe from California. (One indication of the rapid growth of the new generation was the failure to mention Norman Weinstein of Allston, Massachusetts, when this book was being prepared for publication. Weinstein, at twenty-two, won the 1973 U.S. Open on tie-breaking points and followed this four months later by winning his first international tournament at Chicago in December. Also, John Grefe tied for first place in the 1973 U.S. Invitational Championship; and James Tarjan met the requirements for the International Master title.)

In many ways the new generation stands apart from its predecessors. For one thing, the young masters of the 1970s were the first to benefit from the vast increase in inexpensive, English-language chess literature. In 1973 a player could buy a library well stocked with more than forty books covering every aspect of the game—from opening monographs to endgame tomes to tournament books—for less than $100. Despite inflation, the same library might have cost twice as much to the player of 1933—and many of these hardcover books might have been only in Russian or German.

One natural result of this is the growing sophistication of American players. The story is often told of how during the 1945 United States–USSR radio match, after a complex opening in the Smyslov-Reshevsky game, the Americans transmitted a request to see how much time the Russian had consumed. Reshevsky, who was viewing for the first time a complicated variation of the Open Defense to the Ruy Lopez, had taken one hour and a half. But Smyslov had taken only one minute, the Soviets wired back. The entire line had been analyzed in a recent Russian magazine.

When Bobby Fischer was attending high school in Brooklyn he would carry copies of *Shakmatny Bulletin* in his back pocket, the story goes. The post-Fischer generation is equally familiar with the latest wrinkles from the opening innovation factories of Eastern Europe. Their memory and familiarity with important recent games is impressive—especially so, as the number of international tournaments and the corresponding number of important recent games has doubled since the 1930s. During the 1970 World Student Team Championship in Haifa, Israel, Ken Rogoff entered one of the rooms of the U.S. team and glanced at a position which two team members were analyzing. "That's Uhlmann-Vasiukov, isn't it?" Rogoff said, referring to a game that had been played more than a year before. "And here Black played his knight up attacking the queen and White responded with queen to rook four. . .," he continued, giving the next several moves played.

The new generation was also weaned on five-minute chess, which perhaps accounts for a slight superficiality of style. Americans were no longer the "coffeehouse players" they once seemed. But, perhaps because of their youth, the new generation appears at this writing to be less willing to spend five hours of intense concentration at the board than to spend the same amount of time and energy preparing for a game. The result is a sense of hastiness and underdeveloped potential. How this group of talented players grows is, in 1974, a matter of conjecture.

Ken Rogoff

Ken Rogoff, twenty-one years old at this writing, is considered by most close watchers of the chess scene to be the most promising young American since Fischer roamed the Manhattan Chess Club in sneakers. Rogoff, currently a student at Yale, is an excellent example of the Fischer influence. His style is at once solid, dynamic, and simple. His opening knowledge is encyclopedic, the result of having played over thousands of games. His calculating ability is deep, and it is not uncommon for Ken to mention an unplayed fifteen-move variation during a postmortem analysis of a game. His weaknesses are those of most young players. Inexperience makes it difficult for him to play well in bad positions—yet playing well in bad positions is the hallmark of every great American player.

Ken began playing tournament chess in 1966 and within three years he had won the U.S. junior championship for the first of three times. In 1971 Rogoff placed third in the world junior championship, the highest an American had scored since 1957. Rogoff has played on three U.S. student teams and played first board for the victorious Americans in 1970. The following game was played in the last round, when the United States needed a sweep of Scotland to clinch first place.

STUDENT OLYMPIADE, Haifa, 1970

	ROGOFF	LEVY
1	**N-KB3**	**P-QB4**
2	**P-QB4**	**P-KN3**
3	**P-Q4**	**PxP**

With this, White gets a most favorable Maroczy bind. 3 . . . B-N2 contains more chances for Black.

4	**NxP**	**B-N2**

Attempting to transpose into the more popular Gurgenidze equalizing line with 4 . . . N-KB3; 5 N-QB3, N-B3 (6 P-K4, NxN!; 7 QxN, P-Q3) can be met now by 6 N-B2 before P-K4.

5	**P-K4**	**N-QB3**
6	**B-K3**	**N-B3**
7	**N-QB3**	**N-KN5**

Otherwise White will play 8 B-K2, leaving Black without any of the freeing exchanges that are considered best for him.

Notice that 7 . . . P-Q3; 8 B-K2, N-KN5?? loses a piece to 9 BxN, BxB; 10 NxN!

8	QxN	NxN
9	Q-Q1	N-K3

Bronstein's 9 . . . P-K4 is nowhere near sufficient: 10 N-N5, 0-0; 11 Q-Q2, Q-R5; 12 B-Q3, P-Q4?!; 13 BPxP, NxN; 14 BxN, QxKP; 15 P-B3!

10	Q-Q2	Q-R4
11	R-B1	. . .

White would prefer his rook on Q1 but should not allow his pawns to be doubled with . . . BxN.

11	. . .	P-N3
12	B-Q3	B-N2
13	0-0	P-KN4?!

This is an old idea of Larsen's, whose purpose is to exploit black squares via 14 . . . B-K4 and 15 . . . B-B5. If White plays P-KN3, Black continues the attack with . . . P-KR4-5 or . . . P-N5. The move, however, burns Black's positional bridges. He gives up a great many white squares in the hope of exploiting the black ones.

14	P-QR3!	. . .

A strong preparation for 15 P-QN4, which, if allowed, may lead to 15 . . . QxRP; 16 N-Q5, P-KR3; 17 R-B2!, threatening to win the queen. White's move also protects the rook pawn and allows White to move N-Q5 in some cases.

14	. . .	**Q-K4**
15	**P-QN4**	**R-QB1**
16	**N-Q5**	. . .

White has a clear edge because of his advantage in space, the discomfiture of the Black queen, and the lag in Black's development. However, Rogoff realizes that his position requires several moves of preparation before anything can be done with his edge. Remarkably solid judgment for a young player.

16	. . .	**B-QB3**
17	**KR-Q1**	**P-KR4**
18	**B-N1**	**R-Q1**
19	**Q-K2!**	. . .

Preparing for B-Q2-B3, which weakens rather than strengthens Black's control of black squares. The maneuver will also remove the Black queen from its key position and stop its holding action in the center.

19	. . .	**P-N5**

Levy, an enterprising Scot, is an expert in the Sicilian Dragon and is more at home in dynamic, free-flowing tactical positions. Having been denied . . . B-KB5, he has been unable to develop another positional plan and is here reduced to speculation. His only open line—the long black diagonal—is about to be taken from him.

20	**B-Q2**	**B-R5**
21	**R-K1**	**N-Q5**
22	**Q-B1**	. . .

On 22 Q-Q3 Black can continue 22 . . . N-N6; 23 B-B3?, NxR. Having won a small concession in White's queen retreat Black should meet the danger of 23 B-B4 with 22 . . . B-R3!— for example, 23 BxB, RxB; 24 P-B5, P-R5; 25 PxP, PxP; 26 Q-R6, and now not 26 . . . P-R6?; 27 R-B8! but 26 . . . B-B3.

22	. . .	N-N6
23	B-B4	Q-R8

24	R-B2!	. . .

White has maneuvered quite skillfully in an odd position and here prepares to meet 24 . . . N-Q5 with 25 R-R2. The R8 square is the only safe square for the Black queen.

24	. . .	P-K3
25	B-Q6!	. . .

Threatening mate for starters. And 25 . . . PxN naturally opens the file for a devastating discovery. White's move is the beginning of a fine combination that leads to the capture of the queen.

25	. . .	R-QB1
26	R-R2!	Q-Q5
27	R-Q1!	QxBP
28	B-Q3	Q-B3
29	R-B2	QxR

On 29 . . . Q-N2; 30 B-R6, or 29 . . . Q-R1; 30 N-B7ch, Black can resign.

30	**BxQ**	**RxB**
31	**Q-R6!**	. . .

A neat conclusion. The bishop cannot retreat and with it Black's material equality collapses.

31	. . .	**PxN**
32	**QxB**	**R-B6**
33	**QxP**	**Resigns**

Mate follows 33 . . . R-QB1; 34 PxP and 35 R-K1ch. In June 1973 Rogoff took first place in the first USCF-sponsored international tournament held in Norristown, Pa.

Andrew Soltis

When Andrew Soltis won the 1972 Reggio Emilia, Italy, international tournament, it was the first time in more than a dozen years that an American besides Fischer or Reshevsky had taken a foreign first prize. Soltis, twenty-six at this writing, had also taken first prizes in the 1969 U.S. intercollegiate championship and four Marshall Chess Club championships. The author of three books, Soltis writes a chess column for the *New York Post*, where he works as a reporter.

A colorful attacker, Soltis concentrates on unpopular opening lines. He is credited with introducing a tricky variation of the Sicilian (1 P-K4, P-QB4; 2 N-KB3, P-Q3; 3 P-Q4, PxP; 4 NxP, N-KB3; 5 N-QB3, P-KN3; 6 B-K3, B-N2; 7 P-B3, 0-0; 8 Q-Q2, N-B3; 9 B-QB4, B-Q2; 10 P-KR4, R-QB1; 11 B-N3, P-KR4!?). He calculates quickly and scores well in tactical positions. Soltis' weakness is defense in passive positions. Soltis has played on six student teams and had the best score (8-1) of the victorious 1970 team.

GOLDWATER-MARSHALL TOURNAMENT,
New York, 1971

	SOLTIS	MCKELVIE
1	**P-K4**	**P-K4**
2	**N-KB3**	**N-KB3**
3	**P-Q4**	**NxP**
4	**B-Q3**	**P-Q4**
5	**NxP**	**B-K2**

Considered slightly inferior to the symmetrical 5 . . . B-Q3, this move is useful in closing the king file and preparing . . . N-Q2. McKelvie's variation has been recommended as an equalizing line in Hooper's *Complete Defense to 1 P-K4.*

6	**0-0**	**N-Q2**
7	**P-QB4!**	**NxN**
8	**PxN**	**B-KB4?!**

A new, not very good move. Hooper considers 8 . . . B-K3; 9 PxP, BxP but doesn't mention 10 Q-K2, N-B4; 11 B-N5ch, P-B3; 12 R-Q1!, PxB; 13 N-B3 and also suggests 9 . . . QxP??, overlooking 10 Q-R4ch.

9	**P-B3!?**	. . .

A good idea involving a sacrifice of the Exchange for a massive pawn sacrifice. But there was better: 9 Q-K2! so that White threatens to win material with 10 P-B3, and if 9 . . . B-N3; 10 R-Q1, P-QB3; 11 BxN, BxB; 12 N-B3, White wins a pawn.

9	. . .	**B-B4ch**
10	**K-R1**	**N-B⁻:h**
11	**RxN**	**BxB!**
12	**QxB**	**BxR**
13	**PxP**	**0-0**
14	**N-B3**	. . .

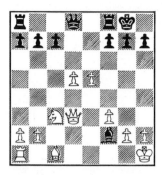

White has very graphic compensation in the pawn center. His center counts for control of important squares more than the ability to convert the pawns into a passed danger. Black's game is not easy to develop: for example, 14 . . . B-B4; 15 N-K4, B-K2; 16 B-B4, or 14 . . . B-N3; 15 N-K4, Q-K2; 16 N-N5, or 14 . . . Q-R5; 15 N-K4, B-N3; 16 B-N5, Q-R4; 17 P-KN4, Q-N3; 18 P-KR4, P-KR4; 19 B-K3, with good play.

14	. . .	R-K1
15	B-B4	B-R5
16	P-KN3	B-N4
17	N-K4	BxB?

Black needs this piece to defend his kingside and should avoid opening the file that leads to his king. White's advantage grows considerably now that he has an attacking line.

| 18 | PxB | P-KR3 |

This stops 19 N-N5, but 18 . . . Q-R5, also protecting KR2, was more useful in restraining White. On 19 Q-Q4, K-R1; 20 N-N3, Q-R6, Black's queen is surprisingly active as a defensive piece.

| 19 | R-KN1 | K-R1 |
| 20 | N-N3! | . . . |

The knight goes to B5 or R5 and supports the advance of White's central pawns. Now 20 . . . P-KN3; 21 Q-Q4, or 20 . . . Q-R5; 21 Q-Q4 is too strong for White. White has a winning advantage within a few moves.

20	. . .	Q-Q2
21	N-R5	R-KN1
22	P-B5!	QR-Q1
23	N-B4	. . .

Now P-K6 is a threat or Q-Q4 first. On 23 . . . Q-K2, for example, 24 P-K6, KR-B1; 25 PxP, QxP; 26 N-N6ch, K-N1; 27 NxR, RxN is still a fight, but 25 Q-Q4!, Q-B3; 26 QxQ, PxQ; 27 P-K7 wins. Also winning is 24 . . . Q-B3; 25 PxP, QxP(2); 26 N-N6ch, K-R2; 27 P-B6!, followed by a discovery.

| 23 | . . . | KR-K1 |
| 24 | P-K6! | . . . |

And here: (a) 24 . . . Q-Q3; 25 Q-Q4, P-KB3 (25 . . . R-KN1; 26 PxP wins a rook); 26 RxP!!, KxR; 27 N-R5ch, K-N1; 28 NxPch, K-B1; 29 N-R5 and wins; (b) 24 . . . Q-K2; 25 RxP!! (not 25 Q-Q4, Q-B3; 26 QxQ, PxQ; 27 PxP, R-KB1; 28 N-N6ch, K-R2, with an unclear position in which White has weak pawns), KxR; 26 P-B6ch, KxP; 27 Q-Q4ch, K-N4; 28 P-R4ch!, KxP (28 . . . K-B4; 29 Q-K4ch, K-B3; 30 N-R5ch mates); 29 N-N6ch, K-N4; 30 NxQ, RxN; 31 Q-N4ch, K-B3; 32 Q-R4ch wins.

24	. . .	PxP
25	**P-B6!**	. . .

Winning a rook with a threat of 26 RxP and 27 N-N6 mate. If 25 . . . PxP; 26 N-N6ch and 27 N-K5ch, winning the queen.

25	. . .	**P-KN4**
26	**N-N6ch**	**K-N1**
27	**N-K5**	**Q-R2**
28	**P-B7ch**	**K-N2**
29	**PxR(Q)**	**RxQ**
30	**Q-B3**	**Resigns**

Greg DeFotis

Greg DeFotis is the foremost competitor of the Chicago young masters, whose strength he confirmed by finishing in a tie for sixth place with Lombardy ahead of Bisguier and Mednis in the 1972 U.S. championship. Now twenty years old, DeFotis has also won or tied for the U.S. junior championship three times. Most recently he tied for first in the 1973 U.S. Open.

DeFotis is a counterpuncher à la Reshevsky. He is especially adept at finding equalizing counterplay against a good opponent and springing a decisive initiative against unsound attackers. Consequently he often does better with the Black pieces than with White. Here is a typical DeFotis game from the 1971 Student Olympiade.

STUDENT OLYMPIADE,
Mayaguez, Puerto Rico, 1971

	SABOYA	DEFOTIS
1	**P-K4**	**P-QB4**
2	**N-KB3**	**P-Q3**
3	**P-Q4**	**PxP**

4	NxP	N-KB3
5	N-QB3	P-QR3
6	B-QB4	P-K3
7	B-N3	P-QN4
8	Q-K2	. . .

White hopes to transpose into a setup resembling Drasko Velimirovich's attacking line with 0-0-0 and P-KN4-5. Some examples of sharp play follow: (a) 8 . . . B-N2; 9 B-N5, P-N5; 10 N-R4, Q-R4; 11 BxN, PxB; 12 0-0-0, with good chances (Radulov-S. Garcia, Varna, 1970); (b) 8 . . . B-N2; 9 B-N5, B-K2?; 10 BxKP, PxB; 11 NxKP, Q-Q2; 12 NxPch, K-B2; 13 N-B5, with a strong attack; (c) 8 . . . B-N2; 9 B-N5, QN-Q2; 10 0-0-0, P-KR3; 11 B-R4, Q-R4?; 12 KR-K1, P-KN4; 13 B-N3, R-B1; 14 P-K5!, RxN; 15 PxN!, RxKB; 16 NxKP! (Mariotti-Eppinger, Italy, 1970).

8	. . .	P-N5!

Not wasting any time for this almost always good move. Now on 9 N-R4 (best) Black can develop his bishop to Q2 rather than QN2 and concentrate on the offsides knight.

9	N-Q1?!	B-N2
10	P-KB3	QN-Q2
11	N-B2	N-B4

Black already stands very well. He prepares . . . P-QR4-5, gaining further space on the queenside and shooting for . . . P-Q4. White is on the defensive and must keep the game closed.

12	B-K3	P-Q4!

Now 13 0-0-0, Q-R4; 14 K-N1, B-K2 is a slight edge for Black, but he can do better with 14 . . . PxP.

13	P-K5?	KN-Q2
14	N-Q3	. . .

White prays for counterplay with 14 . . . NxNch; 15 PxN, NxP; 16 B-R4ch, N-Q2; 17 N-B6.

14	. . .	P-QR4!
15	NxN	NxN

The endgame after 16 Q-N5ch, Q-Q2 is a kind of superior French Defense for Black.

16	P-QR4	PxP e.p.
17	PxP	B-R3
18	Q-Q2	P-R5
19	B-R2	N-Q2!

To develop the bishop on QB4 (19 . . . B-K2; 20 N-B6) where it is most useful.

20	B-KB4	B-B4
21	P-B3	0-0
22	B-N1	. . .

White has nothing now but the attack. His queen bishop pawn is a horrible weakness, he can't castle, and his white squares are very weak. Note that Black has delayed castling until his twenty-first move and has a strong attack brewing.

22	. . .	Q-R5ch!
23	P-N3	Q-R6

24	**R-N1**	**P-B3!**
25	**PxP**	**RxP**

Black must win once he gets control of another open line. All his pieces can advance now.

26	**B-N5**	**KR-B1**
27	**Q-N2**	**Q-R4**
28	**B-K3**	**N-K4**

Now on 29 P-KB4 White may win with 29 . . . BxN and 30 . . . N-B6ch.

29	**P-N4**	**Q-R5ch**
30	**B-B2**	**Q-N4!**

Against the threats of 30 . . . BxN; 31 PxB, NxPch, and 30 . . . Q-B8 mate, there is no defense. White's next is a tactical spasm.

31	**BxPch**	**KxB**
32	**NxP**	**N-Q6ch**
33	**K-Q1**	**N-N7ch!**

Now 34 K-K1, Q-K4ch is no different.

34	**K-B2**	**B-Q6ch**
35	**KxN**	**Q-Q7 mate**

Afterward: The American School of Chess?

It would be reassuring if we could point out a common trait found in all American masters. We have heard of the Soviet School and how the new Soviet Man has brought a wholly different scientific approach to this ancient game. But such generalizations just don't hold up. The Russian who tries to find specific similarities in Petrosian, Tal, Korchnoi, and Spassky will be as unlucky as the American who seeks the common bond linking Morphy, Reshevsky, and Fischer. It would be easier to try, as the late New England master Weaver Adams did, to prove that White has a forced win after 1 P-K4.

We have seen the evolution of a style here. In Morphy's games the application of basic principles brought success in open games. In Pillsbury's career we saw the element of planning added to the Morphy legacy and also the ability to attack on both sides of the board when the center is semiclosed. From Marshall we have the germ of the philosophy that "no one ever won a game by resigning." Capablanca refined Morphy's development theory and showed how this early placement of pieces must be part of Pillsbury's planning. Reshevsky and Fine enriched the art of defense with a tactical skill that would bring Morphy's admiration. And in the play of Fischer we see the "complete chessplayer," bringing all of this national chess legacy together.

Not enough for a separate American School, perhaps. The age of schools is dead. Chess knowledge is so widely distributed today that all masters are to some degree eclectics. We can only point to slight regional characteristics of style.

The fortunes of a country's players go up and down. Italy and Spain dominated chess during the Renaissance but have only produced one or two players of grandmaster rank since. The French hegemony of the eighteenth century died with Philidor and Labourdonnais. Only now in the 1970s do we see a revival of the British mastery that led the chess world in the early nineteenth century.

Since then the game has been enriched by contributions from Russia, America, Eastern Europe, and the German-speaking countries chiefly. Perhaps Mecking of Brazil and Quinteros of Argentina mark the entrance of future masters of Latin America. Or we may see a procession of new grandmasters from Canada, or Asia, or Central America. We can only wait and see.

No, there isn't an American School of Chess. But as long as there is the keen interest in the game that has nurtured a Morphy, a Reshevsky, and a Fischer, American masters will be heard from.

APPENDIX A

An American Sampler: Twenty-five Remarkable Games by U. S. Masters

1. MARACHE-MORPHY, *Casual Game, New York, 1857*
1 P-K4, P-K4; 2 N-KB3, N-QB3; 3 B-B4, B-B4; 4 P-QN4, BxP; 5 P-B3, B-R4; 6 P-Q4, PxP; 7 P-K5? (7 0-0), P-Q4!; 8 PxP e.p., QxP; 9 0-0, KN-K2; 10 N-N5? (as in Meek-Morphy, Chapter 1, White's attack should not succeed because it involves only two pieces), 0-0; 11 B-Q3, B-B4!; 12 BxB, NxB; 13 B-R3, Q-N3; 14 BxR, QxN; 15 B-R3, PxP (Black has excellent compensation); 16 B-B1, Q-N3; 17 B-B4, R-Q1; 18 Q-B2, N(3)-Q5! (now 19 Q-B1 loses to 19 . . . N-K7ch, and 19 R-Q1 fails to 19 . . . N-K6!!; 20 QxQ, N-K7ch and mates; the longest line—19 Q-R4, P-N4!; 20 QxB, N-K7ch; 21 K-R1, NxB; 22 P-N3, Q-B3ch; 23 P-B3, QxPch!); 19 Q-K4, N-KN6!!; 20 Resigns.

Final Position

2. BIRD-MORPHY, *Casual Game, London, 1858*

1 P-K4, P-K4; 2 N-KB3, P-Q3; 3 P-Q4, P-KB4?!; 4 N-B3 (4 B-QB4, BPxP; 5 NxP! refutes one of Morphy's favorite variations), BPxP; 5 QNxP, P-Q4?!; 6 N-N3? (6 NxP!, PxN; 7 Q-R5ch), P-K5; 7 N-K5, N-KB3; 8 B-N5, B-Q3; 9 N-R5, 0-0; 10 Q-Q2, Q-K1; 11 P-KN4? (a miscalculation—Bird didn't like 11 NxNch, PxN; 12 BxP, RxB; 13 Q-N5ch, R-N3), NxP; 12 NxN, QxN (Bird had only figured on 12 . . . BxN; 13 NxP!, KxN; 14 B-R6ch and Q-N5); 13 N-K5, N-B3; 14 B-K2, Q-R6; 15 NxN, PxN; 16 B-K3, R-N1; 17 0-0-0, RxBP?!! (objectively best was 17 . . . B-KN5 or 17 . . . B-QN5, but who could blame Black?); 18 BxR, Q-R6!!; 19 P-B3 (19 PxQ, BxP is mate, of course; Steinitz's suggestion, 19 Q-N5, fails to 19 . . . QxPch; 20 K-Q2, B-N5ch; 21 K-K3, Q-R6ch!; 22 B-Q3, B-R3; 23 KR-N1, B-KB1!), QxP; 20 P-N4 (20 Q-B2, RxP!; 21 QxR, B-QR6 favors the active queen), Q-R8ch; 21 K-B2, Q-R5ch; 22 K-N2? (22 K-B1! draws because Black must take a half point with 22 . . . Q-R8ch; the alternative, 22 . . . BxNP?; 23 PxB, RxP, loses after 24 Q-N5!, Q-R6ch; 25 K-Q2, R-N7ch; 26 K-K1, RxBch; 27 KxR, Q-B6ch; 28 K-K1, QxKRch; 29 Q-N1!), BxNP!!; 23 PxB, RxPch; 24 QxR, QxQch; 25 K-B2 (Steinitz said 25 K-R2 draws, but more than half a century later Euwe showed 25 . . . P-B4!; 26 R-QN1, Q-R4ch; 27 K-N3, B-Q2!, or 26 PxP, P-Q5 would decisively activate the bishop), P-K6!!; 26 BxP, B-B4ch;

27 R-Q3, Q-B5ch; 28 K-Q2, Q-R7ch!; 29 K-Q1, Q-N8ch; 30 Resigns. This was Morphy's most impressive sacrificial combination despite its objective failing.

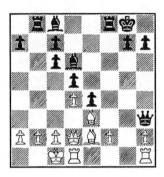

Position after 17 0-0-0

3. LOYD-ROSENTHAL, *Paris, 1867*

1 P-K4, P-K4; 2 N-KB3, N-QB3; 3 B-B4, B-B4; 4 P-Q3, N-B3; 5 B-K3, B-N3; 6 N-B3, P-Q3; 7 P-KR3, N-QR4; 8 B-N3, NxB; 9 RPxN, B-K3; 10 N-QN5, BxB; 11 PxB, P-B3; 12 N-B3, Q-B2; 13 P-KN4 (White has misplayed the opening and could get a bad game after 13 . . . P-Q4), P-QR3?; 14 P-Q4!, 0-0-0; 15 P-Q5!, B-Q2; 16 P-N5, N-K1; 17 N-Q2, P-QB4; 18 N-B4, P-R3!; 19 Q-R5, R-B1?!; 20 PxP, R-R1; 21 PxP, RxQ; 22 P-N8(Q), RxP; 23 RxR, BxR; 24 N-N5! (the beginning of a brilliant attack), Q-K2; 25 Q-R7, B-N5; 26 N-R7ch!, K-N1; 27 RxP!, N-B2; 28 R-R5, Q-B3! (threatening 29 . . . R-R1 and 29 . . . Q-B6); 29 Q-R1!, R-R1; 30 Q-B1, B-B6; 31 N-N6!, Q-R5ch; 32 K-Q2, Q-N5; 33 QxB!!, QxQ; 34 N-Q7ch, K-R1; 35 N-B6ch, N-R3; 36 N-N6 mate. On another occasion Loyd announced a mate in eight moves. His opponent resigned on the spot but both players were embarrassed when it was discovered that not only was the mate avoidable but Loyd's opponent stood an excellent chance of winning.

Position after 32 . . . Q-N5

4. PILLSBURY-WINAWER, *Budapest, 1896*

1 P-Q4, P-Q4; 2 P-QB4, P-K3; 3 N-QB3, P-QB3; 4 P-K3, N-B3; 5 N-B3, QN-Q2; 6 B-Q3, B-Q3; 7 0-0, 0-0; 8 P-K4, PxKP; 9 NxP, NxN; 10 BxN, N-B3? (10 . . . P-QB4!; 11 B-B2, Q-B2; 12 Q-Q3, P-B4! is equal); 11 B-B2, P-KR3; 12 B-K3, R-K1; 13 Q-Q3, Q-B2?; 14 P-B5!, B-B1; 15 N-K5! (threatening 16 N-N4; best is 16 . . . P-KN3), BxP?; 16 BxP!, BxP (16 . . . PxB; 17 Q-N3ch and N-N6ch wins the queen); 17 QxB, PxB; 18 Q-KB4, N-Q4; 19 QxRP!, P-B3 (White mates in four with 20 B-R7ch otherwise); 20 P-B4!, R-K2; 21 N-N6, Resigns.

Position after 13 . . . Q-B2?

5. TCHIGORIN-PILLSBURY, *London, 1899*

1 P-K4, P-K4; 2 N-KB3, N-QB3; 3 B-B4, B-B4; 4 P-QN4, BxP; 5 P-B3, B-B4; 6 0-0, P-Q3; 7 P-Q4, B-N3! (Lasker's Defense, with which the world champion defeated Tchigorin in its first game at St. Petersburg, 1896; White can win his pawn back now but Black is better in the ending); 8 PxP, PxP; 9 QxQch, NxQ; 10 NxP, B-K3; 11 N-Q2, N-K2; 12 B-R3, P-KB3; 13 N-Q3, N-N3; 14 QR-N1, K-B2; 15 B-Q5, R-K1; 16 P-QB4?, P-B3; 17 BxBch, NxB; 18 N-N3, QR-Q1; 19 N(N)-B1, R-Q2!; 20 P-B5, B-B2; 21 P-N3, N-K4!; 22 NxNch, BxN; 23 N-N3, P-KN4; 24 KR-Q1, KR-Q1; 25 RxRch, RxR; 26 P-R3, B-B2; 27 K-B1, P-N4! (Black handles the queenside majority beautifully for the rest of the game); 28 B-N4, P-KR4; 29 K-N2, R-Q6; 30 R-QB1, N-Q5; 31 R-B3, RxR; 32 BxR, NxN; 33 PxN, P-R4; 34 K-B3, K-K3; 35 K-K3, P-KN5! (cripples the adverse majority); 36 PxP, PxP; 37 K-Q3, P-R5; 38 PxP, PxP; 39 B-N4, B-K4!; 40 B-R3, B-R8! (Black's king must enter to attack the weak White pawns now); 41 B-B1, P-B4; 42 B-R3, K-K4; 43 PxP, KxP; 44 K-K3, K-K4; 45 P-B4ch (or 45 P-B3, B-Q5ch; 46 K-K2, PxPch; 47 KxP, K-Q4; 48 P-N4, BxP, and the advance of the rook pawn must win), K-Q4!; 46 P-B5, B-K4; 47 K-B2, K-K5; 48 Resigns.

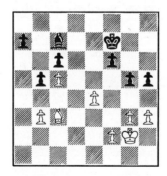

Position after 33 PxN

6. MARSHALL-PILLSBURY, *Vienna, 1903*

1 P-K4, P-K4; 2 P-KB4, PxP; 3 N-KB3, P-KN4; 4 B-B4, B-N2; 5

P-KR4, P-KR3; 6 P-Q4, P-Q3; 7 Q-Q3, P-N5 (the threat was 8 PxP, PxP; 9 RxR, BxR; 10 P-K5 and 11 Q-R7; but 7 . . . N-QB3 or 7 . . . K-B1 was better); 8 N-N1, Q-B3; 9 P-B3, P-KR4; 10 N-QR3, N-K2; 11 N-K2, N-N3; 12 P-KN3!, PxP!; 13 R-B1? (13 QxP, B-K3; 14 N-B4 was best), QxRP; 14 BxPch, K-Q1; 15 BxN, P-N7ch; 16 R-B2, R-B1!; 17 B-K3, B-R3!; 18 BxB (or 18 N-KN1, R-B6!), P-N8(Q)ch; 19 NxQ, QxRch; 20 K-Q1, QxNch; 21 K-B2, R-B7ch; 22 B-Q2, QxR; 23 Q-K3! (White still has dangerous chances, which may be handled by 23 . . . Q-B8), RxBch; 24 QxR, B-Q2; 25 Q-N5ch, K-B1; 26 B-B5!, P-N3! (White can draw with 26 . . . BxB; 27 Q-N8ch, K-Q2; 28 Q-B7ch, K-B3; 29 Q-Q5ch); 27 Q-N8ch, K-N2; 28 BxB, NxB; 29 Q-Q5ch, P-B3? (29 . . . K-N1!; 30 Q-N8ch, N-B1! ends the attack; Marshall is preparing a great swindle); 30 QxQP, R-Q1; 31 P-Q5!, R-KB1? (the winning line was 31 . . . N-B4!!; 32 QxR, Q-B8!; 33 PxPch, KxP, and Black should win with his kingside pawns); 32 PxPch, K-R1; 33 PxN, R-B7ch; 34 K-N3, QxNPch; 35 K-R4, Resigns! Black had probably miscalculated the king hunt, which would end with 35 . . . P-N4ch; 36 K-R5, QxPch; 37 K-R6!. Not until the Fine-Reshevsky games was the country to see such a rivalry.

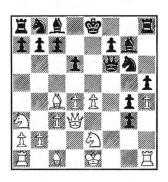

Position after 12 . . . PxP

7. MARSHALL-TCHIGORIN, *Ostend, 1905*
1 P-Q4, P-KB4; 2 P-K4, PxP; 3 N-QB3, N-KB3; 4 B-KN5, P-B3

(today 4 . . . N-B3 is considered Black's best); 5 BxN?!, KPxB; 6 NxP, Q-N3? (6 . . . P-Q4! equalizes at least); 7 R-N1, P-Q4; 8 N-N3, B-K3; 9 B-Q3, N-Q2; 10 Q-K2, K-B2; 11 N-B3, R-K1; 12 0-0, B-Q3; 13 P-B3, N-B1; 14 N-R4, B-KB4? (14 . . . BxN); 15 N(4)xB!!, RxQ; 16 NxBch, K-K3 (Black must attack the knight or he will be overrun by material—for example, 16 . . . K-N1; 17 NxR, P-N3; 18 P-QB4!, P-QB4; 19 QPxP, QxBP; 20 N-N5!, PxP; 21 KR-B1!, as given by Marshall); 17 N-B8!, Q-B2; 18 BxR, K-B2 (it is hard to believe that White's advanced horse can survive behind enemy lines; Marshall gives 18 . . . P-KN3; 19 KR-K1!, P-KB4; 20 B-B3ch, K-B3; 21 N-K7, N-K3; 22 BxP!, among many lines that turn out to be sound); 19 N-B5, N-K3; 20 N(5)-Q6ch, K-N3; 21 B-Q3ch, K-R4; 22 QR-K1, N-B5; 23 R-K7, Q-R4; 24 B-N1, P-KN3; 25 P-KN3, N-R6ch; 26 K-N2, N-N4; 27 B-Q3, RxN; 28 NxR, Q-Q1; 29 P-KR4!, QxN (29 . . . N-K5; 30 RxPch, K-N5; 31 P-B3ch, or 29 . . . N-B2; 30 RxN, QxN; 31 RxPch, K-N5; 32 P-B3 mate would have been fitting ends); 30 PxN, Resigns. Marshall's gift for the purely combinational part of chess was enormous.

Position after 14 . . . B-KB4?

8. CAPABLANCA-MIESES, *Berlin, 1913*

1 P-Q4, N-KB3; 2 N-KB3, P-B4; 3 P-Q5, P-Q3; 4 P-B4, P-KN3; 5 N-B3, B-N2; 6 P-K4, 0-0; 7 B-K2, P-K3; 8 0-0, PxP; 9 KPxP, N-K1; 10 R-K1, B-N5?!; 11 N-KN5!, BxN; 12 PxB, BxB; 13 QxB,

N-N2; 14 N-K4!, P-B3; 15 B-B4, N-K1; 16 B-R6, N-N2 (How does White increase his advantage? The usual Capablanca answer would be to use the open files better.); 17 QR-Q1, N-R3; 18 R-Q3!, P-B4; 19 N-N5, N-B2 (to stop BxN and N-K6ch); 20 Q-K7!, QxQ; 21 RxQ, N(B)-K1; 22 R-R3!, P-B5; 23 BxN, NxB; 24 RxRP, N-B4; 25 R-K6!, KR-K1; 26 RxPch, Resigns. Mate in two. So little effort, it seems, and such results.

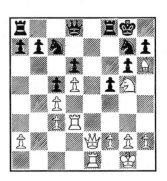

Position after 19 . . . N-B2

9. JANOWSKI–EDWARD LASKER, *New York, 1924*
1 P-Q4, P-Q4; 2 B-B4, N-KB3; 3 P-K3, P-K3; 4 B-Q3, P-B4; 5 P-QB3, Q-N3; 6 Q-B2, QN-Q2; 7 N-Q2, B-Q3; 8 BxB?, QxB; 9 P-KB4, N-N5!; 10 N-B1, PxP; 11 BPxP, Q-N5ch; 12 K-K2, N-N3; 13 P-QR3, Q-K2; 14 N-B3, B-Q2; 15 P-R3, R-QB1?; 16 QxRch!, NxQ; 17 PxN, N-Q3; 18 R-B1, N-B5!; 19 BxN, PxB; 20 N(1)-Q2, P-QN4; 21 R-R5, P-B3; 22 P-N5, K-Q1?!; 23 QR-KR1, B-K1; 24 RxP, RxR; 25 RxR, PxP; 26 NxP, K-B1; 27 R-R8, K-N2; 28 QN-K4, K-N3; 29 N-B5, B-B3 (29 . . . P-K4, as suggested by Alekhine, runs into problems after 30 N[N]-K6, PxQP; 31 PxP— for example, 31 . . . B-B2??; 32 R-N8ch, K-R4; 33 R-N7); 30 N(N)xP, B-Q4; 31 N-N5, K-R4; 32 P-K4, B-B3; 33 K-K3, B-K1; 34 N-B3, P-N5; 35 N-K5, B-N4; 36 P-R4!, BxP; 37 NxPch, K-N4; 38 N-K5, K-R4; 39 R-QN8, B-N4; 40 P-KN3, P-N4; 41 N-B3, PxPch; 42 PxP, Q-R2; 43 P-B5, Q-R8; 44 N-N3ch, K-R5; 45

N(N)-Q2, Q-R3ch; 46 K-B2, B-Q6; 47 R-N8, Q-B5; 48 R-KR8, P-N6 (it is not clear who is winning this bizarre ending; White's minor pieces seem to be more than enough for the queen but Black has chances to hold); 49 R-R4, Q-B2; 50 P-B6, B-B5; 51 R-R5, B-K3; 52 R-K5!, Q-KB2; 53 RxB!!, QxR; 54 P-K5, K-N5; 55 K-K3, P-R4; 56 K-B4, P-R5; 57 N-N5, Q-Q2; 58 P-B7, Q-K2 (not 58 . . . QxQPch; 59 QN-K4, Q-Q1; 60 N-K6; the two knights and three pawns are crushing); 59 P-Q5, P-R6; 60 PxPch, K-B6!; 61 P-Q6, Q-B1; 62 N(5)-K4ch, K-Q6; 63 P-K6, Q-R3ch; 64 K-B5, P-N7; 65 P-Q7, Q-B1; 66 P-R4, Q-QR1; 67 P-K7, Q-Q4ch; 68 K-B6, Q-Q5ch; 69 K-K6?? (tragedy—On 69 K-N6 both players queen and White wins), P-N8(Q); 70 NxQ (now 70 P-Q8[Q], Q-R7ch; 71 K-B5, QxBPch is a perpetual check), QxNch; 71 K-B6, Q-R5ch; Draw!! A long game but surely the weirdest duel in any American tournament.

Position after 68 . . . Q-Q5ch

10. CAPABLANCA-SPIELMANN, *New York, 1927*

1 P-Q4, P-Q4; 2 N-KB3, P-K3; 3 P-B4, N-Q2; 4 N-B3, KN-B3; 5 B-N5, B-N5 (this was the defense that Spielmann and Vidmar had prepared during the Atlantic voyage on the liner "Westphalia"; the opening has since been known as the Westphalia Defense); 6 PxP, PxP; 7 Q-R4, BxNch? (7 . . . P-B4!; 8 P-K3, 0-0 is fine for Black); 8 PxB, 0-0; 9 P-K3, P-B4; 10 B-Q3, P-B5; 11 B-B2, Q-K2;

12 0-0, P-QR3; 13 KR-K1, Q-K3; 14 N-Q2, P-N4; 15 Q-R5!
(Black's queenside is penetrated; now 15 . . . B-N2; 16 P-B3 and
P-K4 would give White a good game in the center also), N-K5?!;
16 NxN, PxN; 17 P-QR4!, Q-Q4; 18 PxP!, QxB; 19 BxP, R-N1
(19 . . . R-R2; 20 P-N6!, QxQ; 21 PxR!); 20 PxP, R-N4 (a trade
of queens costs Black a piece to stop the rook pawn); 21 Q-B7,
N-N3; 22 P-R7, B-R6; 23 KR-N1!, RxRch; 24 RxR, P-B4; 25
B-B3, P-B5; 26 PxP!, Resigns. Because of 26 . . . RxP; 27 RxN,
R-B1; 28 QxBPch, K-R1; 29 R-N8. Black weakened the queenside
black squares and that was enough.

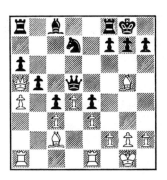

Position after 17 . . . Q-Q4

11. STAHLBERG-KASHDAN, *Hamburg, 1930*

1 P-Q4, N-KB3; 2 P-QB4, P-K3; 3 N-QB3, B-N5; 4 Q-N3, P-B4;
5 PxP, N-B3 (5 . . . N-R3! is even better); 6 N-B3, N-K5; 7
B-Q2, NxQBP!; 8 Q-B2, 0-0 (not bad but 8 . . . P-B4!; 9 P-QR3,
BxN; 11 BxB, 0-0; 12 P-QN4, N-K5 was a bit better); 9 P-K4?,
Q-B3!; 10 0-0-0, P-QN3! (Stahlberg, an expert in this opening, has
weakened his black squares too much; but Black had to avoid the
trap in 10 . . . BxN; 11 BxB, Q-B5ch; 12 N-Q2, QxBP?; 13
P-QN4!); 11 B-Q3, P-QR4; 12 K-N1, Q-N3; 13 KR-N1, B-R3; 14
B-K3, NxB; 15 QxN, BxN; 16 PxB, P-Q4! (Black finds a way to a
winning attack in the ending); 17 KPxP, QxQch; 18 RxQ, BxP; 19
R-Q2, BxQP; 20 BxP, KR-N1; 21 R-N2, P-R5! (So 22 B-B5,
P-R6!; 23 RxRch, RxRch; 24 K-R1, R-N7!); 22 B-B7, R-QB1; 23
B-B4, N-R4; 24 R-QB1, B-K5ch; 25 K-R1, N-N6ch!; 26 Resigns.

Position after 16 PxB

12. DAKE-ALEKHINE, *Pasadena, 1932*

1 P-K4, P-QB3; 2 P-Q4, P-Q4; 3 PxP, PxP; 4 P-QB4, N-KB3; 5 N-QB3, N-B3; 6 N-B3, B-K3? (a typical Alekhine experiment that backfires); 7 P-B5!, P-KN3; 8 B-QN5, B-N2; 9 N-K5, Q-B1; 10 Q-R4, B-Q2; 11 0-0, 0-0; 12 B-KB4, P-QR3; 13 BxN, PxB; 14 KR-K1, N-R4; 15 B-Q2, R-R2; 16 R-K2, B-K1; 17 QR-K1, P-B4?; 18 N-B3!, N-B3 (18 . . . Q-Q1; 19 N-KN5); 19 RxP, RxR; 20 RxR, P-B5?!; 21 BxP!, N-K5; 22 B-K5, B-R3; 23 NxN, PxN; 24 N-N5!, Q-B4; 25 Q-N3ch, B-B2; 26 NxB, RxN; 27 RxR, QxR; 28 Q-N8ch!, Q-B1; 29 P-Q5!, P-K6!; 30 P-B4! (now White wins easily), QxQ; 31 BxQ, K-B2; 32 PxP, K-K1; 33 P-QN4, P-N4; 34 P-N3, PxP; 35 PxP, K-Q1; 36 P-QR4, K-B1; 37 B-Q6, B-N2; 38 K-B1, Resigns. Dake finished in a tie for third place behind Alekhine and Kashdan and ahead of Fine.

Position after 17 . . . P-B4?

13. RESHEVSKY-CAPABLANCA, *Margate England, 1935*
1 P-Q4, N-KB3; 2 P-QB4, P-K3; 3 N-QB3, P-Q4; 4 B-N5, QN-Q2;
5 PxP, PxP; 6 P-K3, B-K2; 7 B-Q3, 0-0; 8 Q-B2, P-B4?! (8 . . .
P-B3); 9 N-B3, P-B5; 10 B-B5, R-K1; 11 0-0, P-KN3; 12 B-R3,
N-B1; 13 BxB, RxB; 14 BxN!, BxB; 15 P-QN3!, Q-R4? (15 . . .
PxP; 16 QxP would cost a pawn, but 15 . . . Q-Q2 was better);
16 P-QN4!, Q-Q1; 17 Q-R4, P-QR3; 18 P-N5, R-K3; 19 QR-N1
(stops 19 . . . P-QR4 with 20 P-N6; White's queenside play is
impressive in the Pillsbury tradition), R-N1; 20 R-N2, B-K2; 21
PxP, RxP; 22 Q-B2, N-K3; 23 KR-N1, R-R2; 24 P-QR4, N-B2;
25 N-K5, Q-K1; 26 P-B4, P-B3; 27 N-N4, Q-Q2; 28 P-R3, K-N2;
29 N-B2, B-R6; 30 R-R2, B-Q3; 31 N(2)-Q1, P-B4; 32 N-N5,
R-R4; 33 NxN, BxN; 34 N-B3, Q-K3; 35 Q-B2, P-N3; 36 Q-B3,
R-Q1; 37 R(R)-N2, Q-K2! (hoping for 38 R-N5, RxR; 39 RxR,
Q-R6!); 38 R-N4, R-Q2; 39 K-R1, B-Q1; 40 P-N4! (after twenty
moves of maneuver against the queen pawn, Reshevsky feels pre-
pared to cash in on his advantages), PxP; 41 PxP, Q-Q3; 42 K-N1,
B-B2; 43 K-B2! (heading for QB2 now that the kingside is opened),
R-B2; 44 P-N5, B-Q1; 45 K-K2, BxP? (45 . . . Q-K3!); 46 RxP,
Q-R6; 47 K-Q2, B-K2; 48 R-N7, RxRP; 49 QxP (49 NxR?,
Q-Q6ch), R-R4; 50 QxP, R-R4; 51 K-Q3, Q-R1; 52 Q-K6, Q-R6;
53 R-Q7, R(4)-KB4; 54 R-N3!, Q-R8; 55 RxB, Q-B8ch; 56 K-Q2,
Resigns.

Position after 15 . . . Q-R4?

14. RESHEVSKY-FINE, *New York State Championship, Hamilton, N.Y., 1941*

1 P-Q4, N-KB3; 2 P-QB4, P-K3; 3 N-QB3, B-N5; 4 P-K3, P-Q4; 5 P-QR3, BxNch; 6 PxB, P-B4; 7 BPxP, KPxP; 8 B-Q3, 0-0; 9 N-K2, P-QN3; 10 0-0, B-R3; 11 BxB, NxB; 12 Q-Q3, Q-B1 (13 . . . P-B5 is a notorious positional error that has given White many winning positions; then Black has no queenside play, while White plays P-B3 and P-K4); 13 B-N2, PxP; 14 BPxP, N-B2; 15 KR-B1! (stops 15 . . . Q-R3 because the ending after 16 QxQ, NxQ; 17 R-B6 is great for White), Q-Q2; 16 P-B3, KR-K1; 17 N-N3, N-K3; 18 R-K1, QR-B1; 19 QR-Q1 (19 P-K4, PxP; 20 PxP, N-B4!; 21 Q-KB3, N-R5 is good for Black; Fine restrains White in the center but now counts too heavily on the open file), Q-R5; 20 R-Q2, Q-B5; 21 Q-N1, Q-N6?; 22 N-B5, R-B2; 23 P-K4, KR-QB1; 24 R-Q3, Q-R5; 25 P-K5, N-K1; 26 N-K3, Q-N4; 27 R-Q2, Q-N6; 28 R-Q3, Q-N4; 29 R-Q2, Q-R4 (White wasn't inviting the draw; he intended P-N3 and P-B4 or Q-B5 after 29 . . . Q-N6); 30 Q-Q1, Q-N4; 31 P-N3, P-N3; 32 P-B4, P-B4; 33 Q-B3, R-Q1; 34 P-N4, N(1)-N2; 35 PxP, N(2)xP; 36 N-N4, R-B2; 37 N-B6ch, K-R1; 38 R-QB1, RxN!? (Fine has withheld the attack so far and places his hopes in the strong knights; the game was adjourned at move 40 with fascinating play); 39 PxR, R-KB1; 40 R-K1, RxP; 41 P-QR4! (now 41 . . . QxP; 42 QxP will open up the game for

his bishop), Q-Q2; 42 R-KB2, N-B2; 43 R-B2, R-B2; 44 R(1)-QB1, N-K1; 45 B-R3!, N-B3? (Black may hold after 45 . . . K-N2; 46 R-B8, R-B3, or 46 Q-K2, N-B3; 47 Q-K5, N-R5); 46 R-B8ch, K-N2; 47 B-B8ch! (nice: 47 . . . RxB; 48 R[8]-B7), K-N1; 48 B-Q6ch? (only in problems do you find a winning move such as 48 QxP!!—for example, 48 . . . QxQ; 49 B-R6ch, 48 . . . QxR; 49 RxQ, NxQ; 50 B-R6ch, and 48 . . . N-Q3; 49 BxNch, K-N2; 50 B-B8ch; best is 48 . . . N-N2; 49 QxQ, RxQ; 50 BxNch, with an easy win), N-K1; 49 B-K5, N-K2; 50 R-R8 (50 R[1]-B7! should have won but Reshevsky was short of time), N-B3; 51 P-R3, NxB; 52 QPxN, QxQRP; 53 R(1)-B8, R-B1; 54 P-K6, K-N2; 55 P-K7? (55 Q-K3 wins), RxP; 56 Q-Q3, R-B4! (threatening 57 . . . Q-R8ch and . . . R-N4ch); 57 R-B2, Q-R5? (a blunder that turns the winning position that could have been reached with 57 . . . Q-R8ch; 58 K-R2, Q-K4ch into a loss); 58 K-R2? (and here 58 RxN wins because Black runs out of checks, as Vera Menchik observed: 58 . . . Q-K8ch; 59 K-R2, Q-K4ch; 60 Q-N3, or 58 . . . R-N4ch; 59 K-R2, Q-B5ch; 60 K-R1), R-N4ch; 59 R-N2, RxRch; 60 KxR, QxP; 61 QxP, Draw. Since on 61 . . . Q-K7ch White wisely plays 62 K-N1! One of a great series.

Position after 46 . . . K-N2

15. RESHEVSKY-VASCONCELLOS, *U.S. Open, Boston, 1944*

1 P-K4, P-K3; 2 P-Q4, P-Q4; 3 P-K5, P-QB4; 4 PxP, N-Q2 (4 . . . BxP; 5 Q-N4 is troublesome); 5 N-KB3, BxP; 6 B-Q3, N-K2;

7 0-0, N-QB3; 8 B-KB4, Q-B2; 9 N-B3, P-QR3; 10 R-K1, Q-N3? (in connection with his next move, this is one of the oldest errors; better was 10 . . . N-N3 and . . . B-Q2); 11 B-N3, QxP?; 12 NxP!, PxN; 13 R-N1, Q-R6; 14 P-K6!, N-B3 (or 14 . . . PxP; 15 N-N5!); 15 PxPch, KxP; 16 B-R4!, N-QN5 (best was 16 . . . B-K2; 17 BxN, PxB; 18 N-R4, N-K4, except that White can improve with 17 P-B4, P-Q5; 18 N-N5ch, K-B1; 19 Q-K2, Reshevsky said); 17 N-K5ch, K-B1; 18 BxN, NxB; 19 BxPch!, KxB; 20 RxPch!, B-K2; 21 Q-R5! (now 21 . . . BxR loses to 22 Q-B7ch, K-R3; 23 N-N4ch, K-N4; 24 Q-N7ch and mates), R-B1; 22 Q-N5ch, K-R1; 23 N-N6ch!, PxN; 24 Q-R6ch, K-N1; 25 QxPch, K-R1; 27 R(7)xB, Resigns. Mate follows. The combinational Reshevsky as attacker.

Position after 18 . . . NxB

16. DENKER-PINKUS, *Manhattan Chess Club Championship, 1945–46*

1 P-Q4, P-Q4; 2 P-QB4, P-K3; 3 N-QB3, P-QB3; 4 P-K4, PxKP; 5 NxP, B-N5ch; 6 N-QB3?! (6 B-Q2, QxP; 7 BxB, QxNch is the more complicated line that the analysts consider more dangerous for Black), P-QB4; 7 P-QR3, BxNch (7 . . . B-R4; 8 B-K3, PxP; 9 BxP and P-QN4 favors White); 8 PxB, N-KB3; 9 N-B3, N-B3; 10 B-Q3!, PxP; 11 PxP, NxP; 12 0-0!, N-B3; 13 B-N2, B-Q2; 14 R-K1, Q-B2?; 15 N-K5, P-KR4 (having been stopped from castling queenside, Black plays for . . . N-KN5); 16 Q-B3!, R-R3; 17 Q-N3, NxN; 18 BxN, Q-B4; 19 P-R3 (19 QxP, N-N5; 20 B-Q4, Q-B2; 21 P-R3 wins but, the winner wrote, "I discarded this varia-

tion at the time, for I felt the position warranted a more artistic finish"), Q-KB1; 20 B-Q6, Q-R1; 21 B-N4, 0-0-0; 22 B-R5, P-QN3; 23 P-B5!, K-N2; 24 PxP, R-QB1 (24 . . . PxP; 25 BxP!, KxB; 26 QR-N1ch mates); 25 PxP, N-Q4; 26 Q-Q6, B-B3; 27 B-R6ch!, KxB; 28 P-R8(Q)ch, RxQ; 29 QxBch, K-R2 (29 . . . KxB; 30 R-K4, N-N3; 31 R-QN4 wins); 30 QR-N1, R-QN1; 31 B-B7, Resigns. The "show me" game.

Position after 10 B-Q3!

17. MENGARINI-BISGUIER, *U.S. Open, Baltimore, 1948*

1 P-Q4, P-Q4; 2 P-QB4, PxP; 3 N-KB3, P-QR3; 4 P-K3, N-KB3; 5 BxP, P-K3; 6 0-0, P-B4; 7 Q-K2, N-B3; 8 R-Q1, P-QN4; 9 B-N3, P-B5!?; 10 B-B2, N-QN5; 11 P-QR4? (11 N-B3), NxB; 12 QxN, B-N2; 13 P-QN3, BPxP; 14 QxNP, B-Q4; 15 Q-N2, P-N5; 16 P-R5, Q-B2; 17 B-Q2, Q-N2; 18 N-K1, Q-N4!; 19 P-B3, Q-K7!; 20 R-B1, P-R4!!; 21 P-K4, N-N5! (threatens 22 . . . Q-B7ch; if 22 B-B3 Black checks at K6; probably best is 22 N-Q3); 22 PxN, PxP!; 23 Q-B2 (23 PxB, B-Q3!), P-QN6!; 24 Q-Q3, QxQ; 25 NxQ, BxP; 26 N-N2, B-Q3 (Black has only two pawns for the piece but maintains the attack); 27 P-N3, K-Q2; 28 N-B3, B-B6; 29 N(3)-R4, RxP!! (White can avoid mate now only by returning material); 30 N-N6ch, K-K2; 31 B-N5ch, P-B3; 32 KxR, R-R1ch; 33 K-N1, BxP; 34 R-B7ch, BxR; 35 K-B2, R-R7ch; 36 K-K3, RxN; 37 B-R4, R-K7ch; 38 K-Q3, P-N7; 39 R-QN1, B-K5ch; 40 KxR, BxR; 41 N-B4, B-Q6ch; 42 Resigns. Bisguier at nineteen.

Position after 20 R-B1

18. EVANS-PILNICK, *Marshall Chess Club Championship, 1947–48*

1 P-K4, P-K3; 2 P-Q4, P-Q4; 3 N-QB3, N-KB3; 4 B-KN5, B-K2; 5 BxN (Kurt Richter won many fine games with this variation of Anderssen's), BxB; 6 P-K5, B-K2; 7 Q-N4, 0-0; 8 0-0-0, P-QB4 (better is 8 . . . P-KB4; 9 Q-R3, P-B4; 10 PxP, N-Q2); 9 P-KR4!?, PxP; 10 QN-K2, N-B3; 11 P-KB4, Q-R4; 12 K-N1, P-Q6!; 13 PxP, B-Q2; 14 R-R3, QR-B1? (this was Black's last chance for . . . P-B4, which gains defensive space on the kingside); 15 R-N3, P-KN3; 16 P-Q4, P-QN4; 17 P-R5, N-N5; 18 P-QR3, N-B3; 19 PxP, BPxP; 20 N-QB3, P-N5; 21 B-Q3!, B-K1; 22 N-B3, PxP (Who gets there first? In retrospect 22 . . . R-B4 appears better.); 23 QxKPch!, B-B2; 24 BxP!! (now 24 . . . BxQ; 25 BxPch, K-R1; 26 R-R1!, RxP; 27 B-Q3ch, B-R5; 28 NxB, B-N5; 29 N-N6ch should win), PxP; 25 BxPch, K-R1; 26 Q-R6, Q-R8ch; 27 K-B2, P-N8(Q)ch; 28 RxQ, N-N5ch; 29 K-Q1, Resigns. Evans at fifteen.

Position after 23 . . . B-B2

19. D. BYRNE–FISCHER, *Rosenwald Tournament, New York, 1956*

1 N-KB3, N-KB3; 2 P-B4, P-KN3; 3 N-B3, B-N2; 4 P-Q4, 0-0; 5 B-B4, P-Q4; 6 Q-N3, PxP; 7 QxBP, P-B3; 8 P-K4, QN-Q2 (better is 8 . . . P-QN4, as in game 22); 9 R-Q1, N-N3; 10 Q-B5?!, B-N5; 11 B-KN5?, N-R5!!; 12 Q-R3 (Black is winning after 12 NxN, NxP; 13 Q-N4, NxB; 14 NxN, BxR; 15 KxB, BxP), NxN; 13 PxN, NxP!; 14 BxP, Q-N3; 15 B-B4, NxQBP!; 16 B-B5, KR-K1ch; 17 K-B1, B-K3!! (not 17 . . . N-N4; 18 BxPch!); 18 BxQ (or 18 BxB, Q-N4ch and mates via Philidor's Legacy; 18 QxN, QxB! also wins), BxBch; 19 K-N1, N-K7ch; 20 K-B1, NxPch; 21 K-N1, N-K7ch; 22 K-B1, N-B6ch; 23 K-N1, PxB; 24 Q-N4, R-R5!; 25 QxP, NxR; 26 P-KR3, RxP; 27 K-R2, NxP; 28 R-K1, RxR; 29 Q-Q8ch, B-B1; 30 NxR, B-Q4; 31 N-B3, N-K5; 32 Q-N8, P-QN4; 33 P-R4, P-R4; 34 N-K5, K-N2; 35 K-N1 (Black has had a won game for several moves; now he mates in seven), B-B4ch; 36 K-B1, N-N6ch; 37 K-K1, B-N5ch; 38 K-Q1, B-N6ch; 39 K-B1, N-K7ch; 40 K-N1, N-B6ch; 41 K-B1, R-B7 mate. The Game of the Century.

Position after 17 K-B1

20. LOMBARDY-KRAMER, *U.S. Championship, New York, 1957–58*

1 N-KB3, P-Q4; 2 P-KN3, P-QB4; 3 B-N2, N-QB3; 4 P-Q4 (the Gruenfeld Defense Reversed cannot be bad for White with an extra tempo), PxP; 5 NxP, N-KB3 (5 . . . P-K3); 6 P-QB4, Q-N3?; 7 NxN, PxN; 8 N-B3, P-K3; 9 0-0, B-K2; 10 PxP, BPxP (taking with the king pawn was better, as now Black is overrun by superior development); 11 P-K4!, 0-0 (11 . . . PxP; 12 NxP, NxN; 13 BxN, B-N2; 14 Q-R4ch, or 12 . . . N-Q4; 13 N-B3! is worse); 12 PxP, B-R3; 13 R-K1, B-B4; 14 B-K3, BxB; 15 RxB, QR-Q1; 16 Q-N3, PxP; 17 NxP, NxN; 18 BxN, Q-KB3; 19 QR-K1, R-Q2; 20 Q-R3 (the threat is 21 QxRch! and mates), Q-Q3?; 21 B-B6!! (resigns was a good reply, as 21 . . . QxQ; 22 RxQ costs the Exchange), B-B1; 22 BxR, QxB; 23 R-Q3, Q-B2; 24 Q-Q6, Resigns.

Position after 21 B-B6!!

21. R. BYRNE–FISCHER, *U.S. Championship, New York, 1963–64*

1 P-Q4, N-KB3; 2 P-QB4, P-KN3; 3 P-KN3, P-B3; 4 B-N2, P-Q4; 5 PxP, PxP; 6 N-QB3, B-N2; 7 P-K3, 0-0; 8 KN-K2, N-B3; 9 0-0, P-N3; 10 P-N3, B-QR3; 11 B-QR3, R-K1; 12 Q-Q2, P-K4!; 13 PxP, NxP; 14 KR-Q1, N-Q6!; 15 Q-B2?, NxP!!; 16 KxN, N-N5ch; 17 K-N1, NxKP; 18 Q-Q2, NxB!; 19 KxN, P-Q5!; 20 NxP, B-N2ch; 21 K-B1, Q-Q2!; 22 Resigns. In the analysis room several strong players were wondering what Fischer had after 21 . . . Q-Q2. They suspected he was in trouble until a messenger brought in Byrne's surrender. On 22 Q-KB2, Q-R6ch; 23 K-N1, Black mates with 23 . . . R-K8ch!; 24 RxR, BxN!

Final Position

22. BISGUIER-BENKO, *U.S. Championship, New York, 1963–64*

1 P-Q4, N-KB3; 2 P-QB4, P-KN3; 3 N-QB3, P-Q4; 4 N-B3, B-N2; 5 Q-N3, PxP; 6 QxBP, 0-0; 7 B-B4, P-B3; 8 P-K4, P-QN4!; 9 Q-Q3, Q-R4; 10 B-K2, P-N5; 11 N-Q1, P-B4; 12 0-0, B-QR3; 13 Q-B2, PxP; 14 NxP? (14 BxB first), R-B1; 15 Q-N1, N-R4!; 16 N-N3 (now 16 BxB, QxB; 17 B-K3, BxN!; 18 BxB, N-B5 is too strong), NxB!!; 17 NxQ, NxBch; 18 K-R1, R-B8!; 19 QxR, NxQ; 20 RxN, BxR; 21 R-B8ch, B-B1; 22 N-K3 (or 22 N-B6, NxN; 23 RxR, B-QR3!; 24 N-K3, P-K3! and . . . B-QN2, trapping the rook!), B-QR3; 23 R-Q8, P-K3; 24 N-N4, K-N2; 25 P-K5, B-K2; 26 R-K8, B-KN4; 27 P-KR4, BxP; 28 P-KN3, B-QN4!; 29 N-KB6, BxR; 30 NxBch, K-B1; 31 N-B7, B-Q1!; 32 Resigns. The knight does not escape and Black is two pieces ahead. Benko's Brilliancy.

Position after 16 N-N3

23. R. BYRNE–EVANS, *U.S. Championship, New York, 1965–66*

1 P-K4, P-QB4; 2 N-KB3, P-Q3; 3 P-Q4, PxP; 4 NxP, N-KB3; 5 N-QB3, P-QR3; 6 B-KN5, P-K3; 7 P-B4, Q-N3; 8 Q-Q2, QxP; 9 R-QN1, Q-R6; 10 P-K5, PxP; 11 PxP, KN-Q2; 12 B-QB4, B-N5!?; 13 R-N3, Q-R4; 14 0-0, 0-0; 15 B-B6!?, PxB? (15 . . . NxB; 16 PxN, R-Q1!; 17 RxB!, QxR; 18 Q-N5, P-KN3!; 19 R-B4, RxN!? is Black's main bid to refute Byrne's prepared line); 16 Q-R6!! (the point Black had overlooked; his game is lost now), QxKP (16 . . . BxN; 17 B-Q3!, BxNch; 18 K-R1, P-B4; 19 BxBP

mates); 17 N-B5!, PxN; 18 N-K4!! (now 18 . . . QxN; 19 R-N3ch, Q-N5; 20 RxQch, PxR; 21 B-Q3, P-B4; 22 BxBP, or 18 . . . P-B5; 19 RxP, P-B4; 20 R-N3ch, K-R1; 21 QxPch! also lose for Black), B-Q7; 19 NxB, Q-Q5ch; 20 K-R1, N-K4; 21 R-N3ch, N-N5; 22 P-KR3, Q-K4; 23 R-B4, Q-K8ch; 24 N-B1, QxR; 25 RxNch, QxR; 26 PxQ, N-Q2; 27 N-N3, K-R1; 28 B-Q3, R-KN1; 29 BxBP, R-N3; 30 BxR, PxB; 31 N-K4, P-QN4; 32 P-N5!, B-N2; 33 NxP, N-B1; 34 Q-R2, B-B1; 35 Q-K5, N-K3; 36 N-Q7ch, Resigns.

Position after 15 . . . PxB?

24. KAUFMAN-KAVALEK, *U.S. Championship, New York, 1972*

1 P-QB4, P-K4; 2 N-QB3, P-Q3; 3 N-B3, B-N5; 4 P-Q4, N-Q2; 5 P-K3, KN-B3; 6 B-K2, P-B3; 7 P-KR3, B-R4; 8 PxP? (8 P-KN4!, B-N3; 9 N-Q2 and P-B4), PxP; 9 0-0, P-K5!; 10 N-Q2, B-N3; 11 P-QN3, Q-B2; 12 Q-B2? (Black has the edge after this; better was 12 B-N2), Q-K4!; 13 R-Q1, B-Q3; 14 N-B1, 0-0; 15 B-N2, Q-K2; 16 R-Q2, N-K4; 17 QR-Q1, N-B6ch!!; 18 PxN, PxP; 19 B-Q3, Q-K3!; 20 N-N3 (20 N-R2, QxRP; 21 NxP, Q-N5ch; 22 K-B1, QxN; 23 BxB, BPxB; 24 RxB, N-N5 is a winning game), QxRP; 21 B-KB1, Q-R3; 22 B-Q3, N-N5; 23 QN-K4, Q-R6; 24 Resigns.

Position after 17 QR-Q1

25. R. BYRNE–TAIMANOV, *Leningrad Interzonal, 1973*
1 P-K4, P-QB4; 2 N-KB3, N-QB3; 3 N-B3, P-QR3; 4 P-Q4, PxP;
5 NxP, P-K3; 6 P-KN3, KN-K2; 7 N-N3!, P-QN4 (7 . . . N-R4!);
8 B-N2, P-Q3; 9 P-B4, B-N2; 10 B-K3, P-N3; 11 Q-Q2, Q-B2; 12
Q-B2!, B-N2; 13 0-0, 0-0; 14 QR-Q1, KR-K1; 15 R-Q2 (Black's
failure to rid himself of one pair of knights has left White with an
excellent game), N-B1; 16 P-QR3, R-N1; 17 KR-Q1, P-N5; 18
PxP, NxP; 19 B-Q4, BxB; 20 QxB, B-R1; 21 B-B1, P-K4; 22 PxP,
RxP (22 . . . PxP; 23 Q-Q7!, QxQ; 24 RxQ, NxP; 25 B-B4); 23
Q-B2, BxP? (falling into a very deep trap); 24 NxB, RxN; 25
P-B3, N-B3 (25 . . . N-B7; 26 B-Q3, N-K6! was a try); 26 N-B5!!,
PxN (else 27 NxR or NxRP); 27 R-Q7, QxR; 28 RxQ, R-K2; 29
R-Q1, N(1)-R2; 30 BxP, N-K4; 31 B-B1, P-B5; 32 B-N2, N-Q6;
33 Q-Q4, N-N4; 34 QxP, NxNP; 35 Q-B4, QR-K1; 36 R-N1,
N-Q6; 37 Q-Q2!, N-R6; 38 R-R1, R-K8ch; 39 RxR, NxR; 40
Q-Q7, R-K7; 41 B-Q5, K-N2 and Resigns.

107
Position after 23 . . . BxP?

APPENDIX B

Major Tournaments and Matches Held in the United States or Involving U.S. Players

TOURNAMENTS

1857 FIRST AMERICAN CHESS CONGRESS, *New York*
1. Morphy; 2. Paulsen; 3. Lichtenhein (knockout system)

1871 SECOND AMERICAN CHESS CONGRESS, *Cleveland*
1. Mackenzie

1874 THIRD AMERICAN CHESS CONGRESS, *Chicago*
1. Mackenzie

1876 FOURTH AMERICAN CHESS CONGRESS, *Philadelphia*
1. Mason

1880 FIFTH AMERICAN CHESS CONGRESS
1. Mackenzie

280 American Chess Masters

1889 Sixth American Chess Congress
1-2. Tchigorin, Weiss, 29; 3. Gunsberg, 28½; 4. Blackburne, 27; 5. Burn, 26; 6. Lipschutz, 25½ (20 players)

1904 Cambridge Springs, *Pennsylvania*
1. Marshall, 13; 2-3. Janowski, Emanuel Lasker, 11; 4. Marco, 9; 5. Showalter, 8½; 6-7. Schlecter, Tchigorin, 7½; 8-9. Mieses, Pillsbury, 7; 10-11. Fox, Teichmann, 6½; 12-13. Lawrence, Napier, 5½; 14-15. Barry, Hodges, 5; 16. Delmar, 4½

1924 *New York (Double Round)*
1. Emanuel Lasker, 16; 2. Capablanca, 14½; 3. Alekhine, 12; 4. Marshall, 11; 5. Reti, 10½; 6. Maroczy, 10; 7. Bogolyubov, 9½; 8. Tartakover, 8; 9. Yates, 7; 10. Edward Lasker, 6½; 11. Janowski, 5

1927 *New York (Quadruple Round)*
1. Capablanca, 14; 2. Alekhine, 11½; 3. Nimzovich, 10½; 4. Vidmar, 10; 5. Spielmann, 8; 6. Marshall, 6

1936 U.S. Championship i, *New York*
1. Reshevsky, 11½; 2. Simonson, 11; 3-4. Fine, Treysman, 10½; 5. Kashdan, 10; 6-7. Dake, Kupchik, 9; 8. Kevitz, 7½; 9. Horowitz, 7; 10. Factor, 6½; 11-12. Steiner, Denker, 6; 13. Bernstein, 5; 14. Hanauer, 4½; 15-16. Adams, Morton, 3

1938 U.S. Championship ii, *New York*
1. Reshevsky, 13; 2. Fine, 12½; 3. Simonson, 11; 4. Horowitz, 10; 5. Kashdan, 9½; 6-7. Dake, Polland, 9; 8. Kupchik, 8½; 9. Bernstein, 7½; 10-11. Santasiere, Treysman, 7; 12-14. Cohen, Hanauer, Reinfeld, 6½; 15. Shainswit, 5½; 16. Morton, 5; 17. Suesman, 2

1940 U.S. Championship iii, *New York*
1. Reshevsky, 13; 2. Fine, 12½; 3. Kashdan, 10½; 4-5. Pinkus, Simonson, 10; 6-7. Kupchik, Denker, 9½; 8-11. Bernstein, Polland, Reinfeld, Shainswit, 7½; 12-13. Adams,

Seidman, 7; 14-15. Green, Hanauer, 6; 16. Woliston, 3; 17. Littman, 2

1942 U.S. CHAMPIONSHIP IV, *New York*
1-2. Kashdan, Reshevsky, $12\frac{1}{2}$; 3-4. Denker, Pinkus, $10\frac{1}{2}$; 5. Steiner, 10; 6. Horowitz, 9; 7. Seidman, 7; 8-9. Levin, Levy, $6\frac{1}{2}$; 10-11. Chernev, Pilnick, 6; 12-13. Baker, Lessing, $5\frac{1}{2}$; 14-16. Altman, Green, Halhbohm, 4. Playoff match won by Reshevsky.

1944 U.S. CHAMPIONSHIP V, *New York*
1. Denker, $15\frac{1}{2}$; 2. Fine, $14\frac{1}{2}$; 3-4. Horowitz, Steiner, 14; 5. Pinkus, $13\frac{1}{2}$; 6. Shainswit, $10\frac{1}{2}$; 7. Altman, 9; 8-9. Adams, Almgren, 8; 10-11. DiCamillo, Weinstock, 7, 12-14. Isaacs, Neidich, Rothman, $6\frac{1}{2}$; 15. Stromberg, 5; 16. Chernev, $4\frac{1}{2}$; 17. Goldstone, $2\frac{1}{2}$; 18. Persinger, $\frac{1}{2}$

1946 U.S. CHAMPIONSHIP VI, *New York*
1. Reshevsky, 16; 2. Kashdan, $13\frac{1}{2}$; 3. Santasiere, 13; 4. Levin, $12\frac{1}{2}$; 5-6. Denker, Horowitz, 12; 7. Steiner, 11; 8. Pinkus, $10\frac{1}{2}$; 9. Kramer, $9\frac{1}{2}$; 10. Sandrin, 8; 11. Ulvestad, $7\frac{1}{2}$; 12. Rubinow, 7; 13-16. Adams, DiCamillo, Rothman, Suesman, $6\frac{1}{2}$; 17. Drexel, 5; 18. Fink, 4; 19. Kowalski, $3\frac{1}{2}$

1948 NEW YORK INTERNATIONAL
1. Fine, 8; 2. Najdorf, $6\frac{1}{2}$; 3-4. Euwe, Pilnick, 5; 5-6. Horowitz, Kramer, $4\frac{1}{2}$; 7-8. Bisguier, Kashdan, 4; 9. Denker, 2; 10. Steiner, $1\frac{1}{2}$

1948 U.S. CHAMPIONSHIP VII, *South Fallsburg, New York*
1. Steiner, 15; 2. Kashdan, $14\frac{1}{2}$; 3-4. Kramer, Ulvestad, 13; 5-7. Hesse, Rubinow, Shainswit, 12; 8-10. Adams, Evans, Shipman, $11\frac{1}{2}$; 11-12. Sandrin, Santasiere, $10\frac{1}{2}$; 13. Poschel, 8; 14. Platz, $7\frac{1}{2}$; 15. Heitner, 7; 16. Whitaker, 6; 17. Howard, $5\frac{1}{2}$; 18. Almgren, 4; 19. Suraci, 3; 20. James, 2

1951 U.S. CHAMPIONSHIP VIII, *New York*
1. Evans, $9\frac{1}{2}$; 2. Reshevsky, $8\frac{1}{2}$; 3. Pavey, 7; 4. Seidman, $6\frac{1}{2}$; 5. Horowitz, $5\frac{1}{2}$; 6-7. Bernstein, Santasiere, 5; 8.

Mengarini, $4\frac{1}{2}$; 9. Shainswit, 4; 10-12. Hanauer, Pinkus, Simonson, $3\frac{1}{2}$

1951   NEW YORK INTERNATIONAL
1. Reshevsky, 8; 2-3. Euwe, Najdorf, $7\frac{1}{2}$; 4. Fine, 7; 5. Evans, $6\frac{1}{2}$; 6-7. R. Byrne, Horowitz, 6; 8. Guimard, 5; 9. O'Kelly, $4\frac{1}{2}$; 10. Bisguier, $3\frac{1}{2}$; 11. Kramer, 3; 12. Shainswit, $1\frac{1}{2}$

1954   U.S. CHAMPIONSHIP IX, *New York*
1. Bisguier, 10; 2. Evans, 9; 3. Seidman, 8; 4-5. Pavey, Sherwin, $7\frac{1}{2}$; 6-7. Bernstein, Rossolimo, 7; 8-9. Berliner, Wachs, $6\frac{1}{2}$; 10. Hearst, 6; 11. Burger, $5\frac{1}{2}$; 12. Pilnick, 5; 13. Brandts, 3; 14. Mengarini, $2\frac{1}{2}$

1954   ROSENWALD I, *New York*
1. Reshevsky, $7\frac{1}{2}$; 2. Evans, $6\frac{1}{2}$; 3. Bisguier, 6; 4. D. Byrne, 5; 5. Sherwin, 3; 6. Kramer, 2

1955   ROSENWALD II, *New York*
1-2. Bisguier, Evans, 6; 3. Reshevsky, $5\frac{1}{2}$; 4. Horowitz, $4\frac{1}{2}$; 5-6. Shipman, Lombardy, 4

1956   ROSENWALD III, *New York*
1. Reshevsky, 9; 2. Bisguier, 7; 3-4. Feuerstein, Mednis, $6\frac{1}{2}$; 5-7. Bernstein, D. Byrne, Turner, $5\frac{1}{2}$; 8-9. Fischer, Seidman, $4\frac{1}{2}$; 10-11. Hearst, Pavey, 4; 12. Shainswit, $2\frac{1}{2}$

1957–58   U.S. CHAMPIONSHIP X, *New York*
1. Fischer, $10\frac{1}{2}$; 2. Reshevsky, $9\frac{1}{2}$; 3. Sherwin, 9; 4. Lombardy, $7\frac{1}{2}$; 5. Berliner, 7; 6-8. Denker, Feuerstein, Mednis, $6\frac{1}{2}$; 9. Seidman, 6; 10-11. Bernstein, Bisguier, 5; 12-13. DiCamillo, Turner, $4\frac{1}{2}$; 14. Kramer, 3

1957   DALLAS INTERNATIONAL *(Double Round)*
1-2. Reshevsky, Gligorich, $8\frac{1}{2}$; 3-4. Larsen, Szabo, $7\frac{1}{2}$; 5. Yanofsky, 7; 6. Olafsson, $6\frac{1}{2}$; 7. Najdorf, $5\frac{1}{2}$; 8. Evans, 5

1958–59   U.S. CHAMPIONSHIP XI, *New York*
1. Fischer, $8\frac{1}{2}$; 2. Reshevsky, $7\frac{1}{2}$; 3. Sherwin, $6\frac{1}{2}$; 4-7.

Bisguier, D. Byrne, Evans, Lombardy, 6; 8. Benko, 5½;
9-10. R. Byrne, Kalme, 4; 11-12. Mednis, Weinstein, 3

1959–60 U.S. CHAMPIONSHIP XII, *New York*
1. Fischer, 9; 2. R. Byrne, 8; 3. Reshevsky, 7½; 4. Benko,
7; 5. Bisguier, 6½; 6. Weinstein, 6; 7. Seidman, 5½; 8.
Sherwin, 5; 9. Mednis, 4½; 10. Bernstein, 4; 11. Denker, 3;
12. Ault, 0

1960–61 U.S. CHAMPIONSHIP XIII, *New York*
1. Fischer, 9; 2. Lombardy, 7; 3. Weinstein, 6½; 4-6.
Reshevsky, Bisguier, Sherwin, 6; 7. Kalme, 5; 8-11. Benko,
Berliner, R. Byrne, Saidy, 4½; 12. Seidman, 2½

1961–62 U.S. CHAMPIONSHIP XIV, *New York*
1. Evans, 7½; 2. R. Byrne, 7; 3-6. Benko, Mednis, Seidman,
Sherwin, 6½; 7. Hearst, 5½; 8. D. Byrne, 5; 9. Weinstein, 4½; 10. Turner, 4; 11. Kramer, 3½; 12. Bernstein, 3

1962–63 U.S. CHAMPIONSHIP XV, *New York*
1. Fischer, 8; 2. Bisguier, 7; 3-5. Addison, Evans, Reshevsky,
6½; 6. R. Byrne, 6; 7-8. Berliner, Mednis, 5; 9-10. Benko,
Rossolimo, 4½; 11. Steinmeyer, 4; 12. Sherwin, 2½

1963 PIATIGORSKY CUP I, *Los Angeles (Double Round)*
1-2. Keres, Petrosian, 8½; 3-4. Najdorf, Olafsson, 7½; 5.
Reshevsky, 7; 6. Gligorich, 6; 7-8. Benko, Panno, 5½

1963–64 U.S. CHAMPIONSHIP XVI, *New York*
1. Fischer, 11; 2. Evans, 7½; 3. Benko, 7; 4-5. Saidy,
Reshevsky, 6½; 6. R. Byrne, 5½; 7. Weinstein, 5; 8.
Bisguier, 4; 9-10. Addison, Mednis, 3½; 11. Steinmeyer, 3;
12. D. Byrne, 2½

1965–66 U.S. CHAMPIONSHIP XVII, *New York*
1. Fischer, 8½; 2-3. R. Byrne, Reshevsky, 7½; 4-5. Addison, Zuckerman, 6½; 6. Rossolimo, 6; 7-9. Benko, Evans,
Saidy, 5; 10-11. Bisguier, Burger, 3; 12. Suttles, 2½

1966 PIATIGORSKY CUP II, *Santa Monica (Double Round)*
1. Spassky, 11½; 2. Fischer, 11; 3. Larsen, 10; 4-5. Portisch,

Unzicker, 9½; 6-7. Petrosian, Reshevsky, 9; 8. Najdorf, 8; 9. Ivkov, 6½; 10. Donner, 6

1966–67   U.S. CHAMPIONSHIP XVIII, *New York*
1. Fischer, 9½; 2. Evans, 7½; 3-4. Benko, Sherwin, 6; 5. Bisguier, 5½; 6-7. Addison, Saidy, 5; 8-10. R. Byrne, Reshevsky, Rossolimo, 4½; 11-12. D. Byrne, Zuckerman, 4

1968   U.S. CHAMPIONSHIP XIX, *New York*
1. Evans, 8½; 2. R. Byrne, 8; 3. Reshevsky, 7; 4. Benko, 6½; 5-6. Lombardy, Bisguier, 6; 7-9. Rossolimo, Saidy, Zuckerman, 5½; 10. Horowitz, 4; 11. Weinburger, 2; 12. Seidman, 1½

1969   U.S. CHAMPIONSHIP XX, *New York*
1. Reshevsky, 8; 2. Addison, 7½; 3. Benko, 7; 4. Lombardy, 6; 5-8. D. Byrne, Evans, Mednis, Zuckerman, 5½; 9-11. R. Byrne, Bisguier, Saidy, 4½; 12. Burger, 2

1972   U.S. CHAMPIONSHIP XXI, *New York*
1-3. R. Byrne, Kavalek, Reshevsky, 9; 4. Evans, 8½; 5. Benko, 8; 6-7. DeFotis, Lombardy, 7½; 8. Mednis, 7; 9-10. Bisguier, Martz, 6½; 11. Kaufman, 5; 12. Feuerstein, 3; 13. Horowitz, 2½; 14. Popovych, 2. Byrne won the playoff held in early 1973, with Reshevsky second.

1972   SAN ANTONIO INTERNATIONAL
1-3. Karpov, Petrosian, Portisch, 10½; 4. Gligorich, 10; 5. Keres, 9½; 6-7. Hort, Suttles, 9; 8-9. Larsen, Mecking, 8½; 10. D. Byrne, 7; 11-12. Browne, Evans, 6½; 13. Kaplan, 5; 14-15. Campos-Lopez, Saidy, 3½; 16. Smith, 2

1973   NORRISTOWN, PENNSYLVANIA, INTERNATIONAL
1-4. Rogoff, Biyaisas, Pilnick, Parma, 7½; 5-6. Soltis, Bisguier, 6; 7-8. Commons, Martz, 5; 9. Mednis, 4½; 10-11. Uzman, Chellstorp, 3½; 12. Paoli, 1½

MATCHES *(First named player is winner of match)*

1892   U.S. CHAMPIONSHIP: Lipschutz-Showalter, 7-1 (7 draws), New York

1894   U.S. CHAMPIONSHIP: Hodges-Showalter, won by Hodges, New York

1895   U.S. CHAMPIONSHIP: Showalter-Lipschutz, 7-4 (3 draws), New York

1896   U.S. CHAMPIONSHIP: Showalter-Kemeny, won by Showalter, Philadelphia

1896   U.S. CHAMPIONSHIP: Showalter-Barry, 7-2 (4 draws), New York

1897   U.S. CHAMPIONSHIP: Pillsbury-Showalter, 10-8 (4 draws), New York

1898   U.S. CHAMPIONSHIP: Pillsbury-Showalter, 7-3 (2 draws), New York

1907   WORLD CHAMPIONSHIP: Emanuel Lasker–Marshall, 8-0 (7 draws), New York

1909   Capablanca-Marshall, 8-1 (14 draws), New York

1909   U.S. CHAMPIONSHIP: Marshall-Showalter, 7-2 (3 draws), Lexington, Ky.

1921   WORLD CHAMPIONSHIP: Capablanca–Emanuel Lasker, 4-0 (14 draws), Havana

1923   U.S. CHAMPIONSHIP: Marshall–Edward Lasker, 5-4 (9 draws), New York–Chicago

1927   WORLD CHAMPIONSHIP: Alekhine-Capablanca, 6-3 (25 draws), Buenos Aires

1941   U.S. CHAMPIONSHIP: Reshevsky-Horowitz, 3-0 (13 draws), New York

1942   U.S. CHAMPIONSHIP: Reshevsky-Kashdan, 6-2 (13 draws), played at four Army camps

1946   U.S. CHAMPIONSHIP: Denker-Steiner, 3-1 (6 draws), New York

1952   U.S. CHAMPIONSHIP: Evans-Steiner, 10-4

1956   Reshevsky-Lombardy, 1-0 (5 draws), New York

1957   Reshevsky-Bisguier, 4-2 (4 draws), New York

1957   Reshevsky–D. Byrne, 7-3, New York

1960   Reshevsky-Benko, 3-2 (5 draws), New York

1961   Reshevsky-Fischer, 2-2 (7 draws), New York–Los Angeles

1962   Evans-Lombardy, 4-3 (3 draws), New York

1972   WORLD CHAMPIONSHIP: Fischer-Spassky, 6-3 (12 draws), Reykjavik

INDEX OF GAMES AND GAME SEGMENTS

CHAPTER 3

Pillsbury-Gunsberg, Hastings, 1895
Pillsbury–Emanuel Lasker, Nuremberg, 1896
Pillsbury-Tarrasch, Vienna, 1898
Pillsbury-Marco, Paris, 1900
Pillsbury-Janowski, Vienna, 1898
Pillsbury-Maroczy, Budapest, 1896
Pillsbury-Tarrasch, Hastings, 1895
Pillsbury–Emanuel Lasker, Cambridge Springs, 1904
Pillsbury-Marshall, Paris, 1900
Tchigorin-Marshall, Vienna, 1903
Marshall-Burn, Ostend, 1907
Marshall-Atkins, Cable Match, 1903
Marshall-Bogolyubov, New York, 1924

CHAPTER 4

Capablanca-Vidmar, New York, 1927
Janowski-Capablanca, New York, 1916
Capablanca-Alekhine, St. Petersburg, 1913
Capablanca-Schroeder, New York, 1916
Nimzovich-Capablanca, New York, 1927
Colle-Capablanca, Carlsbad, 1929
Capablanca-Tartakover, New York, 1924
Capablanca-Marshall, New York, 1918
Kashdan-Mikenas, Folkestone, 1933
Rellstab-Kashdan, Stockholm, 1930

CHAPTER 5

Landau-Reshevsky, Kemeri, 1937
Reshevsky-Kashdan, Western Championship, 1934
Botvinnik-Reshevsky, The Hague, 1948
Emanuel Lasker–Reshevsky, Nottingham, 1936
Reshevsky-Polugayevsky, Palma de Mallorca, 1970

Pillsbury-Winawer, Budapest, 1896
Tchigorin-Pillsbury, London, 1899
Marshall-Pillsbury, Vienna, 1903
Marshall-Tchigorin, Ostend, 1905
Capablanca-Mieses, Berlin, 1913
Janowski–Edward Lasker, New York, 1924
Capablanca-Spielmann, New York, 1927
Stahlberg-Kashdan, Hamburg, 1930
Dake-Alekhine, Pasadena, 1932
Reshevsky-Capablanca, Margate, 1935
Reshevsky-Fine, New York State Championship, Hamilton, N.Y.,
    1941
Reshevsky-Vasconcellos, Boston, 1944
Denker-Pinkus, New York, 1945
Mengarini-Bisguier, Baltimore, 1948
Evans-Pilnick, New York, 1947
D. Byrne–Fischer, New York, 1956
Lombardy–Kramer, New York, 1958
R. Byrne–Fischer, New York, 1963
Bisguier-Benko, New York, 1963
R. Byrne–Evans, New York, 1965
Kaufman-Kavalek, New York, 1972
R. Byrne–Taimanov, Leningrad, 1973

ANSWERS TO LOYD'S PROBLEMS

No. 1

It's the queen knight pawn: 1 P-N4, R-B4 (to stop 2 R-KB5);
2 PxR, P-R7; 3 P-B6, B-B2; 4 PxP and 5 PxN(Q) mate.

No. 2

Mate in three: 1 RxP, BxR; 2 N-B3 and 3 P-N4, or 1 . . . BxN;
2 R-R3ch, B-R5; 3 P-N4 mate.

Mate in four: 1 PxP, B-K8; 2 R-N4, BxP; 3 RxB and 4 R-R3
mate, or 1 . . . B-K6; 2 R-N4, B-N4; 3 R-R4ch, BxR; 4 P-N4 mate.

Mate in five: 1 R-N7, B-N8; 2 R-N1, B-R7; 3 R-K1, K-R5; 4 K-N6, or 1 . . . B-K6; 2 R-N1, B-N4; 3 R-R1ch, B-R5; 4 R-R2.

Mate in six: 1 N-B3, B-K8; 2 NxB, K-R5; 3 P-R3, K-R4; 4 N-Q3, K-R5; 5 N-B4, P-R4; 6 N-B3 mate. Two Nantucket players in 1966 found an alternate mate in 4 K-B6, K-R5; 5 K-N6, P-R4; 6 N-B3 mate.